DESIGNS ON PREHISTORIC HOPI POTTERY

Jesse Walter Fewkes

DOVER PUBLICATIONS, INC.

NEW YORK

Published in Canada by General Publishing Company, Ltd., 30 Lesmill Road, Don Mills, Toronto, Ontario.

Published in the United Kingdom by Constable and Company, Ltd., 10 Orange Street, London WC 2.

This Dover edition, first published in 1973, is an unabridged republication of the following two articles:

"Designs on Prehistoric Hopi Pottery," an Accompanying Paper to the *Thirty-third Annual Report of the Bureau of American Ethnology to the Secretary of the Smithsonian Institution 1911-12*, published by the Government Printing Office, Washington D. C., in 1919 (pp. 207-284).

"Sikyatki and Its Pottery," an excerpt (pp. 631-728) from "Archeological Expedition to Arizona in 1895," an Accompanying Paper to the *Seventeenth Annual Report of the Bureau of American Ethnology to the Secretary of the Smithsonian Institution, 1895-96, by J. W. Powell, Director*, published by the Government Printing Office, Washington D. C., in 1898. The following plates, which appear in black and white in the present edition, were in color in the original edition: CXXI through CXXVIII, CXXX, CXXXII through CXXXIX, CXLI, CXLIII through CXLIX, CLII through CLVI, CLVIII, CLXIII through CLXV.

International Standard Book Number: 0-486-22959-9
Library of Congress Catalog Card Number:73-81507

Manufactured in the United States of America
Dover Publications, Inc.
180 Varick Street
New York, N.Y. 10014

PUBLISHER'S NOTE

The present volume is comprised of two sections. The first appeared in 1898 as part of an Accompanying Paper to the *Seventeenth Annual Report of the Bureau of American Ethnology to the Secretary of the Smithsonian Institution, 1895-96* under the title "Archeological Expedition to Arizona in 1895." The present edition uses only that section of the report which concerns itself with Sikyatki and its pottery. The second section reprints, in its entirety, "Designs on Prehistoric Hopi Pottery" which appeared in the *Thirty-Third Annual Report.*

Plates which appeared in color in the original editions are here reproduced in black and white. As an aid to the scholar, the plate numbers and pagination of the originals have been retained (in brackets), but a consecutive pagination has been added for convenience.

CONTENTS

                                                    PAGE
1. Sikyatki and Its Pottery   1
2. Designs on Prehistoric Hopi Pottery 105

SIKYATKI AND ITS POTTERY

CONTENTS

The ruins of Sikyatki... 631
  Traditional knowledge of the pueblo................................... 631
  Nomenclature.. 636
  Former inhabitants of Sikyatki 636
  General features 637
  The acropolis 643
  Modern gardens 646
  The cemeteries.. 646
  Pottery.. 650
    Characteristics—Mortuary pottery 650
    Coiled and indented ware 651
    Smooth undecorated ware.. 652
    Polished decorated ware 652
  Paleography of the pottery 657
    General features 657
    Human figures.. 660
    The human hand... 666
    Quadrupeds 668
    Reptiles 671
    Tadpoles 677
    Butterflies or moths.. 678
    Dragon-flies 680
    Birds 682
    Vegetal designs.. 698
    The sun 699
    Geometric figures... 701
      Interpretation of the figures................................. 701
      Crosses 702
      Terraced figures 703
      The crook 703
      The germinative symbol 704
      Broken lines... 704
    Decorations on the exterior of food bowls 705

ILLUSTRATIONS

PLATE   PAGE

     CXV. Sikyatki mounds from the Kanelba trail 636

    CXVI. Ground plan of Sikyatki 638

  CXVII. Excavated rooms on the acropolis of Sikyatki 642

 CXVIII. Plan of excavated rooms on the acropolis of Sikyatki 644

   CXIX. Coiled and indented pottery from Sikyatki 650

    CXX. Saucers and slipper bowls from Sikyatki 652

   CXXI. Decorated pottery from Sikyatki 654

  CXXII. Decorated pottery from Sikyatki 655

 CXXIII. Decorated pottery from Sikyatki 656

 CXXIV. Decorated pottery from Sikyatki 660

  CXXV. Flat dippers and medicine box from Sikyatki 662

 CXXVI. Double-lobe vases from Sikyatki 664

CXXVII. Unusual forms of vases from Sikyatki 666

CXXVIII. Medicine box and pigment pots from Sikyatki 668

 CXXIX. Designs on food bowls from Sikyatki 670

  CXXX. Food bowls with figures of quadrupeds from Sikyatki 671

 CXXXI. Ornamented ladles from Sikyatki 674

CXXXII. Food bowls with figures of reptiles from Sikyatki 675

CXXXIII. Bowls and dippers with figures of tadpoles, bird, etc. from
        Sikyatki 676

CXXXIV. Food bowls with figures of sun, butterfly, and flower from
        Sikyatki 677

 CXXXV. Vases with figures of butterflies from Sikyatki 678

CXXXVI. Vases with figures of birds and feathers from Sikyatki ... 679

CXXXVII. Vessels with figures of human hand, birds, turtle, etc. from
        Sikyatki 680

CXXXVIII. Food bowls with figures of birds from Sikyatki 682

CXXXIX. Food bowls with figures of birds from Sikyatki 684

   CXL. Figures of birds from Sikyatki 686

  CXLI. Food bowls with figures of birds and feathers from Sikyatki 688

 CXLII. Vases, bowls, and ladle with figures of feathers from
        Sikyatki·.. 689

CXLIII. Vase with figures of birds from Sikyatki 690

CXLIV. Vase with figures of birds from Sikyatki 691

 CXLV. Vases with figures of birds from Sikyatki 691

 CXLVI. Bowls and potsherd with figures of birds from Sikyatki ... 692

CXLVII. Food bowls with figures of birds from Sikyatki 693

CXLVIII. Food bowls with symbols of feathers from Sikyatki 694

CXLIX. Food bowls with symbols of feathers from Sikyatki 695

   CL. Figures of birds and feathers from Sikyatki 696

  CLI. Figures of birds and feathers from Sikyatki 697

 CLII. Food bowls with bird, feather, and flower symbols from
        Sikyatki 698

CLIII. Food bowls with figures of birds and feathers from Sikyatki 699

CLIV. Food bowls with figures of birds and feathers from Sikyatki 700

CLV. Food bowls with figures of birds and feathers from Sikyatki   701
CLVI. Food bowls with figures of birds and feathers from Sikyatki   702
CLVII. Figures of birds and feathers from Sikyatki   703
CLVIII. Food bowls with figures of sun and related symbols from
        Sikyatki   704
CLIX. Cross and related designs from Sikyatki   705
CLX. Cross and other symbols from Sikyatki   705
CLXI. Star, sun, and related symbols from Sikyatki   705
CLXII. Geometric ornamentation from Sikyatki   706
CLXIII. Food bowls with geometric ornamentation from Sikyatki .   707
CLXIV. Food bowls with geometric ornamentation from Sikyatki .   710
CLXV. Food bowls with geometric ornamentation from Sikyatki .   714
CLXVI. Linear figures on food bowls from Sikyatki   718
CLXVII. Geometric ornamentation from Awatobi   719

FIGURE

262. The acropolis of Sikyatki   644
263. War god shooting an animal (fragment of food bowl)   665
264. Mountain sheep   669
265. Mountain lion   670
266. Plumed serpent   672
267. Unknown reptile   674
268. Unknown reptile   675
269. Unknown reptile   676
270. Outline of plate CXXXV, a   678
271. Butterfly design on upper surface of plate CXXXV, b   679
272. Man-eagle   683
273. Pendent feather ornaments on a vase   690
274. Upper surface of vase with bird decoration   691
275. Kwataka eating an animal   692
276. Decoration on the bottom of plate CXLVI, f   694
277. Oblique parallel line decoration   706
278. Parallel lines fused at one point   706
279. Parallel lines with zigzag arrangement   706
280. Parallel lines connected by middle bar   707
281. Parallel lines of different width; serrate margin   707
282. Parallel lines of different width; median serrate   707
283. Parallel lines of different width; marginal serrate   707
284. Parallel lines and triangles   708
285. Line with alternate triangles   708
286. Single line with alternate spurs   708
287. Single line with hourglass figures   708
288. Single line with triangles   709
289. Single line with alternate triangles and ovals   709
290. Triangles and quadrilaterals   709
291. Triangle with spurs   709
292. Rectangle with single line   709
293. Double triangle; multiple lines   710
294. Double triangle; terraced edges   710
295. Single line; closed fret   710
296. Single line; open fret   711
297. Single line; broken fret   711
298. Single line; parts displaced   711
299. Open fret; attachment displaced   711
300. Simple rectangular design   711

FIGURE

301. Rectangular S-form 712
302. Rectangular S-form with crooks 712
303. Rectangular S-form with triangles 712
304. Rectangular S-form with terraced triangles 712
305. S-form with interdigitating spurs 713
306. Square with rectangles and parallel lines 713
307. Rectangles, triangles, stars, and feathers 713
308. Crook, feathers, and parallel lines 713
309. Crooks and feathers 714
310. Rectangle, triangles, and feathers 714
311. Terraced crook, triangle, and feathers 714
312. Double key 715
313. Triangular terrace 715
314. Crook, serrate end 715
315. Key pattern; rectangle and triangles 716
316. Rectangle and crook 716
317. Crook and tail-feathers 716
318. Rectangle, triangle, and serrate spurs 717
319. W-pattern; terminal crooks 717
320. W-pattern; terminal rectangles 717
321. W-pattern; terminal terraces and crooks 718
322. W-pattern; terminal spurs 718
323. W-pattern; bird form 719
324. W-pattern; median triangle 719
325. Double triangle; two breath feathers 720
326. Double triangle; median trapezoid 720
327. Double triangle; median rectangle 720
328. Double compound triangle; median rectangle 720
329. Double triangle; median triangle 721
330. Double compound triangle 721
331. Double rectangle; median rectangle 721
332. Double rectangle; median triangle 721
333. Double triangle with crooks 722
334. W-shape figure; single line with feathers 722
335. Compound rectangles, triangles, and feathers 722
336. Double triangles 722
337. Double triangles and feathers 723
338. Twin triangles 723
339. Triangle with terraced appendages 723
340. Mosaic pattern 723
341. Rectangles, stars, crooks, and parallel lines 724
342. Continuous crooks 724
343. Rectangular terrace pattern 724
344. Terrace pattern with parallel lines 725
345. Terrace pattern 725
346. Triangular pattern with feathers 725
347. S-pattern 726
348. Triangular and terrace figures 726
349. Crook, terrace, and parallel lines 726
350. Triangles, squares, and terraces 726
351. Bifurcated rectangular design 727
352. Lines of life and triangles 727
353. Infolded triangles 727
354. Human hand 728
355. Animal paw, limb, and triangle 728

SIKYATKI AND ITS POTTERY

THE RUINS OF SIKYATKI

TRADITIONAL KNOWLEDGE OF THE PUEBLO

Very vague ideas are current regarding the character of Hopi culture prior to Tobar's visit to Tusayan in 1540, and with the exception of the most meager information nothing concerning it has come down to us from early historical references in the sixteenth century. It is therefore interesting to record all possible information in regard to these people prior to the period mentioned, and this must be done mainly through archeology.

Although there are many Tusayan ruins which we have every reason to believe are older than the time of Coronado, no archeologist has gathered from them the evidences bearing on prehistoric Tusayan culture which they will undoubtedly yield. Large and beautiful collections of pottery ascribed to Tusayan ruins have shown the excellent artistic taste of the ancient potters of this region, indicating that in the ceramic art they were far in advance of their descendants. But these collections have failed to teach the lesson they might have taught, from the fact that data concerning the objects composing them are so indefinite. Very little care had been taken to label these collections accurately or to collect any specimens but those which were strikingly beautiful or commercially valuable. It was therefore with the hope of giving a more precise and comprehensive character to our knowledge of Tusayan antiquities that I wished to excavate one of the ruins of this province which was undoubtedly prehistoric. Conditions were favorable for success at the mounds called by the Indians Sikyatki.[1] These ruins are situated near the modern Tusayan pueblos of East Mesa, from which I could hire workmen, and not far from Keam's Canyon, which could be made a base of supplies. The existing legends bearing on these ruins, although obscure, are sufficiently definite for all practical purposes.

I find no mention of Sikyatki in early historical documents, nor can the name be even remotely identified with any which has been given to a Tusayan pueblo. My knowledge of the mounds which mark the site of this ancient village dates back to 1892, when I visited them with one of the old men of Walpi, who then and there narrated the legend of its destruction by the Walpians previously to the advent of the Spaniards. I was at that time impressed by the extent of the mounds, and prepared a rough sketch of the ground plan of the former houses, but from lack of means was unable to conduct any systematic excavation of the ruin.

Comparatively nothing concerning the ruin of Sikyatki has been published, although its existence had been known for several years previously to my visit. In his brief account Mr Victor Mindeleff[2] speaks of it as two prominent knolls, "about 400 yards apart," the summits of which are covered with house walls. He also found portions of walls on intervening hummocks, but gives no plan of the ruin. The name, Sikyatki, is referred to the color of the sandstone of which the walls were built. He found some of the rooms were constructed of small stones, dressed by rubbing, and laid in mud. The largest chamber was stated to be 9½ by 4½ feet, and it was considered that many of the houses were "built in excavated places around the rocky summits of the knolls."[3] Mr Mindeleff identified the former inhabitants with the ancestors of the Kokop people, and mentioned the more important details of their legend concerning the destruction of the village.

---

[1] Many of the specimens in the well-known Keam collection, now in the Tusayan room of the Peabody Museum at Cambridge, are undoubtedly from Sikyatki, and still more are from Awatobi. Since the beginning of my excavations at Sikyatki it has come to be a custom for the Hopi potters to dispose of, as Sikyatki ware, to unsuspecting white visitors, some of their modern objects of pottery. These fraudulent pieces are often very cleverly made.

[2] Architecture of Tusayan and Cibola, op. cit., pp. 20, 21.

[3] These rooms I failed to find. One of the rocky knolls may be that called by me the "acropolis." The second knoll I cannot identify, unless it is the elevation in continuation of the same side toward the east. Possibly he confounded the ruin of Küküchomo with that of Sikyatki.

We can rely on the statement that Sikyatki was inhabited by the Kokop or Firewood people of Tusayan, who were so named because they obtained fire from wood by the use of drills. These people are represented today at Walpi by Katci, whose totem is a picture of Masauwû, the God of Fire. It is said that the home of the Firewood people before they built Sikyatki was at Tebuñki, or Fire-house, a round ruin northeastward from Keam's canyon. They were late arrivals in Tusayan, coming at least after the Flute people, and probably before the Honani or Badger people, who brought, I believe, the *katcina* cult. Although we can not definitely assert that this cultus was unknown at Sikyatki, it is significant that in the ruins no ornamental vessel was found with a figure of a *katcina* mask, although these figures occur on modern bowls. The original home of the Kokop people is not known, but indefinite legends ascribe their origin to Rio Grande valley. They are reputed to have had kindred in Antelope valley and at the Fire-house, above alluded to, near Eighteen-mile spring.

The ruin of Fire-house, one of the pueblos where the Kokop people are reputed to have lived before they built Sikyatki, is situated on the periphery of Tusayan. It is built of massive stones and differs from all other ruins in that province in that it is circular in form. The round type of ruin is, however, to be seen in the two conical mounds on the mesa above Sikyatki, which was connected in some way with the inhabitants who formerly lived at its base.

The reason the Kokop people left Fire-house is not certain, but it is said that they came in conflict with Bear clans who were entering the province from the east. Certain it is that if the Kokop people once inhabited Fire-house they must have been joined by other clans when they lived at Sikyatki, for the mounds of this pueblo indicate a village much larger than the round ruin on the brink of the mesa northeast of Keam's canyon. The general ground plan of the ruin indicates an inclosed court with surrounding tiers of houses, suggesting the eastern type of pueblo architecture.

The traditional knowledge of the destruction of Sikyatki is very limited among the present Hopi, but the best folklorists all claim that it was destroyed by warriors from Walpi and possibly from Middle Mesa. Awatobi seems not to have taken part in the tragedy, while Hano and Sichomovi did not exist when the catastrophe took place.

The cause of the destruction of Sikyatki is not clearly known, and probably was hardly commensurate with the result. Its proximity to Walpi may have led to disputes over the boundaries of fields or the ownership of the scanty water supply. The people who lived there were intruders and belonged to clans not represented in Walpi, which in all probability kept hostility alive. The early Tusayan peoples did not readily assimilate, but quarreled with one another even when sorely oppressed by common enemies.

There is current in Walpi a romantic story connected with the over-throw of Sikyatki. It is said that a son of a prominent chief, disguised as a *katcina*, offered a prayer-stick to a maiden, and as she received it he cut her throat with a stone knife. He is said to have escaped to the mesa top and to have made his way along its edge to his own town, taunting his pursuers. It is also related that the Walpians fell upon the village of Sikyatki to avenge this bloody deed, but it is much more likely that there was ill feeling between the two villages for other reasons, probably disputes about farm limits or the control of the water supply, inflamed by other difficulties. The inhabitants of the two pueblos came into Tusayan from different directions, and as they may have spoken different languages and thus have failed to understand each other, they may have been mutually regarded as interlopers. Petty quarrels no doubt ripened into altercations, which probably led to bloodshed. The forays of the Apache from the south and the Ute from the north, which began at a later period, should naturally have led to a defensive alliance; but in those early days confederation was not dreamed of and the feeling between the two pueblos culminated in the destruction of Sikyatki. This was apparently the result of a quarrel between two pueblos of East Mesa, or at least there is no inti-mation that the other pueblos took prominent part in it. It is said that after the destruction some of those who escaped fled to Oraibi, which would imply that the Walpi and Oraibi peoples, even at that early date, were not on very friendly terms. If, however, the statement that Oraibi was then a distinct pueblo be true, it in a way affords a suggestion of the approximate age [1] of this village.

There was apparently a more or less intimate connection between the inhabitants of old Sikyatki and those of Awatobi, but whether or not it indicates that the latter was founded by the refugees from the former I have not been able definitely to make out. All my informants agree that on the destruction of Sikyatki some of its people fled to Awatobi, but no one has yet stated that the Kokop people were represented in the latter pueblo. The distinctive clans of the pueblo of Antelope mesa are not mentioned as living in Sikyatki, and yet the two pueblos are said to have been kindred. The indications are that the inhabitants of both came from the east—possibly were intruders, which may have been the cause of the hostility entertained by both toward the Walpians. The problem is too complex to be solved with our present limited knowledge in this direction, and archeology seems not to afford very satisfactory evidence one way or the other. We may never know whether the Sikyatki refugees founded Awatobi or simply fled to that pueblo for protection.

---

[1] The legends of the origin of Oraibi are imperfectly known, but it has been stated that the pueblo was founded by people from Old Shuñopovi. It seems much more likely, however, that our knowledge is too incomplete to accept this conclusion without more extended observations. The composition of the present inhabitants indicates amalgamation from several quarters, and neighboring ruins should be studied with this thought in mind.

There appears to be no good evidence that Sikyatki was destroyed by fire, nor would it seem that it was gradually abandoned. The larger beams of the houses have disappeared from many rooms, evidently having been appropriated in building or enlarging other pueblos.

There is nothing to show that any considerable massacre of the people took place when the village was destroyed, in which respect it differs considerably from Awatobi. There is little doubt that many Sikyatki women were appropriated by the Walpians, and in support of this it is stated that the Kokop people of the present Walpi are the descendants of the people of that clan who dwelt at Sikyatki. This conclusion is further substantiated by the statements of one of the oldest members of the Kókop phratry who frequently visited me while the excavations were in progress.

The destruction of Sikyatki and its consequent abandonment doubt-less occurred before the Spaniards obtained a foothold in the country. The aged Hopi folklorists insist that such is the case, and the excavations did not reveal any evidence to the contrary. If we add to the negative testimony that Sikyatki is not mentioned in any of the early writings, and that no fragment of metal, glass, or Spanish glazed pottery has been taken from it, we appear to have substantial proof of its prehistoric character.

In the early times when Sikyatki was a flourishing pueblo, Walpi was still a small settlement on the terrace of the mesa just below the present town that bears its name. Two ruins are pointed out as the sites of Old Walpi, one to the northward of the modern town, and a second more to the westward. The former is called at present the Ash-heap house or pueblo, the latter Kisakobi. It is said that the people whose ancestors formed the nucleus of the more northerly town moved from there to Kisakobi on account of the cold weather, for it was too much in the shadow of the mesa. Its general appearance would indicate it to be older than the more westerly ruin, higher up on the mesa. It was a pueblo of some size, and was situated on the edge of the terrace. The refuse from the settlement was thrown over the edge of the decline, where it accumulated in great quantities. This débris contains many fragments of characteristic pottery, similar to that from Sikyatki, and would well repay systematic investigation. No walls of the old town rise more than a few feet above the surface, for most of the stones have long ago been used in rebuilding the pueblo on other sites. Kisakobi was situated higher up on the mesa, and bears every appearance of being more modern than the ruin below. Its site may readily be seen from the road to Keam's canyon, on the terrace-like prolongation of the mesa. Some of the walls are still erect, and the house visible for a great distance is part of the old pueblo. This, I believe, was the site of Walpi at the time the Spaniards visited Tusayan, and I have found here a fragment of pottery which I believe is of Spanish origin. The ancient pueblo crowned the ridge of the terrace which narrows here to 30 or 40 feet, so that ancient Walpi was an elongated pueblo, with narrow passageways and no rectangular court. I should judge, however, that the pueblo was not inhabited for a great period, but was moved to its present site after a few generations of occupancy. The Ash-hill village was inhabited contemporaneously with Sikyatki, but Kisakobi was of later construction. Neither Sichomovi nor Hano was in existence when Sikyatki was in its prime, nor, indeed, at the time of its abandonment. In 1782 Morfi spoke of Sichomovi as a pueblo recently founded, with but fifteen families. Hano, although older, was certainly not established before 1700.[1]

The assertions of all Hopi traditionists that Sikyatki is a prehistoric ruin, as well as the scientific evidence looking the same way, are most important facts in considering the weight of deductions in regard to the character of prehistoric Tusayan culture.

Although we have no means of knowing how long a period has elapsed since the occupancy and abandonment of Sikyatki, we are reasonably sure that objects taken from it are purely aboriginal in character and antedate the inception of European influence. It is certain, however, that the Sikyatki people lived long enough in that pueblo to develop a ceramic art essentially peculiar to Tusayan.

NOMENCLATURE

The commonly accepted definition of Sikyatki is "yellow house" (*sikya*, yellow; *ki*, house). One of the most reliable chiefs of Walpi, however, called my attention to the fact that the hills in the locality were more or less parallel, and that there might be a relationship between the parallel valleys and the name. The application of the term "yellow" would not seem to be very appropriate so far as it is distinctive of the general color of the pueblo. The neighboring spring, however, contains water which after standing some time has a yellowish tinge, and it was not unusual to name pueblos from the color of the adjacent water or from some peculiarity of the spring, which was one of the most potent factors in the determination of the site of a village. Although the name may also refer to a cardinal point, a method of nomenclature followed in some regions of the Southwest, if such were the case in regard to Sikyatki it would be exceptional in Tusayan.

FORMER INHABITANTS OF SIKYATKI

The origin of the pueblo settlement at Sikyatki is doubtful, but as I have shown in my enumeration of the clans of Walpi, the Kokop (Firewood) and the Isauûh (Coyote) phratries which lived there are supposed

---

[1] It is distinctly stated that the Tanoan families whose descendants now inhabit Hano were not in Tusayan when Awatobi fell. To be sure they may have been sojourning in some valley east of the province, which, however, is not likely, since they were "invited" to East Mesa for the specific purpose of aiding the Hopi against northern nomads. Much probability attaches to a suggestion that they belonged to the emigrants mentioned by contemporary historians as leaving the Rio Grande on account of the unsettled condition of the country after the great rebellion of 1680.

SIKYATKI MOUNDS FROM THE KANELBA TRAIL

to have come into Tusayan from the far east or the valley of the Rio
Grande. The former phratry is not regarded as one of the earliest
arrivals in Tusayan, for when its members arrived at Walpi they
found living there the Flute, Snake, and Water-house phratries. It is
highly probable that the Firewood, or as they are sometimes called the
Fire, people, once lived in the round pueblo known as Fire-house, and as
the form of this ruin is exceptional in Tusayan, and highly characteristic of the region east of this province, there is archeological evidence
of the eastern origin of the Fire people. Perhaps the most intelligent
folklorist of the Kokop people was Nasyuñweve, who died a few years
ago—unfortunately before I had been able to record all the traditions
which he knew concerning his ancestors. At the present day Katci,
his successor[1] in these sacerdotal duties in the Antelope-Snake mys-
teries, claims that his people formerly occupied Sikyatki, and indeed the
contiguous fields are still cultivated by members of that phratry.

It is hardly possible to do more than estimate the population of
Sikyatki when in its prime, but I do not believe that it was more
than 500;[2] probably 300 inhabitants would be a closer estimate if we
judge from the relative population to the size of the pueblo of Walpi
at the present time. On the basis of population given, the evidences
from the size of the Sikyatki cemeteries would not point to an occupancy of the village for several centuries, although, of course, the
strict confines of these burial places may not have been determined
by our excavations. The comparatively great depth at which some
of the human remains were found does not necessarily mean great
antiquity, for the drifting sands of the region may cover or uncover
the soil or rocks in a very short time, and the depth at which an object
is found below the surface is a very uncertain medium for estimating
the antiquity of buried remains.

GENERAL FEATURES

The ruin of Sikyatki (plates CXV, CXVI) lies about three miles east of
the recent settlement of Tanoan families at Isba or Coyote spring,
near the beginning of the trail to Hano. Its site is in full view from
the road extending from the last-mentioned settlement to Keam's
canyon, and lies among the hills just below the two pyramidal elevations
called Küküchomo, which are visible for a much greater distance.
When seen from this road the mounds of Sikyatki are observed to be
elevated at least 300 feet above the adjacent cultivated plain, but at
the ruin itself this elevation is scarcely appreciable, so gradual is the

---

[1] The succession of priests is through the clan of the mother, so that commonly, as in the case of
Katci, the nephew takes the place of the uncle at his death. Some instances, however, have come to
my knowledge where, the clan having become extinct, a son has been elevated to the position made
vacant by the death of a priest. The Kokop people at Walpi are vigorous, numbering 21 members if we include the Coyote and Wolf clans, the last mentioned of which may be descendants of
the former inhabitants of Küküchomo, the twin ruins on the mesa above Sikyatki.

[2] In this census I have used also the apparently conservative statement of Vetancurt that there
were 800 people in Awatobi at the end of the seventeenth century.

southerly decline to the arroyo which drains the plain. The ruin is situated among foothills a few hundred yards from the base of the mesa, and in the depression between it and the mesa there is a stretch of sand in which grow peach trees and a few stunted cedars. At this point, likewise, there is a spring, now feeble in its flow from the gradually drifting sand, yet sufficient to afford a trickling stream by means of which an enterprising native, named Tcino, irrigates a small garden of melons and onions. On all sides of the ruin there are barren stretches of sand relieved in some places by stunted trees and scanty vegetation similar to that of the adjacent plains. The soil in the plaza of the ruin is cultivated, yielding a fair crop of squashes, but is useless for corn or beans.

Here and there about the ruins stand great jagged bowlders, relieving what would otherwise be a monotonous waste of sand. One of these stony outcrops forms what I have called the "acropolis" of Sikyatki, which will presently be described. On the eastern side the drifting sand has so filled in around the elevation on which the ruin stands that the ascent is gradual, and the same drift extends to the rim of the mesa, affording access to the summit that otherwise would necessitate difficult climbing. Along the ridge of this great drift there runs a trail which passes over the mesa top to a beautiful spring, on the other side, called Kanelba.[1]

The highest point of the ruin as seen from the plain is the rocky eminence rising at the western edge, familiarly known among the members of my party as the "acropolis." As one approaches the ruin from a deep gulch on the west, the acropolis appears quite lofty, and a visitor would hardly suspect that it marks the culminating point of a ruin, so similar does it appear to surrounding hills of like geologic character where no vestiges of former house-walls appear.

The spring from which the inhabitants of the old pueblo obtained their water supply lies between the ruin and the foot of the mesa, nearer the latter. The water is yellow in color, especially after it has remained undisturbed for some time, and the quantity is very limited. It trickles out of a bed of clay in several places and forms a pool from which it is drawn to irrigate a small garden and a grove of peach trees. It is said that when Sikyatki was in its prime this spring was larger than at present, and I am sure that a little labor spent in digging out the accumulation of sand would make the water more wholesome and probably sufficiently abundant for the needs of a considerable population.

The nearest spring of potable water available for our excavation camp at Sikyatki was Kanelba, or Sheep spring, one af the best sources of water supply in Tusayan. The word Kanelba, containing a Spanish element, must have replaced a Hopi name, for it is hardly to be supposed that this spring was not known before sheep were brought into

---

[1] *Kanel* = Spanish *carnero*, sheep; *ba* = water, spring.

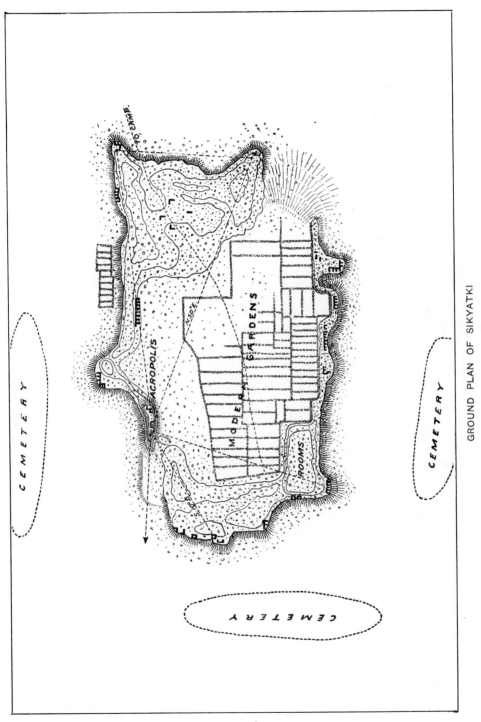

GROUND PLAN OF SIKYATKI

the country.   There is a legend that formerly the site of this spring was
dry, when an ancient priest, who had deposited his *tiponi*, or chieftain's
badge, at the place, caused the water to flow from the ground; at present however the water rushes from a hole as large as the arm in the
face of the rock, as well as from several minor openings.   It is situated
on the opposite side of the mesa from Sikyatki, a couple of miles
northeastward from the ruin.

Half-way up the side of the mesa, about opposite Sikyatki, there is a
large reservoir, used as a watering place for sheep.   The splash of the
water, as it falls into this reservoir, is an unusual sound in this arid
region, and is worth a tramp of many miles.   There are many evidences that this spring was a popular one in former times.   As it
is approached from the top of the mesa, a brief inspection of the
surroundings shows that for about a quarter of a mile, on either side,
there are signs of ancient terraced gardens, walled in with rows of
stones.   These gardens have today greatly diminished in size, as compared with the ancient outlines, and only that portion which is occupied by a grove of peach trees is now under cultivation, although
there is plenty of water for the successful irrigation of a much larger
tract of land than the gardens now cover.[1]   Judging from their size,
many of the peach trees are very old, although they still bear their
annual crop of fruit.   Everything indicates, as the legends relate, that
these Kanelba gardens, the walls of which now form sheep corrals,
were long ago abandoned.

The terraces south of the Kanelba peach grove resemble the lower
terraces of Wipo.   About 100 rods farther south, along the foot of
the mesa, on the same level, are a number of unused fields, and a
cluster of house remains.   The whole of this terrace is of a type which
shows greater action of the weather than the others, but the boundaries
of the fields are still marked with rows of stones.   The adjacent foothills
contain piles of ashes in several places, as if the sites of ancient pottery
kilns, and very old stone inclosures occur on the top of the mesa above
Kanelba.   All indications seem to point to the ancient occupancy of
the region about Kanelba by many more farmers than today.   Possibly
the inhabitants of Sikyatki, which is only two or three miles away, fre-
quented this place and cultivated these ancient gardens.   Kanelba is
regarded as a sacred spring by several Hopi religious societies of East
Mesa.   The Snake priests of Walpi always celebrate a feast there on
the day of the snake hunt to the east in odd years,[2] while in the alternate years it is visited by the Flute men.

---

[1] Wipo spring, a few miles northward from the eastern end of the mesa, would be an excellent site
for a Government school.   It is sufficiently convenient to the pueblos, has an abundant supply of
potable water at all seasons, and cultivable fields in the neighborhood.

[2] The boy who brought our drinking water from Kanelba could not be prevailed upon to visit it on
the day of the snake hunt to the east in 1895, on the ground that no one not a member of the society
should be seen there or take water from it at that time.   This is probably a phase of the taboo of all
work in the world-quarter in which the snake hunts occur, when the Snake priests are engaged in
capturing these reptilian "elder brothers."

The present appearance of Sikyatki (plate CXV) is very desolate, and when visited by our party previously to the initiation of the work, seemed to promise little in the way of archeological results. No walls were standing above ground, and the outlines of the rooms were very indistinct. All we saw at that time was a series of mounds, irregularly rectangular in shape, of varying altitude, with here and there faint traces of walls. Prominent above all these mounds, however, was the pinnacle of rock on the northwestern corner, rising abruptly from the remainder of the ruin, easily approached from the west and sloping more gradually to the south. This rocky elevation, which we styled the acropolis, was doubtless once covered with houses.

On the western edge of the ruin a solitary farmhouse, used during the summer season, had been constructed of materials from the old walls, and was inhabited by an Indian named Lelo and his family during our excavations. He is the recognized owner of the farm land about Sikyatki and the cultivator of the soil in the old plaza of the ruins. Jakwaina, an enterprising Tewan who lives not far from Isba, the spring near the trail to Hano, has also erected a modern house near the Sikyatki spring, but it had not been completed at the time of our stay. Probably never since its destruction in prehistoric times have so many people as there were in our party lived for so long a time at this desolate place.

The disposition of the mounds show that the ground plan of Sikyatki (plate CXVI) was rectangular in shape, the houses inclosing a court in which are several mounds that may be the remains of kivas. The highest range of rooms, and we may suppose the most populous part of the ancient pueblo, was on the same side as the acropolis, where a large number of walled chambers in several series were traced.

The surface of what was formerly the plaza is crossed by rows of stones regularly arranged to form gardens, in which several kinds of gourds are cultivated. In the sands north of the ruin there are many peach trees, small and stunted, but yearly furnishing a fair crop. These are owned by Tcino,[1] and of course were planted long after the destruction of the pueblo.

In order to obtain legends of the former occupancy and destruction of Sikyatki, I consulted Nasyuñweve, the former head of the Kokop people, and while the results were not very satisfactory, I learned that the land about Sikyatki is still claimed by that phratry. Nasyuñweve,[2]

---

[1] Tcino lives at Sichomovi, and in the Snake dance at Walpi formerly took the part of the old man who calls out the words, "Awahaia," etc, at the kisi, before the reptiles are carried about the plaza. These words are Keresan, and Tcino performed this part on account of his kinship. He owns the grove of peach trees because they are on land of his ancestors, a fact confirmatory of the belief that the people of Sikyatki came from the Rio Grande.

[2] Nasyuñweve, who died a few years ago, formerly made the prayer-stick to Masauwûh, the Fire or Death god. This he did as one of the senior members of the Kokop or Firewood people, otherwise known as the Fire people, because they made fire with the fire-drill. On his death his place in the kiva was taken by Katci. Nasyuñweve was Intiwa's chief assistant in the Walpi katcinas, and wore the mask of Eototo in the ceremonials of the Niman. All this is significant, and coincides with the theory that katcinas are incorporated in the Tusayan ritual, that Eototo is their form of Masauwûh, and that he is a god of fire, growth, and death, like his dreaded equivalent.

Katci, and other prominent Kokop people occupy and cultivate the land about Sikyatki on the ground of inheritance from their ancestors who once inhabited the place.

Two routes were taken to approach Sikyatki—one directly across the sandy plain from the entrance to Keam's canyon, following for some distance the road to East Mesa; the other along the edge of the mesa, on the first terrace, to the cluster of houses at Coyote spring. The trail to the pueblos of East Mesa ascends the cliff just above Sikyatki spring, and joins that to Kanelba or Sheep spring, not far from Küküchomo, the twin mounds. By keeping along the first terrace a well traveled trail, with interesting views of the plain and the ruin, joins the old wagon road to *Wala*, the "gap" of East Mesa, at a higher level than the cluster of Tewan houses at Isba. In going and returning from their homes our Hopi workmen preferred the trail along the mesa, which we also often used; but the climb to the mesa top from the ruin is very steep and somewhat tiresome.

We prosecuted our excavations at Sikyatki for a few days over three weeks, choosing as a site for our camp a small depression to the east of the ruin near a dwarf cedar at the point where the trail to Kanelba passes the ruin. The place was advantageously near the cemeteries, and not too far from water. For purposes other than cooking and drinking the Sikyatki spring was used, the remainder of the supply being brought from Kanelba by means of a burro.

I employed Indian workmen at the ruin, and found them, as a rule, efficient helpers. The zeal which they manifested at the beginning of the work did not flag, but it must be confessed that toward the close of the excavations it became necessary to incite their enthusiasm by prizes, and, to them, extraordinary offers of overalls and calico. They at first objected to working in the cemeteries, regarding it as a desecration of the dead, but several of their number overcame their scruples, even handling skulls and other parts of skeletons. The Snake chief, Kopeli, however, never worked with the others, desiring not to dig in the graves. Respecting his feelings, I allotted him the special task of excavating the rooms of the acropolis, which he performed with much care, showing great interest in the results. At the close of our daily work prayer-offerings were placed in the trenches by the Indian workmen, as conciliatory sacrifices to Masauwûh, the dread God of Death, to offset any malign influence which might result from our desecration of his domain. A superstitious feeling that this god was not congenial to the work which was going on, seemed always to haunt the minds of the laborers, and once or twice I was admonished by old men, visitors from Walpi, not to persist in my excavations. The excavators, at times, paused in their work and called my attention to strange voices echoing from the cliffs, which they ascribed, half in earnest, to Masauwûh.

The Indians faithfully delivered to me all objects which they found in their digging, with the exception of turquoises, many of which, I have good reason to suspect, they concealed while our backs were turned and, in a few instances, even before our eyes.

The accompanying plan of Sikyatki (plate CXVI) shows that it was a rectangular ruin with an inclosed plaza. It is evident that the ancient pueblo was built on a number of low hills and that the eastern portion was the highest. In this respect it resembled Awatobi, but apparently differed from the latter pueblo in having the inclosed plaza. In the same way it was unlike Walpi or the ancient and modern pueblos of Middle Mesa and Oraibi. In fact, there is no Tusayan ruin which resembles it in ground plan, except Payüpki, a Tanoan town of much later construction. The typical Tusayan form of architecture is the pyramidal, especially in the most ancient pueblos. The ground plan of Sikyatki is of a type more common in the eastern pueblo region and in those towns of Tusayan which were built by emigrants from the Rio Grande region. Sikyatki and some of the villages overlooking Antelope valley are of this type.

In studying the ground plans of the three modern villages on East Mesa, the fact is noted that both Sichomovi and Hano differ architecturally from Walpi. The forms of the former smaller pueblos are primarily rectangular with an inclosed plaza in which is situated the kiva; Walpi, on the other hand, although furnished with a small plaza at the western end, has kivas located peripherally rather than in an open space between the highest house clusters. Sichomovi is considered by the Hopi as like Zuñi, and is sometimes called by the Hano people, Sionimone, "Zuñi court," because to the Tewan mind it resembles Zuñi; but the term is never applied to Walpi.[1] The distinction thus recognized is, I believe, architecturally valid. The inclosed court or plaza in Tusayan is an intrusion from the east, and as eastern colonists built both Hano and Sichomovi, they preserved the form to which they were accustomed. The Sikyatki builders drew their architectural inspiration likewise from the east, hence the inclosed court in the ruins of that village.

The two most considerable house clusters of Sikyatki are at each end of a longer axis, connected by a narrow row of houses on the other sides. The western rows of houses face the plain, and were of one story, with a gateway at one point. The opposite row was more elevated, no doubt overlooking cultivated fields beyond the confines of the ruin. No kivas were discovered, but if such exist they ought to be found in the mass of houses at the southern end. I thought we had found circular rooms in that region, but cursory excavations did not demonstrate their existence. As there is no reason to suspect the existence of circular kivas in ancient Tusayan, it would be difficult to decide whether or not any one of the large rectangular rooms was used for ceremonial purposes, for it is an interesting fact that some of the oldest secret

---

[1] The Hano people call the Hopi *Koco* or *Koso;* the Santa Clara (also Tewa) people call them *Khoso,* according to Hodge.

EXCAVATED ROOMS ON THE ACROPOLIS OF SIKYATKI

rites in the Hopi villages occur, not in kivas, but in ordinary dwelling
rooms in the village. It has yet to be shown that there were special
kivas in prehistoric Tusayan.

The longer axis of the ruin is about north and south; the greatest
elevation is approximately 50 feet. Rocks outcrop only at one place,
the remainder of the ruin being covered with rubble, sand, stones, and
fragments of pottery. The mounds are not devoid of vegetation, for
sagebrush, cacti, and other desert genera grow quite profusely over
their surface; but they are wholly barren of trees or large bushes, and
except in the plaza the ruin area is uncultivated. As previously stated,
Sikyatki is situated about 250 or 300 feet above the plain, and when
approached from Keam's canyon appears to be about halfway up the
mesa height. On several adjacent elevations evidences of former fires,
or places where pottery was burned, were found, and one has not to go
far to discover narrow seams of an impure lignite. Here and there are
considerable deposits of selenite, which, as pointed out by Sitgreaves in
his report on the exploration of the Little Colorado, looks like frost
exuding from the ground in early spring.

THE ACROPOLIS

During the limited time devoted to the excavation of Sikyatki it was
impossible, in a ruin so large, to remove the soil covering any considerable number of rooms. The excavations at different points over
such a considerable area as that covered by the mounds would have
been more or less desultory and unsatisfactory, but a limited section
carefully opened would be much more instructive and typical. While,
therefore, the majority of the Indian workmen were kept employed at
the cemeteries, Kopeli, the Snake chief, a man in whom I have great
confidence, was assigned to the excavation of a series of rooms at the
highest point of the ruin, previously referred to as the acropolis (figure
262). Although his work in these chambers did not yield such rich
results as the others, so far as the number of objects was concerned,
he succeeded in uncovering a number of rooms to their floors, and
unearthed many interesting objects of clay and stone. A brief description of these excavations will show the nature of the work at that
point.

The acropolis, or highest point of Sikyatki, is a prominent rocky elevation at the western angle, and overlooks the entire ruin. On the side
toward the western cemetery it rises quite abruptly, but the ascent is
more gradual from the other sides. The surface of this elevation, on
which the houses stood, is of rock, and originally was as destitute of
soil as the plaza of Walpi. This surface supported a double series
of rooms, and the highest point is a bare, rocky projection.

From the rooms of the acropolis there was a series of chambers,
probably terraced, sloping to the modern gardens now occupying
the old plaza, and the broken walls of these rooms still protrude from

the surface in many places (plate CXVIII). When the excavations on the acropolis were begun, no traces of the biserial rows of rooms were detected, although the remains of the walls were traceable. The surface was strewn with fragments of pottery and other evidences of former occupancy.

On leveling the ground and throwing off the surface stones, it was found that the narrow ridge which formed the top of the acropolis was occupied by a double line of well-built chambers which show every evidence of having been living rooms. The walls were constructed of squared stones set in adobe, with the inner surface neatly plastered. Many of the rooms communicated by means of passageways with adja-

Fig. 262—The acropolis of Sikyatki

cent chambers, some of them being provided with niches and shelves. The average height of the standing walls revealed by excavation, as indicated by the distance of the floor below the surface of the soil, was about 5 feet.

The accompanying illustration (plate CXVIII) shows a ground plan of nine of these rooms, which, for purposes of reference, are lettered *a* to *l*. A description of each, it is hoped, will give an idea of a typical room of Sikyatki. Room *a* is rectangular in shape, 5 feet 3 inches by 6 feet 8 inches, and is 5 feet 8 inches deep. It has two depressions in the floor at the southeastern corner, and there is a small niche in the side wall above them. Some good specimens of mural plastering,

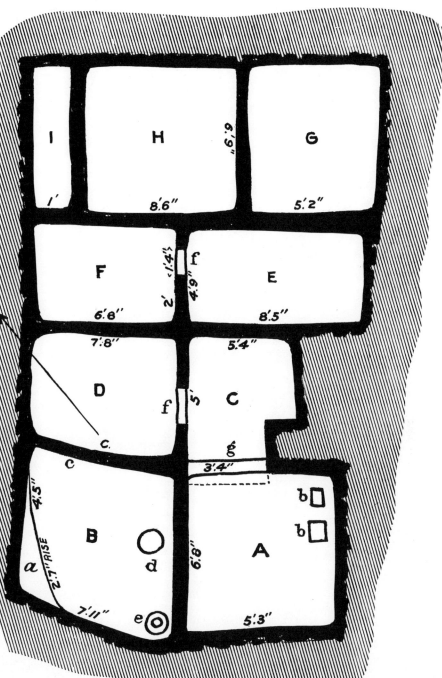

PLAN OF EXCAVATED ROOMS ON THE ACROPOLIS OF SIKYATKI
(Dimensions in feet and inches)

much blackened by soot, are found on the eastern wall. Room *a* has no passageway into room *b*, but it opens into the adjoining room *c* by an opening in the wall 3 feet 4 inches wide, with a threshold 9 inches high.

The shape of room *b* is more irregular. It is 8 feet 1 inch long by 4 feet 5 inches wide, and the floor is 5 feet 2 inches below the surface. In one corner there is a raised triangular platform 2 feet 7 inches above the floor. A large cooking pot, blackened with soot, was found in one corner of this room, and near it was a circular depression in the floor 17 inches in diameter, evidently a fireplace.

Room *c* is smaller than either of the preceding, and is the only one with two passageways into adjoining chambers. Remains of wooden beams in a fair state of preservation were found on the floors of rooms *c* and *b*, but they were not charred, as is so often the case, nor were there any ashes except in the supposed fireplace.

Room *d* is larger than those already mentioned, being 7 feet 8 inches by 5 feet, and connects with room *c* by means of a passageway. Rooms *e* and *f* communicate with each other by an opening 16 inches wide. We found the floors of these rooms 4 feet below the surface. The length of room *e* is 8 feet.

Room *f* is 6 feet 8 inches long and of the same width as *e*. The three chambers *g*, *h*, and *i* are each 6 feet 9 inches wide, but of varying width. Room *g* is 5 feet 2 inches, *h* is 8 feet 6 inches, and *i*, the smallest of all, only a foot wide. These three rooms have no intercommunication.

The evidence of former fires in some of these rooms, afforded by soot on the walls and ashes in the depressions identified as old fireplaces, is most important. In one or two places I broke off a fragment of the plastering and found it to be composed of many strata of alternating black and adobe color, indicating successive plasterings of the room. Apparently when the surface wall became blackened by smoke it was renewed by a fresh layer or wash of adobe in the manner followed in renovating the kiva walls today.[1]

An examination of the dimensions of the rooms of the acropolis will show that, while small, they are about the average size of the chambers in most other southwestern ruins. They are, however, much smaller than the rooms of the modern pueblo of Walpi or those of the cliff ruins in the Red-rock region, elsewhere described. Evidently the roof was 2 or 3 feet higher than the top of the present walls, and the absence of external passageways would seem to indicate that entrance was through the roof. The narrow chamber, *i*, is no smaller than some of those which were excavated at Awatobi, but unless it was a storage bin or dark closet for ceremonial paraphernalia its function is not known to me.

---

[1] The replastering of kivas at Walpi takes place during the *Powamu*, an elaborate *katcina* celebration. I have noticed that in this renovation of the kivas one corner, as a rule, is left unplastered, but have elicited no satisfactory explanation of this apparent oversight, which, no doubt, has significance. Someone, perhaps overimaginative, suggested to me that the unplastered corner was the same as the break in encircling lines on ancient pottery.

The mural plastering was especially well done in rooms *g* and *h*, a section thereof showing many successive thin strata of soot and clay, implying long occupancy. No chimneys were found, the smoke, as is the case with that from kiva fires today, doubtless finding an exit through the hatchway in the roof.

MODERN GARDENS

The whole surface of the ancient plaza of Sikyatki is occupied by rectangular gardens outlined by rows of stones. These are of modern construction and are cultivated by an enterprising Hopi who, as previously mentioned, has erected a habitable dwelling on one of the western mounds from the stones of the old ruin. These gardens are planted yearly with melons and squashes, and stones forming the outlines serve as wind-breaks to protect the growing plants from drifting sand. The plotting of the plan of these gardens was made in 1891, when a somewhat larger part of the plaza was under cultivation than in 1895.[1]

There is a grove of dwarf peach trees in the sands between the northern side of the ruin and the mesa along the run through which sometimes trickles a little stream from the spring. These trees belong to an inhabitant of Sichomovi named Tcino, who, it is claimed, is a descendant of the ancient Sikyatkians. The trees were of course planted there since the fall of the village, on land claimed by the Kokop phratry by virtue of their descent from the same phratral organization of the ancient pueblo.[2] The spring shows no evidence of having been walled up, but apparently has been filled in by drifting sand since the time that it formed the sole water supply of the neighboring pueblo. It still preserves the yellow color mentioned in traditions of the place.

THE CEMETERIES

By far the largest number of objects found at Sikyatki were gathered from the cemeteries outside the ruin, and were therefore mortuary in character. It would seem that the people buried their dead a short distance beyond the walls, at the three cardinal points. The first of these cemeteries was found in the dune between the ruin and the peach trees below the spring, and from its relative position from the pueblo has been designated the northern cemetery. The cemetery proper lies on the edge of the sandy tract, and was first detected by the finding of the long-bones of a human skeleton projecting from the soil. The position of individual graves was indicated usually by small, oblong piles of stones; but, as this was not an invariable sign, it was

---

[1] I was aided in making this plan by the late J. G. Owens, my former assistant in the field work of the Hemenway Expedition. It was prepared with a few simple instruments, and is not claimed to be accurate in all particulars.

[2] The existence of these peach trees near Sikyatki suggests, of course, an abandonment of the neighboring pueblo in historic times, but I hardly think it outweighs other stronger proofs of antiquity.

deemed advisable to extend long trenches across the lower part of the dune. As a rule, the deeper the excavations the more numerous and elaborate were the objects revealed. Most of the skeletons were in a poor state of preservation, but several could have been saved had we the proper means at our disposal to care for them.

No evidence of cremation of the dead was found, either at Awatobi or Sikyatki, nor have I yet detected any reference to this custom among the modern Hopi Indians. They have, however, a strange concept of the purification of the breath-body, or shade of the dead, by fire, which, although I have always regarded it as due to the teaching of Christian missionaries, may be aboriginal in character. This account of the judgment of the dead is as follows:

There are two roads from the grave to the Below. One of these is a straight way connected with the path of the sun into the Underworld. There is a branch trail which divides from this straight way, passing from fires to a lake or ocean (*patübha*). At the fork of the road sits Tokonaka, and when the breath-body comes to this place this chief looks it over and, if satisfied, he says " *Üm-pac lo-la-mai, ta ai*," "You are very good; go on." Then the breath-body passes along the straight way to the far west, to the early *Sipapû*, the Underworld from which it came, the home of Müiyinwû. Another breath-body comes to the fork in the road, and the chief says, "You are bad,"and he conducts it along the crooked path to the place of the first fire pit, where sits a second chief, Tokonaka, who throws the bad breath-body into the fire, and after a time it emerges purified, for it was not wholly bad. The chief says, "You are good now," and carries it back to the first chief, who accepts the breath-body and sends it along the straight road to the west.

If, on emerging from the first fire, the soul is still unpurified, or not sufficiently so to be accepted, it is taken to the second fire pit and cast into it. If it emerges from this thoroughly purified, in the opinion of the judge, it is immediately transformed into a *ho-ho-ya-üh*, or prayer-beetle. All the beetles we now see in the valleys or among the mesas were once evil Hopi. If, on coming out of the second fire pit, the breath-body is still considered bad by the chief, he takes it to the third fire, and, if there be no evil in it when it emerges from this pit, it is metamorphosed into an ant, but if unpurified by these three fires—that is, if the chief still finds evil left in the breath-body—he takes it to a fourth fire and again casts it into the flames, where it is utterly consumed, the only residue being soot on the side of the pit.

I have not recorded this as a universal or an aboriginal belief among the Hopi, but rather to show certain current ideas which may have been brought to Tusayan by missionaries or others. The details of the purification of the evil soul are characteristic.

The western cemetery of Sikyatki is situated among the hillocks covered with surface rubble below a house occupied in summer by a

Hopi and his family. From the nature of the soil the excavation of this cemetery was very difficult, although the mortuary objects were more numerous. Repeated attempts to make the Indians work in a systematic manner failed, partly on account of the hard soil and partly from other reasons. Although the lower we went the more numerous and beautiful were the objects exhumed, the Indians soon tired of deep digging, preferring to confine their work to within two or three feet of the surface. At many places we found graves under and between the huge bowlders, which are numerous in this cemetery.

The southern cemetery lies between the outer edge of the ruin on that side and the decline to the plain, a few hundred feet from the southern row of houses. Two conspicuous bowlders mark the site of most of the excavations in that direction. The mortuary objects from this cemetery are not inferior in character or number to those from the other burial places. All attempts to discover a cemetery on the eastern side of the pueblo failed, although a single food basin was brought to the camp by an Indian who claimed he had dug it out of the deep sand on the eastern side of the ruins. Another bowl was found in the sand drift near the trail over the mesa to Kanelba, but careful investigation failed to reveal any systematic deposit of mortuary vessels east of the ruin.[1]

The method of excavation pursued in the cemeteries was not so scientific as I had wished, but it was the only practicable one to be followed with native workmen. Having found the location of the graves by means of small prospecting holes sunk at random, the workmen were aligned and directed to excavate a single long, deep trench, removing all the earth as they advanced. It was with great difficulty that the Indians were taught the importance of excavating to a sufficient depth, and even to the end of the work they refused to be taught not to burrow. In their enthusiasm to get the buried treasures they worked very well so long as objects were found, but became at once discouraged when relics were not so readily forthcoming and went off prospecting in other places when our backs were turned. A shout that anyone had discovered a new grave in the trench was a signal for the others to stop work, gather around the place, light cigarettes, and watch me or my collaborators dig out the specimens with knives. This we always insisted on doing, for the reason that in their haste the Indians at first often broke fragile pottery after they had discovered it, and in spite of all precautions several fine jars and bowls were thus badly damaged by them. It is therefore not too much to say that most of the vessels which are now entire were dug out of the impacted sand by Mr Hodge or myself.

---

[1] The position of the cemeteries in ancient Tusayan ruins is by no means uniform. They are rarely situated far from the houses, and are sometimes just outside the walls. While the dead were seldom carried far from the village, a sandy locality was generally chosen and a grave excavated a few feet deep. Usually a few stones were placed on the surface of the ground over the burial place, evidently to protect the remains from prowling beasts.

No rule could be formulated in regard to the place where the pottery would occur, and often the first indication of its presence was the stroke of a shovel on the fragile edge of a vase or bowl. Having once found a skeleton, or discolored sand which indicated the former presence of human remains, the probability that burial objects were near by was almost a certainty, although in several instances even these signs failed.

A considerable number of the pottery objects had been broken when the soil and stones were thrown on the corpse at interment. So many were entire, however, that I do not believe any considerable number were purposely broken at that time, and none were found with holes made in them to "kill" or otherwise destroy their utility.

No evidences of cremation—no charred bones of man or animal in or near the mortuary vessels—were found. From the character of the objects obtained from neighboring graves, rich and poor were apparently buried side by side in the same soil. Absolutely no evidence of Spanish influence was encountered in all the excavations at Sikyatki—no trace of metal, glass, or other object of Caucasian manufacture such as I have mentioned as having been taken from the ruins of Awatobi—thus confirming the native tradition that the catastrophe of Sikyatki antedated the middle of the sixteenth century, when the first Spaniards entered the country.

It is remarkable that in Sikyatki we found no fragments of basketry or cloth, the fame of which among the Pueblo Indians was known to Coronado before he left Mexico. That the people of Sikyatki wore cotton kilts no one can doubt, but these fabrics, if they were buried with the dead, had long since decayed. Specimens of strings and ropes of yucca, which were comparatively abundant at Awatobi, were not found at Sikyatki; yet their absence by no means proves that they were not used, for the marks of the strings used to bind feathers to the mortuary pahos, on the green paint with which the wood was covered, may still be readily seen.

The insight into ancient beliefs and practices afforded by the numerous objects found at Sikyatki is very instructive, and while it shows the antiquity of some of the modern symbols, it betrays a still more important group of conventionalized figures, the meaning of which may always remain in doubt. This is particularly true of the decoration on many specimens of the large collection of highly ornamented pottery found in the Sikyatki cemeteries.

If we consider the typical designs on modern Hopi pottery and compare them with the ancient, as illustrated by the collections from Awatobi and Sikyatki, it is noted, in the first place, how different they are, and secondly, how much better executed the ancient objects are than the modern. Nor is it always clear how the modern symbols are derived from the ancient, so widely do they depart from them in all their essential characters.

POTTERY

CHARACTERISTICS—MORTUARY POTTERY

The pottery exhumed from the burial places of Sikyatki falls in the divisions known as—

 I—Coiled and indented ware.

 II—Smooth undecorated ware.

 III—Polished decorated ware.

  a. Yellow.

  b. Red.

  c. Black-and-white.

By far the largest number of ancient pottery objects from this locality belong to the yellow-ware group in the above classification. This is the characteristic pottery of Tusayan, although coiled and indented ware is well represented in the collection. The few pieces of red ware are different from that found in the ruins of the Little Colorado, while the black-and-white pottery closely resembles the archaic ware of northern cliff houses. Although the Sikyatki pottery bears resemblance to that of Awatobi, it can be distinguished from it without difficulty. The paste of both is of the finest character and was most carefully prepared. Some of the ancient specimens are much superior to those at present made, and are acknowledged by the finest potters of East Mesa to be beyond their power of ceramic production. The coloration is generally in red, brown, yellow, and black. Decorative treatment by spattering is common in the food basins, and this was no doubt performed, Chinese fashion, by means of the mouth. The same method is still employed by the Hopi priests in painting their masks.

The Sikyatki collection of pottery shows little or no duplication in decorative design, and every ornamented food basin bears practically different symbols. The decoration of the food basins is mainly on the interior, but there is almost invariably a geometrical design of some kind on the outside, near the rim. The ladles, likewise, are ornamented on their interior, and their handles aiso are generally decorated. When the specimens were removed from the graves their colors, as a rule, were apparently as well preserved as at the time of their burial; nor, indeed, do they appear to have faded since their deposit in the National Museum.

The best examples of ceramic art from the graves of Sikyatki, in texture, finish, and decoration, are, in my judgment, superior to any pottery made by ancient or modern Indians north of Mexico. Indeed, in these respects the old Tusayan pottery will bear favorable comparison even with Central American ware. It is far superior to the rude pottery of the eastern pueblos, and is also considerably better than that of the great villages of the Gila and Salado. Among the Hopi themselves the ceramic art has degenerated, as the few remaining potters

COILED AND INDENTED POTTERY FROM SIKYATKI

confess. These objects can hardly be looked upon as products of a savage people destitute of artistic feeling, but of a race which has developed in this line of work, through the plane of savagery, to a high stage of barbarism. While, as a whole, we can hardly regard the modern Hopi as a degenerate people with a more cultured ancestry, certainly the entire Pueblo culture in the Southwest, judged by the character of their pottery manufacture, has greatly deteriorated since the middle of the sixteenth century.

Coiled and Indented Ware

The rudest type of pottery from Sikyatki has been classed as coiled and indented ware. It is coarse in texture, not polished, and usually not decorated. Although the outer surface of the pottery of this class is rough, the general form of the ware is not less symmetrical than that of the finer vessels. The objects belonging to this group are mostly jars and moccasin-shape vessels, there being no bowls of this type. As a rule, the vessels are blackened with soot, although some of the specimens are light-brown in color. The former variety were undoubtedly once used in cooking; the latter apparently for containing water or food. In the accompanying illustration (plate CXIX, a) is shown one of the best specimens of indented ware, the pits forming an equatorial zone about the vessel. All traces of the coil of clay with which the jar was built up have been obliterated save on the bottom. The vessel is symmetrical and the indentations regular, as if made with a pointed stone, bone, or stick.

In another form of coarse pottery (plate CXIX, b) the rim merges into two ears or rudimentary handles on opposite sides. Traces of the original coiling are readily observable on the sides of this vessel.

Another illustration (plate CXIX, c) shows an amphora or jar with diametrically opposite handles extending from the rim to the side of the bowl. The surface of this rude jar is rough and without decoration, but the form is regular and symmetrical. In another amphora (plate CXIX, d) the opposite handles appear below the neck of the vessel; they are broader and apparently more serviceable.

The jar shown in plate CXIX, e, has two ear-like extensions or projections from the neck of the jar, which are perforated for suspension. This vessel is decorated with an incised zigzag line, which surrounds it just above its equator. This is a fair example of ornamented rough ware.

Several of the vessels made of coarse clay mixed with sand, the grains of which make the surface very rough, are of slipper or moccasin shape. These are covered with soot or blackened by fire, indicating their former use as cooking pots. By adopting this form the ancients were practically enabled to use the principle of the dutch-oven, the coals being piled about the vessels containing the food to be cooked much more advantageously than in the vase-like forms.

The variations in slipper-shape cooking pots are few and simple. The blind end is sometimes of globular form, as in the example illustrated in plate CXX, *a*, and sometimes pointed as in figures *b* and *c* of the same plate. One of the specimens of this type has a handle on the rim and another has a flaring lip. Slipper-form vessels are always of coarse ware for the obvious reason that, being somewhat more porous, they are more readily heated than polished utensils. They are not decorated for equally obvious reasons.

Smooth Undecorated Ware

There are many specimens of undecorated ware of all shapes and sizes, a type of which is shown in plate CXX, *d*. These include food bowls, saucers, ladles, and jars, and were taken from many graves. These utensils differ from the coarse ware vessels not only in the character of the clay from which they are made, but also in their superficial polish, which, in some instances, is as fine as that of vessels with painted designs. Several very good spoons of half-gourd shape were found, and there are many undecorated food bowls and vases. The first attemps at ornamentation appear to have been a simple spattering of the surface with liquid pigment or a drawing of simple encircling bands. In one instance (plate CXX, *d*) a blackening of the surface by exposure to smoke was detected, but no superficial gloss, as in the Santa Clara ware, was noted.

Polished Decorated Ware

By far the greater number of specimens of mortuary pottery from Sikyatki are highly polished and decorated with more or less complicated designs. Of these there are at least three different groups, based on the color of the ware. Most of the vessels are light yellow or of cream color; the next group in point of color is the red ware, the few remaining specimens being white with black decorations in geometric patterns. These types naturally fall into divisions consisting of vases, jars, bowls, square boxes, cups, ladles, and spoons.

In the group called vases (plates CXXI, CXXII) many varieties are found; some of these are double, with an equatorial constriction; others are rounded below, flat above, with an elevated neck and a recurved lip. It is noteworthy that these jars or vases are destitute of handles, and that their decoration is always confined to the equatorial and upper sections about the opening. In the specimens of this group which were found at Sikyatki there is no basal rim and no depression on the pole opposite the opening. No decoration is found on the interior of the vases, although in several instances the inside of the lip bears lines or markings of various kinds. The opening is always circular, sometimes small, often large; the neck of a vessel is occasionally missing, although the specimens bear evidence of use after having been thus broken. In one or two instances the equatorial constriction is so deep that the jar is practically double; in other

SAUCERS AND SLIPPER BOWLS FROM SIKYATKI

cases the constriction is so shallow that it is hardly perceptible (plate CXXVI, *a, b*). The size varies from a simple globular vessel not larger than a walnut to a jar of considerable size. Many show marks of previous use; others are as fresh as if made but yesterday.

One of the most fragile of all the globular vessels is a specimen of very thin black-and-white ware, perforated near the rim for suspension (plate CXXXII). This form, although rare at Sikyatki, is represented by several specimens, and in mode of decoration is very similar to the cliff-house pottery. From its scarcity in Tusayan I am inclined to believe that this and related specimens were not made of clay found in the immediate vicinity of Sikyatki, but that the vessels were brought to the ancient pueblo from distant places. As at least some of the cliff houses were doubtless inhabited contemporaneously with and long after the destruction of Sikyatki, I do not hesitate to say that the potters of that pueblo were familiar with the cliff dweller type of pottery and acquainted with the technic which gave the black and-white ware its distinctive colors.

By far the largest number of specimens of smooth decorated pottery from Sikyatki graves are food bowls or basins, evidently the dishes in which food was placed on the floor before the members of a family at their meals. As the mortuary offerings were intended as food for the deceased it is quite natural that this form of pottery should far outnumber any and all the others. In no instance do the food bowls exhibit marks of smoke blackening, an indication that they had not been used in the cooking of food, but merely as receptacles of the same.

The beautiful decoration of these vessels speaks highly for the artistic taste of the Sikyatki women, and a feast in which they were used must have been a delight to the native eye so far as dishes were concerned. When filled with food, however, much of the decoration of the bowls must have been concealed, a condition avoided in the mode of ornamentation adopted by modern Tusayan potters; but there is no doubt that when not in use the decoration of the vessels was effectually exhibited in their arrangement on the floor or convenient shelves.

The forms of these food bowls are hemispherical, gracefully rounded below, and always without an attached ring of clay on which to stand to prevent rocking. Their rims are seldom flaring, but sometimes have a slight constriction, and while the rims of the majority are perfectly circular, oblong variations are not wanting. Many of the bowls are of saucer shape, with almost vertical sides and flat bases; several are double, with rounded or flat base.

The surface, inside and out, is polished to a fine gloss, and when exteriorly decorated, the design is generally limited to one side just below the rim, which is often ornamented with double or triple parallel lines, drawn in equidistant, quaternary, and other forms. Most of the bowls show signs of former use, either wear on the inner surface or on the base where they rested on the floor in former feasts.

These mortuary vessels were discovered generally at one side of the chest or neck of the person whose remains they were intended to accompany, and a single specimen was found inverted over the head of the deceased. The number of vessels in each grave was not constant, and as many as ten were found with one skeleton, while in other graves only one or two were found. In one instance a nest of six of these basins, one inside another, was exhumed. While many of these mortuary offerings were broken and others chipped, there were still a large number as perfect as when made. Some of the bowls had been mended before burial, as holes drilled on each side of a crack clearly indicate. Fragments of various vessels, which evidently had been broken before they were thrown into the graves, were common.

There is a general similarity in the artistic decoration of bowls found in the same grave, as if they were made by the same potter; and persons of distinction, as shown by other mortuary objects, were, as a rule, more honored than some of their kindred in the character and number of pottery objects deposited with their remains. There were also a number of skeletons without ceramic offerings of any kind.

In one or two interments two or more small jars were found placed inside of a food bowl, and in many instances votive offerings, like turquois, beads, stones, and arrowpoints, had been deposited with the dead. The bowls likewise contained, in some instances, prayer-sticks and other objects, which will later be described.

One of the most interesting modifications in the form of the rim of one of these food bowls is shown in plate cxx, e, which illustrates a variation from the circular shape, forming a kind of handle or support for the thumb in lifting the vessel. The utility of this projection in handling a bowl of hot food is apparent. This form of vessel is very rare, it being the only one of its kind in the collection.

A considerable number of cups were found at Sikyatki; these vary in size and shape from a flat-bottom saucer like specimen to a mug-shape variety, always with a single handle (plate cxxv). Many of these resemble small bowls with rounded sides, but there are others in which the sides are vertical, and still others the sides of which incline at an angle to the flattened base.

The handles of these cups are generally smooth, and in one instance adorned with a figure in relief. The rims of these dippers are never flaring, either inward or outward. As a rule they are decorated on the exterior; indeed there is only one instance of interior decoration. The handles of the dippers are generally attached at both ends, but sometimes the handle is free at the end near the body of the utensil and attached at the tip. These handles are usually flat, but sometimes they are round, and often are decorated. Traces of imitations of the braiding of two coils of clay are seen in a single specimen.[1]

---

[1] The excavations at Homolobi in 1896 revealed two beautiful cups with braided handles and one where the clay strands are twisted.

a   ½

b   ½

c   ½

M.W.H.

DECORATED POTTERY FROM SIKYATKI

a 1/2

b 3/10

c 3/10

M.W.H.

DECORATED POTTERY FROM SIKYATKI

Small and large ladles, with long handles, occurred in large numbers in Sikyatki graves, but there was little variation among them except in the forms of their handles. Many of these utensils were much worn by use, especially on the rim opposite the attachment of the handle, and in some specimens the handle itself had evidently been broken and the end rounded off by rubbing long before it was placed in the grave. From the comparatively solid character of the bowls of these dippers they were rarely fractured, and were commonly found to contain smaller mortuary objects, such as paint, arrowheads, or polishing stones.

The ladles, unlike most of the cups, are generally decorated on the interior as well as on the exterior. Their handles vary in size and shape, are usually hollow, and sometimes are perforated at the end. In certain specimens the extremity is prolonged into a pointed, recurved tip, and sometimes is coiled in a spiral. A groove in the upper surface of one example is an unusual variation, and a right-angle bend of the tip is a unique feature of another specimen. The Sikyatki potters, like their modern descendants,[1] sometimes ornamented the tip of a single handle with the head of an animal and painted the upper surface of the shaft with alternate parallel bars, zigzags, terraces, and frets.

Several spoons or scoops of earthenware, which evidently had been used in much the same way as similar objects in the modern pueblos, were found. Some of these have the shape of a half gourd—a natural object which no doubt furnished the pattern. These spoons, as a rule, were not decorated, but on a single specimen bars and parallel lines may be detected. In the innovations of modern times pewter spoons serve the same purpose, and their form is sometimes imitated in earthenware. More often, in modern and probably also in ancient usage, a roll of paper-bread or *piki* served the same purpose, being dipped into the stew and then eaten with the fingers. Possibly the Sikyatkian drank from the hollow handle of a gourd ladle, as is frequently done in Walpi today, but he generally slaked his thirst by means of a clay substitute.[2]

Several box-like articles of pottery of both cream and red ware were found in the Sikyatki graves, some of them having handles, others being without them (plate CXXV). They are ornamented on the exterior and on the rim, and the handle, when not lacking, is attached to the longer side of the rectangular vessel. Not a single bowl was found with a terraced rim, a feature so common in the medicine bowls of Tusayan at the present time.[3]

---

[1] The modern potters commonly adorn the ends of ladle handles with heads of different mythologic beings in their pantheon. The knob-head priest-clowns are favorite personages to represent, although even the Corn-maid and different *katcinas* are also sometimes chosen for this purpose. The heads of various animals are likewise frequently found, some in artistic positions, others less so.

[2] The clay ladles with perforated handles with which the modern Hopi sometimes drink are believed to be of late origin in Tusayan.

[3] The oldest medicine bowls now in use ordinarily have handles and a terraced rim, but there are one or two important exceptions. In this connection it may be mentioned that, unlike the Zuñi, the Hopi never use a clay bowl with a basket-like handle for sacred meal, but always carry the meal in basket trays. This the priests claim is a very old practice, and so far as my observations go is confirmed by archeological evidence. The bowl with a basket-form handle is not found either in ancient or modern Tusayan.

In addition to the various forms of pottery which have been mentioned, there are also pieces made in the form of birds, one of the most typical of which is figured in plate CXII, c. In these objects the wings are represented by elevations in the form of ridges on the sides, and the tail and head by prolongations, which unfortunately were broken off.

Toys or miniature reproductions of all the above-mentioned ceramic specimens occurred in several graves. These are often very roughly made, and in some cases contained pigments of different colors. The finding of a few fragments of clay in the form of animal heads, and one or two rude images of quadrupeds, would seem to indicate that sometimes such objects were likewise deposited with the dead. A clay object resembling the flaring end of a flageolet and ornamented with a zigzag decoration is unique in the collections from Sikyatki, although in the western cemetery there was found a fragment of an earthenware tube, possibly a part of a flute.

In order to show more clearly the association of mortuary objects in single graves a few examples of the grouping of these deposits will be given.

In a grave in the western cemetery the following specimens were found: 1, ladle; 2, paint grinder; 3, paint slab; 4, arrowpoints; 5, fragments of a marine shell (*Pectunculus*); 6, pipe, with fragments of a second pipe, and 7, red paint (sesquioxide of iron).

In the grave which contained the square medicine bowl shown in plate CXXVIII, a, a ladle containing food was also unearthed.

The bowl decorated with a picture of a girl's head was associated with fragments of another bowl and four ladles.

Another single grave contained four large and small cooking pots and a broken metate.

In a grave 8 feet below the surface in the western cemetery we found: 1, decorated food vessel; 2, black shoe-shape cooking pot resting in a food bowl and containing a small rude ladle; 3, coarse undecorated basin.

A typical assemblage of mortuary objects comprised: 1, small decorated bowl containing polishing stones; 2, miniature cooking pot blackened by soot; 3, two small food bowls.

In modern Hopi burials the food bowls with the food for the dead are not buried with the deceased, but are placed on the mound of soil and stones which covers the remains. From the position of the mortuary pottery as regards the skeletons in the Sikyatki interments, it is probable that this custom is of modern origin. Whether in former times food bowls were placed on the burial mounds as well as in the grave I am not able to say. The number of food bowls in ancient graves exceeds those placed on modern burials.

The Sikyatki dead were apparently wrapped in coarse fabrics, possibly matting.

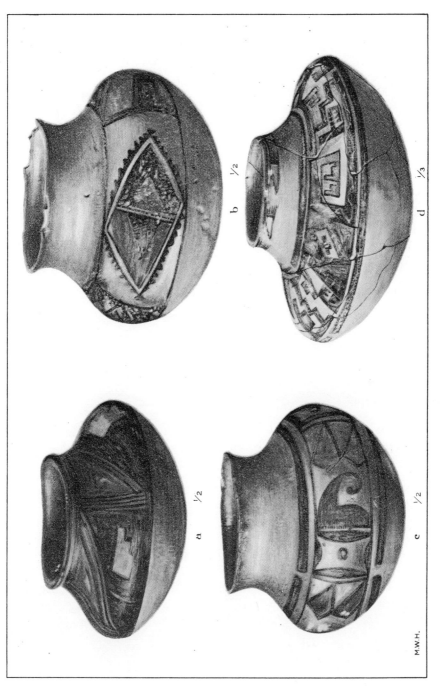

b ½

a ½

d ⅓

c ½

M.W.H.

DECORATED POTTERY FROM SIKYATKI

PALEOGRAPHY OF THE POTTERY

GENERAL FEATURES

The pottery from Sikyatki is especially rich in picture writing, and imperfect as these designs are as a means of transmitting a knowledge of manners, customs, and religious conceptions, they can be interpreted with good results.

One of the most important lessons drawn from the pottery is to be had from a study of the symbols used in its decoration, as indicative of current beliefs and practices when it was made. The ancient inhabitants of Sikyatki have left no written records, for, unlike the more cultured people of Central America, they had no codices; but they have left on their old mortuary pottery a large body of picture writings or paleography which reveals many instructive phases of their former culture. The decipherment of these symbols is in part made possible by the aid of a knowledge of modern survivals, and when interpreted rightly they open a view of ancient Tusayan myths, and in some cases of prehistoric practices.[1]

Students of Pueblo mythology and ritual are accumulating a considerable body of literature bearing on modern beliefs and practices. This is believed to be the right method of determining their aboriginal status, and is therefore necessary as a basis of our knowledge of their customs and beliefs. It is reasonable to suppose that what is now practiced in Pueblo ritual contains more or less of what has survived from prehistoric times, but from Taos to Tusayan there is no pueblo which does not show modifications in mythology and ritual due to European contact. Modern Pueblo life resembles the ancient, but is not a facsimile of it, and until we have rightly measured the effects of incorporated elements, we are more or less inexact in our estimation of the character of prehistoric culture. The vein of similarity in the old and the new can be used in an interpretation of ancient paleography, but we overstep natural limitations if by so doing we ascribe to prehistoric culture every concept which we find current among the modern survivors. To show how much the paleography of Tusayan has changed since Sikyatki was destroyed, I need only say that most of the characteristic figures of deities which are used today in the decoration of pottery are not found on the Sikyatki ware. Perhaps the most common figures on modern food bowls is the head of a mythologic being, the Corn-maid, *Calako-mana*, but this picture, or any which resembles it, is not found on the bowls from Sikyatki. A knowledge of the cult of the Corn-maid possibly came into Tusayan, through foreign influences, after the fall of Sikyatki, and there is no doubt that

---

[1]Symbolism rather than realism was the controlling element of archaic decoration. Thus, while objects of beauty, like flowers and leaves, were rarely depicted, and human forms are most absurd caricatures, most careful attention was given to minute details of symbolism, or idealized animals unknown to the naturalist.

the picture decoration of modern Tusayan pottery, made within a league of Sikyatki, is so different from the ancient that it indicates a modification of the culture of the Hopi in historic times, and implies how deceptive it may be to present modern beliefs and practices as facsimiles of ancient culture.

The main subjects chosen by the native women for the decoration of their pottery are symbolic, and the most abundant objects which bear these decorations are food bowls and water vases. Many mythic concepts are depicted, among which may be mentioned the Plumed Snake, various birds, reptiles, frogs, tadpoles, and insects. Plants or leaves are seldom employed as decorative motives, but the flower is sometimes used. The feather was perhaps the most common object utilized, and it may likewise be said the most highly conventionalized.

An examination of the decorations of modern food basins used in the villages of East Mesa shows that the mythologic personages most commonly chosen for the ornamentation of their interiors are the Corn or Germ goddesses.[1] These assume a number of forms, yet all are reducible to one type, although known by very different names, as Hewüqti, "Old Woman," Kokle, and the like.

Figures of reptiles, birds, the antelope, and like animals do not occur on any of the food bowls from the large collection of modern Tusayan pottery which I have studied, and as these figures are well represented in the decorations on Sikyatki food bowls, we may suppose their use has been abandoned or replaced by figures of the Corn-maids.[2] This fact, like so many others drawn from a study of the Tusayan ritual, indicates that the cult of the Corn-maids is more vigorous today than it was when Sikyatki was in its prime.

Many pictures of masks on modern Tusayan bowls are identified as *Tacab* or Navaho *katcinas*.[3] Their symbolism is well characterized by chevrons on the cheeks or curved markings for eyes. None of these figures, however, have yet been found on ancient Tusayan ceramics. Taken in connection with facts adduced by Hodge indicative of a recent advent of this vigorous Athapascan tribe into Tusayan, it would seem that the use of the *Tacab katcina* pictures was of recent date, and is therefore not to be expected on the prehistoric pottery of the age of that found in Sikyatki.

---

[1] Certainly no more appropriate design could be chosen for the decoration of the inside of a food vessel than the head of the Corn-maid, and from our ideas of taste none less so than that of a lizard or bird. The freshness and absence of wear of many of the specimens of Sikyatki mortuary pottery raises the question whether they were ever in domestic use. Many evidently were thus employed, as the evidences of wear plainly indicate, but possibly some of the vessels were made for mortuary purposes, either at the time of the decease of a relative or at an earlier period.

[2] The figure shown in plate CXXIX, *a*, was probably intended to represent the Corn-maid, or an Earth goddess of the Sikyatki pantheon. Although it differs widely in drawing from figures of Calako-mana on modern bowls, it bears a startling resemblance to the figure of the Germ goddess which appears on certain Tusayan altars.

[3] Hopi legends recount how certain clans, especially those of Tanoan origin, lived in Tségi canyon and intermarried with the Navaho so extensively that it is said they temporarily forgot their own language. From this source may have sprung the numerous so-called Navaho *katcinas*, and the reciprocal influence on the Navaho cults was even greater.

In the decoration of ancient pottery I find no trace of figures of the clown-priests, or *tcukuwympkiya*, who are so prominent in modern Tusayan *katcina* celebrations. These personages, especially the Tat-cukti, often called by a corruption of the Zuñi name Kóyimse (Kóyo-mäshi), are very common on modern bowls, especially at the extremities of ladles or smaller objects of pottery.

Many handles of ladles made at Hano in late times are modeled in the form of the Paiakyamu,[1] a glutton priesthood peculiar to that Tanoan pueblo. From the data at hand we may legitimately conclude that the conception of the clown-priest is modern in Tusayan, so far as the ornamentation of pottery is concerned.

The large collections of so-called modern Hopi pottery in our museums is modified Tanoan ware, made in Tusayan. Most of the component specimens were made by Hano potters, who painted upon them figures of *katcinas*, a cult which they and their kindred introduced.

Several of the food bowls had evidently cracked during their firing or while in use, and had been mended before they were buried in the graves. This repairing was accomplished either by filling the crack with gum or by boring a hole on each side of the fracture for tying. In one specimen of black-and-white ware a perfectly round hole was made in the bottom, as if purposely to destroy the usefulness of the bowl before burial. This hole had been covered inside with a rounded disk of old pottery, neatly ground on the edge. It was not observed that any considerable number of mortuary pottery objects were "killed" before burial, although a large number were chipped on the edges. It is a great wonder that any of these fragile objects were found entire, the stones and soil covering the corpse evidently having been thrown into the grave without regard to care.

The majority of the ancient symbols are incomprehensible to the present Hopi priests whom I have been able to consult, although they are ready to suggest many interpretations, sometimes widely divergent. The only reasonable method that can be pursued in determining the meaning of the conventional signs with which the modern Tusayan Indians are unfamiliar seems, therefore, to be a comparative one. This method I have attempted to follow so far as possible.

There is a closer similarity between the symbolism of the Sikyatki pottery and that of the Awatobi ware than there is between the ceramics of either of these two pueblos and that of Walpi, and the same likewise may be said of the other Tusayan ruins so far as known. It is desirable, however, that excavations be made at the site of Old Walpi in order to determine, if possible, how widely different the ceramics of that village are from the towns whose ruins were studied in 1895. There are certain practical difficulties in regard to work at Old Walpi, one of the greatest of which is its proximity to modern

---

[1] These priests wear a close-fitting skullcap, with two long, banded horns made of leather, to the end of which corn husks are tied. For an extended description see *Journal of American Ethnology and Archæology*, vol. II, No. 1, page 11.

burial places and shrines still used. Moreover, it is probable—indeed, quite certain—that most of the portable objects were carried from the abandoned pueblo to the present village when the latter was founded; but the old cemeteries of Walpi contain many ancient mortuary bowls which, when exhumed, will doubtless contribute a most interesting chapter to the history of modern Tusayan decorative art.

One of the largest, and, so far as form goes, one of the most unique vessels, is shown in plate CXXVI, b. This was not exhumed from Sikyatki, but was said to have been found in the vicinity of that ruin. While the ware is very old, I do not believe it is ancient, and it is introduced in order to show how cleverly ancient patterns may be simulated by more modern potters. The sole way in which modern imitations of ancient vessels may be distinguished is by the peculiar crackled or crazed surface which the former always has. This is due, I believe, to the method of firing and the unequal contraction or expansion of the slip employed. All modern imitations are covered with a white slip which, after firing, becomes crackled, a characteristic unknown to ancient ware. The most expert modern potter at East Mesa is Nampéo, a Tanoan woman who is a thorough artist in her line of work. Finding a better market for ancient than for modern ware, she cleverly copies old decorations, and imitates the Sikyatki ware almost perfectly. She knows where the Sikyatki potters obtained their clay, and uses it in her work. Almost any Hopi who has a bowl to sell will say that it is ancient, and care must always be exercised in accepting such claims.

An examination of the ornamentation of the jar above referred to shows a series of birds drawn in the fashion common to early pottery decoration. This has led me to place this large vessel among the old ware, although the character of the pottery is different from that of the best examples found at Sikyatki. I believe this vessel was exhumed from a ruin of more modern date than Sikyatki. The woman who sold it to me has farming interests near Awatobi, which leads me to conjecture that she or possibly one of her ancestors found it at or near that ruin. She admitted that it had been in the possession of her family for some time, but that the story she had heard concerning it attributed its origin to Sikyatki.

HUMAN FIGURES

Very few figures of men or women are found on the pottery, and these are confined to the interior of food basins (plate CXXIX).[1] They are ordinarily very roughly drawn, apparently with less care and with much less detail than are the figures of animals. From their character I am led to the belief that the drawing of human figures on pottery was a late development in Tusayan art, and postdates the use of animal figures on their earthenware. There are, however, a few decora-

---

[1] The rarity of human figures on such kinds of pottery as are found in the oldest ruins would appear to indicate that decorations of this kind were a late development. No specimen of black-and-white ware on which pictures of human beings are present has yet been figured. The sequence of evolution in designs is believed to be (1) geometrical figures, (2) birds, (3) other animals, (4) human beings.

a   2/5

b   2/5

M.W.H.

DECORATED POTTERY FROM SIKYATKI

tions in which human figures appear, and these afford an interesting
although meager contribution to our knowledge of ancient Tusayan art
and custom.

As is well known, the Hopi maidens wear their hair in two whorls,
one over each ear, and that on their marriage it is tied in two coils
falling on the breast. The whorl is arranged on a U-shape stick called
a gñela; it is commonly done up by a sister, the mother, or some
friend of the maiden, and is stiffened with an oil pressed from squash
seeds. The curved stick is then withdrawn and the two puffs held in
place by a string tightly wound between them and the head. The
habit of dressing the hair in whorls is adopted after certain puberty
ceremonials, which have elsewhere been described. When on betrothal
a Hopi maid takes her gifts of finely ground cornmeal to the house of
her future mother-in-law, her hair is dressed in this fashion for the last
time, because on her return she is attacked by the women of the pueblo,
drawn hither and thither, her hair torn down, and her body smeared
with dirt. If her gifts are accepted she immediately becomes the wife
of her lover, and her hair is thenceforth dressed in the fashion common
to matrons.

The symbolic meaning of the whorls of hair worn by the maidens is
said to be the squash-flower, or, perhaps more accurately speaking, the
potential power of fructification. There is legendary and other evidence
that this custom is very ancient among the Tusayan Indians, and the
data obtainable from their ritual point the same way. In the personification of ancestral "breath-bodies," or spirits by men, called katcinas,
the female performers are termed katcina-manas (katcina-virgins), and
it is their custom to wear the hair in the characteristic coiffure of
maidens. In the personification of the Corn-maid by symbolic figures,
such as graven images,[1] pictures, and the like, in secret rites, the style
of coiffure worn by the maidens is common, as I have elsewhere shown
in the descriptions of the ceremonials known as the Flute, Lalakonti,
Mamzrauti, Palülükoñti, and others. The same symbol is found in
images used as dolls of Calako-mana, the equivalent, as the others, of
the same Corn-maid. From the nature of these images there can
hardly be a doubt of the great antiquity of this practice, and that it
has been brought down, through their ritual, to the present day. This
style of hair dressing was mentioned by the early Spanish explorers,
and is represented in pictographs of ancient date; but if all these evidences of its antiquity are insufficient the testimony afforded by the
pictures on certain food-basins from Sikyatki leaves no doubt on this
point.[2]

---

[1] In some of the figurines used in connection with modern Hopi altars these whorls are represented
by small wheels made of sticks radiating from a common juncture and connected by woolen yarn.

[2] The natives of Cibola, according to Castañeda, "gather their hair over the two ears, making a frame
which looks like an old-fashioned headdress." The Tusayan Pueblo maidens are the only Indians
who now dress their hair in this way, although the custom is still kept up by men in certain sacred
dances at Zuñi. The country women in Salamanca, Spain, do their hair up in two flat coils, one on
each side of the forehead, a custom which Castañeda may have had in mind when he compared the
Pueblo coiffure to an "old-fashioned headdress."

Plate cxxix, *b*, represents a food-basin, on the inside of which is drawn, in brown, the head and shoulders of a woman. On either side the hair is done up in coils which bear some likeness to the whorls worn by the present Hopi maidens. It must be borne in mind, however, that similar coils are sometimes made after ceremonial head-washing, and certain other rites, when the hair is tied with corn husks. The face is painted reddish, and the ears have square pendants similar to the turquois mosaics worn by Hopi women at the present day. Although there is other evidence than this of the use of square ear-pendants, set with mosaic, among the ancient people—and traditions point the same way—this figure of the head of a woman from Sikyatki leaves no doubt of the existence of this form of ornament in that ancient pueblo.

However indecisive the last-mentioned picture may be in regard to the coiffure of the ancient Sikyatki women, plate cxxix, *a*, affords still more conclusive evidence. This picture represents a woman of remarkable form which, from likenesses to figures at present made in sand on an altar in the *Lalakonti* ceremony,[1] I have no hesitation in ascribing to the Corn-maid. The head has the two whorls of hair very similar to those made in that rite on the picture of the Goddess of Germs, and the square body is likewise paralleled in the same figure. The peculiar form is employed to represent the outstretched blanket, a style of art which is common in Mayan codices.[2] On each lower corner representations of feathered strings, called in the modern ritual *nakwákwoci*,[3] are appended. The figure is represented as kneeling, and the four parallel lines are possibly comparable with the prayer-sticks placed in the belt of the Germ goddess on the *Lalakonti* altar. In her left hand (which, among the Hopi, is the ceremonial hand or that in which sacred objects are always carried) she holds an ear of corn, symbolic of germs, of which she is the deity. The many coincidences between this figure and that used in the ceremonials of the September moon, called *Lalakonti*, would seem to show that in both instances it was intended to represent the same mythic being.

There is, however, another aspect of this question which is of interest. In modern times there is a survival among the Hopi of the custom of decorating the inside of a food basin with a figure of the Corn-maid, and this is, therefore, a direct inheritance of ancient methods represented by the specimen under consideration. A large majority of modern food bowls are ornamented with an elaborate figure of Calako-mana, the Corn-maid, very elaborately worked out, but still retaining the essential symbolism figured in the Sikyatki bowl.[4]

---

[1] *American Anthropologist*, April, 1892.

[2] Troano and Cortesiano codices.

[3] A *nakwákwoci* is an individual prayer-string, and consists of one or more prescribed feathers tied to a cotton string. These prayer emblems are made in great numbers in every Tusayan ceremony.

[4] The evidence afforded by this bowl would seem to show that the cult of the Corn-maid was a part of the mythology and ritual of Sikyatki. The elaborate figures of the rain-cloud, which are so prominent in representations of the Corn-maid on modern plaques, bowls, and dolls, are not found in the Sikyatki picture.

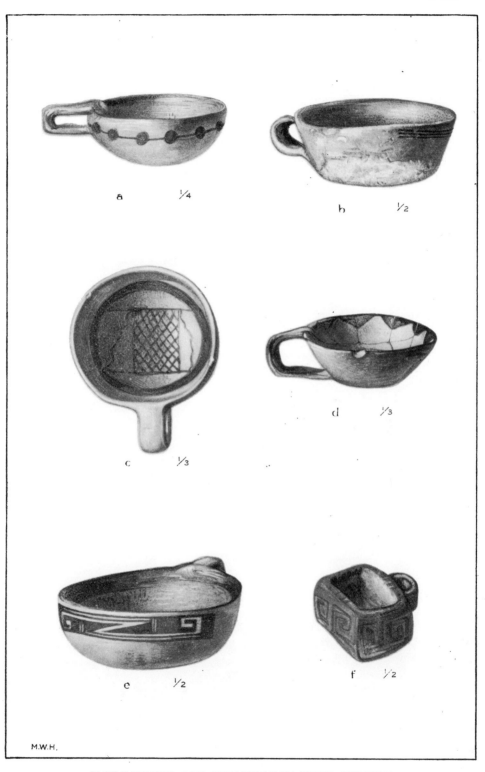

a   1/4

b   1/2

c   1/3

d   1/3

e   1/2

f   1/2

M.W.H.

FLAT DIPPERS AND MEDICINE BOX FROM SIKYATKI

While one of the two figures shown in plate CXXIX, *e*, is valuable as affording additional and corroborative evidence of the character of the ancient coiffure of the women, its main interest is of a somewhat different kind. Two figures are rudely drawn on the inside of the basin, one of which represents a woman, the other, judging from the character of the posterior extremity of the body, a reptilian conception in which a single foreleg is depicted, and the tail is articulated at the end, recalling a rattlesnake. Upon the head is a single feather;[1] the two eyes are represented on one side of the head, and the line of the alimentary tract is roughly drawn. The figure is represented as standing before that of the woman.

With these few lines the potter no doubt intended to depict one of those many legends, still current, of the cultus hero and heroine of her particular family or priesthood. Supposing the reptilian figure to be a totemic one, our minds naturally recall the legend of the Snake-hero and the Corn-mist-maid[2] whom he brought from a mythic land to dwell with his people.

The peculiar hairdress is likewise represented in the figures on the food basin illustrated in plate CXXIX, *c*, which represent a man and a woman Although the figures are partly obliterated, it can easily be deciphered that the latter figure wears a garment similar to the *kwaca* or dark-blue blanket for which Tusayan is still famous, and that this blanket was bound by a girdle, the ends of which hang from the woman's left hip. While the figure of the man is likewise indistinct (the vessel evidently having been long in use), the nature of the act in which he is engaged is not left in doubt.[3]

Among the numerous deities of the modern Hópi Olympus there is one called Kokopeli,[4] often represented in wooden dolls and clay images. From the obscurity of the symbolism, these dolls are never figured in works on Tusayan images. The figure in plate CXXIX, *d*, bears a resemblance to Kokopeli. It represents a man with arms raised in the act of dancing, and the head is destitute of hair as if covered by one of the peculiar helmets used by the clowns in modern ceremonials. As many of the acts of these priests may be regarded as obscene from our point of view, it is not improbable that this figure may represent an ancient member of this archaic priesthood.

---

[1] The reason for my belief that this is a breath feather will be shown under the discussion of feather and bird pictures.

[2] For the outline of this legend see *Journal of American Ethnology and Archæology*, vol. IV. The maid is there called the Tcüa-mana or Snake-maid, a sacerdotal society name for the Germ goddess. The same personage is alluded to under many different names, depending on the society, but they are all believed to refer to the same mythic concept.

[3] The attitude of the male and female here depicted was not regarded as obscene; on the contrary, to the ancient Sikyatki mind the picture had a deep religious meaning. In Hopi ideas the male is a symbol of active generative power, the female of passive reproduction, and representations of these two form essential elements of the ancient pictorial and graven art of that people.

[4] The doll of Kokopeli has a long, bird-like beak, generally a rosette on the side of the head, a hump on the back, and an enormous penis. It is a phallic deity, and appears in certain ceremonials which need not here be described. During the excavations at Sikyatki one of the Indians called my attention to a large Dipteran insect which he called "Kokopeli."

The three human figures on the food basin illustrated in plate CXXIX, *f*, are highly instructive as showing the antiquity of a curious and revolting practice almost extinct in Tusayan.

As an accompaniment of certain religious ceremonials among the Pueblo and the Navaho Indians, it was customary for certain priests to insert sticks into the esophagus. These sticks are still used to some extent and may be obtained by the collector. The ceremony of stick-swallowing has led to serious results, so that now in the decline of this cult a deceptive method is often adopted.

In Tusayan the stick-swallowing ceremony has been practically abandoned at the East Mesa, but I have been informed by reliable persons that it has not wholly been given up at Oraibi. The illustration above referred to indicates its former existence in Sikyatki. The middle figure represents the stick-swallower forcing the stick down his esophagus, while a second figure holds before him an unknown object. The principal performer is held by a third figure, an attendant, who stands behind him. This instructive pictograph thus illustrates the antiquity of this custom in Tusayan, and would seem to indicate that it was once a part of the Pueblo ritual.[1] It is possible that the Navaho, who have a similar practice, derived it from the Pueblos, but there are not enough data at hand to demonstrate this beyond question.

Regarding the pose of the three figures in this picture, I have been reminded by Dr Walter Hough of the performers who carry the wad of cornstalks in the Antelope dance. In this interpretation we have the "carrier," "hugger," and possibly an Antelope priest with the unknown object in his hand. This interpretation appears more likely to be a correct one than that which I have suggested; and yet Kopeli, the Snake chief, declares that the Snake family was not represented at Sikyatki. Possibly a dance similar to the Antelope performance on the eighth day of the Snake dance may have been celebrated at that pueblo, and the discovery of a rattlesnake's rattle in a Sikyatki grave is yet to be explained.

One of the most prominent of all the deities in the modern Tusayan Olympus is the cultus-hero called Püükoñhoya, the Little War God. Hopi mythology teems with legends of this god and his deeds in killing monsters and aiding the people in many ways. He is reputed to have been one of twins, children of the Sun and a maid by parthenogenetic conception. His adventures are told with many variants and he reappears with many aliases.

The symbolism of Püükoñhoya at the present day consists of parallel marks on the face or body, and when personated by a man the figure

---

[1]The practice still exists at Zuñi, I am told, and there is no sign of its becoming extinct. It is said that old Naiutci, the chief of the Priesthood of the Bow, was permanently injured during one of these performances. (Since the above lines were written I have excavated from one of the ruins on the Little Colorado a specimen of one of these objects used by ancient stick-swallowers. It is made of bone, and its use was explained to me by a reliable informant familiar with the practices of Oraibi and other villagers. It is my intention to figure and describe this ancient object in the account of the explorations of 1896.)

a   ½

b   ½

M.W.H.

DOUBLE-LOBE VASES FROM SIKYATKI

is always represented as carrying weapons of war, such as a bow and arrows. Images of the same hero are used in ceremonies, and are sometimes found as household gods or penates, which are fed as if human beings. A fragment of pottery represented in the accompanying illustration (figure 263), shows enough of the head of a personage to indicate that Püükoñhoya was intended, for it bears on the cheek the two parallel marks symbolic of that deity, while in his hands he holds a bow and a jointed arrow as if shooting an unknown animal. All of these features are in harmony with the identification of the figure with that of the cultus hero mentioned, and seem to indicate the truth of the current legend that as a mythologic conception he is of great antiquity in Tusayan.

In this connection it may be instructive to call attention to two figures on a food bowl collected by Mr H. R. Voth from a ruin near Oraibi. It represents a man and a woman, the former with two horns, a crescent on the forehead, and holding in his outstretched hand a staff. The woman has a curious gorget, similar to some which I have found in ruins near Tusayan, and a belt like those still worn by Pueblo Indians. This smaller figure likewise has a crescent on its face and three strange appendages on each side of the head.

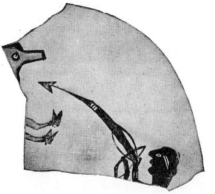

FIG. 263—War god shooting an animal. (Fragment of food bowl)

Another food basin in Mr Voth's collection is also instructive, and is different in its decoration from any which I have found. The character of the ware is ancient, but the figure is decidedly modern. If, however, it should prove to be an ancient vessel it would carry back to the time of its manufacture the existence of the *katcina* cult in Tusayan, no actual proof of the existence of which, at a time when Sikyatki was in its prime, has yet been discovered.

The three figures represent Hahaiwüqti, Hewüqti, and Natacka exactly as these supernatural beings are now personated at Walpi in the *Powamû*, as described and figured in a former memoir.[1]

It is unfortunate that the antiquity of this specimen, suggestive as it is, must be regarded as doubtful, for it was not exhumed from the ruin by an archeologist, and the exact locality in which it was found is not known.

---

[1] "Tusayan Katcinas," Fifteenth Annual Report of the Bureau of Ethnology, 1893-94, Washington, 1897. Hewüqti is also called Soyokmana, a Keresan Hopi name meaning the Natacka-maid. The Keresan (Sia) Skoyo are cannibal giants, according to Mrs Stevenson, an admirable definition of the Hopi Natackas.

The Human Hand

Excepting the figure of the maid's head above described, the human hand, for some unknown reason, is the only part of the body chosen by the ancient Hopi for representation in the decoration of their pottery. Among the present Tusayan Indians the human hand is rarely used, but oftentimes the beams of the kivas are marked by the girls who have plastered them with impressions of their muddy hands, and there is a *katcina* mask which has a hand painted in white on the face. As in the case of the decoration of all similar sacred paraphernalia, there is a legend which accounts for the origin of the *katcina* with the imprint of the hand on its mask. The following tale, collected by the late A. M. Stephen, from whose manuscript I quote, is interesting in this connection:

"The figure of a hand with extended fingers is very common, in the vicinity of ruins, as a rock etching, and is also frequently seen daubed on the rocks with colored pigments or white clay. These are vestiges of a test formerly practiced by the young men who aspired for admission to the fraternity of the Calako. The Calako is a trinity of two women and a man from whom the Hopi obtained the first corn, and of whom the following legend is told:

"In the early days, before houses were built, the earth was devastated by a whirlwind. There was then neither springs nor streams, although water was so near the surface that it could be found by pulling up a tuft of grass. The people had but little food, however, and they besought Masauwûh to help them, but he could not.

"There came a little old man, a dwarf, who said that he had two sisters who were the wives of Calako, and it might be well to petition them. So they prepared an altar, every man making a *paho*, and these were set in the ground so as to encircle a sand hillock, for this occurred before houses were known.

"Masauwûh's brother came and told them that when Calako came to the earth's surface wherever he placed his foot a deep chasm was made; then they brought to the altar a huge rock, on which Calako might stand, and they set it between the two pahos placed for his wives.

"Then the people got their rattles and stood around the altar, each man in front of his own paho; but they stood in silence, for they knew no song with which to invoke this strange god. They stood there for a long while, for they were afraid to begin the ceremonies until a young lad, selecting the largest rattle, began to shake it and sing. Presently a sound like rushing water was heard, but no water was seen; a sound also like great winds, but the air was perfectly still, and it was seen that the rock was pierced with a great hole through the center. The people were frightened and ran away, all save the young lad who had sung the invocation.

"The lad soon afterward rejoined them, and they saw that his back was cut and bleeding and covered with splinters of yucca and willow.

a   ⅜

b   ⅜

c   ⅜

d   ⅜

M.W.H.

UNUSUAL FORMS OF VASES FROM SIKYATKI

The flagellation, he told them, had been administered by Calako, who told him that he must endure this laceration before he could look upon the beings he had invoked; that only to those who passed through his ordeals could Calako become visible; and, as the lad had braved the test so well, he should thenceforth be chief of the Calako altar. The lad could not describe Calako, but said that his two wives were exceedingly beautiful and arrayed with all manner of fine garments. They wore great headdresses of clouds and every kind of corn which they were to give to the Hopi to plant for food. There were white, red, yellow, blue, black, blue-and-white speckled, and red-and-yellow speckled corn, and a seeded grass (*kwapi*).

" The lad returned to the altar and shook his rattle over the hole in the rock, and from its interior Calako conversed with him and gave him instructions. In accordance with these he gathered all the Hopi youths and brought them to the rock, that Calako might select certain of them to be his priests. The first test was that of putting their hands in the mud and impressing them upon the rock. Only those were chosen as novices the imprints of whose hands had dried on the instant.

" The selected youths then moved within the altar and underwent the test of flagellation. Calako lashed them with yucca and willow. Those who made no outcry were told to remain in the altar, to abstain from salt and flesh for ten days, when Calako would return and instruct them concerning the rites to be performed when they sought his aid.

"Calako and his two wives appeared at the appointed time, and after many ceremonials gave to each of the initiated five grains of each of the different kinds of corn. The Hopi women had been instructed to place baskets woven of grass at the foot of the rock, and in these Calako's wives placed the seeds of squashes, melons, beans, and all the other vegetables which the Hopi have since possessed.

" Calako and his wives, after announcing that they would again return, took off their masks and garments, and laying them on the rock disappeared within it.

" Some time after this, when the initiated were assembled in the altar, the Great Plumed Snake appeared to them and said that Calako could not return unless one of them was brave enough to take the mask and garments down into the hole and give them to him. They were all afraid, but the oldest man of the Hopi took them down and was deputed to return and represent Calako.

"Shortly afterward Masauwûh stole the paraphernalia, and with his two brothers masqueraded as Calako and his wives. This led the Hopi into great trouble, and they incurred the wrath of Muiyinwûh, who withered all their grain and corn.

"One of the Hopi finally discovered that the supposed Calako carried a cedar bough in his hand, when it should have been willow; then they knew that it was Masauwûh who had been misleading them.

"The boy hero one day found Masauwûh asleep, and so regained possession of the mask. Muiyinwûh then withdrew his punishments and sent Palülükoñ (the Plumed Snake) to tell the Hopi that Calako would never return to them, but that the boy hero should wear his mask and represent him, and his festival should be celebrated when they had a proper number of novices to be initiated." [1]

Several food basins from Sikyatki have a human hand depicted upon them, and in one of these both hands are represented. On the most perfect of these hand figures (plate CXXXVII, *c*) a wristlet is well represented, with two triangular figures, which impart to it an unusual form. From between the index and second finger there arises a triangular appendage, which joins a graceful curve, extending on one side to the base of the thumb and continued on the other side to the arm. The whole inside of the basin, except the figure of the hand and its appendage, is decorated with spattering,[2] and on the outside there is a second figure, evidently a hand or the paw of some animal. This external decoration also has a triangular figure in which are two terraces, recalling rain-cloud symbols.

One of the most interesting representations of the human hand (figure 354) is found on the exterior of a beautiful bowl. The four fingers and the thumb are shown with representations of nails, a unique feature in such decorations. From between the index finger and the next, or rather from the tip of the former, arises an appendage comparable with that before mentioned, but of much simpler form. The palm of the hand is crossed by a number of parallel lines, which recall a custom of using the palm lines in measuring ceremonial prayer sticks, as I have described in a memoir on the Snake dance. In place of the arm this hand has many parallel lines, the three medial ones being continued far beyond the others, as shown in the figure.

QUADRUPEDS

Figures of quadrupeds are sparingly used in the decoration of food bowls or basins, but the collection shows several fine specimens on which appear some of the mammalia with which the Hopi are familiar. Most of these are so well drawn that there appears to be no question as to their identification.

One of the most instructive of these figures is shown in plate CXXX, *a*, which is much worn, and indistinct in detail, although from what can be traced it was probably intended to represent a mythic creature known as the Giant Elk. The head bears two branched horns, drawn without perspective, and the neck has a number of short parallel marks similar to those occurring on the figure of an antelope on the

---

[1] The celebration occurs in the modern Tusayan pueblos in the *Powamû* where the representative of Calako flogs the children. Calako's picture is found on the *Powamû* altars of several of the villages of the Hopi.

[2] Figures of the human hand have been found on the walls of cliff houses. These were apparently made in somewhat the same way as that on the above bowl, the hand being placed on the surface and pigment spattered about it. See " The Cliff Ruins of Canyon de Chelly," by Cosmos Mindeleff; Sixteenth Annual Report, 1894–95.

a   3/4

b   3/4

c   3/8

d   2/3

e   2/3

f   2/3

g   2/3

M.W.H.

MEDICINE BOX AND PIGMENT POTS FROM SIKYATKI

walls of one of the kivas at Walpi. The hoofs are bifid, and from a short stunted tail there arises a curved line which encircles the whole figure, connecting a series of round spots and terminating in a triangular figure with three parallel lines representing feathers. Perhaps the strangest of all appendages to this animal is at the tail, which is forked, recalling the tail of certain birds. Its meaning is unknown to me.

There can be no doubt that the delineator sought to represent in this figure one of the numerous horned *Cervidæ* with which the ancient Hopi were familiar, but the drawing is so incomplete that to choose between the antelope, deer, and elk seems impossible. It may be mentioned, however, that the Horn people are reputed to have been early arrivals in Tusayan, and it is not improbable that representatives of the Horn clans lived in Sik-yatki previous to its overthrow.

Two faintly drawn animals, evidently intended for quadrupeds, appear on the interior of the food bowl shown in plate CXXX, *b*. These are interesting from the method in which they were drawn. They are not outlined with defined lines, but are of the original color of the bowl, and appear as two ghost-like figures surrounded by a dense spattering of red spots, similar in technic to the figure of the human hand. I am unable to identify these animals, but provisionally refer them to the rabbit. They have no distinctive symbolism, however, and are destitute of the characteristic spots which

FIG. 264—Mountain sheep

members of the Rabbit clan now invariably place on their totemic signatures.

The animal design on the bowl illustrated in plate CXXX, *c*, probably represents a rabbit or hare, quite well drawn in profile, with a feathered appendage from the head. Behind it is the ordinary symbol of the dragon-fly. Several crosses are found in an opposite hemisphere, separated from that occupied by the two animal pictures by a series of geometric figures ornamented with crooks and other designs.

The interior of the food bowl shown in plate CXXX, *d*, as well as the inner sides of the two ladles represented in plate CXXXI, *b*, *d*, are decorated with peculiar figures which suggest the porcupine. The body is crescentic and covered with spines, and only a single leg, with claws, is represented. It is worthy of mention that so many of these animal forms have only one leg, representative, no doubt, of a single pair, and that many of these have plantigrade paws like those of the bear and badger. The appendages to the head in this figure remind one of those of certain forms regarded as reptiles, with which this may be identical.

In another decoration we have what is apparently the same animal furnished with both fore and hind legs, the tail curving upward like that of a cottontail rabbit, which it resembles in other particulars as well. This figure also hangs by a band from a geometric design formed of two crescents and bearing four parallel marks representing

Fig. 265—Mountain lion

feathers. The single crescent depicted on the inside of the ladle shown in plate CXXXI, *b*, is believed to represent the same conception, or the moon; and in this connection the very close phonetic resemblance between the Hopi name for moon[1] and that for the mammal may be mentioned. In the decoration last described the same crescentic figure is elaborated into its zoömorphic equivalent.

_____

[1] *Mu'yi*, mole or gopher; *mu'iyawú*, moon. There may be some Hopi legend connecting the gopher with the moon, but thus far it has eluded my studies, and I can at present do no more than call attention to what appears to be an interesting etymological coincidence.

a

b

c

d

e

f

DESIGNS ON FOOD BOWLS FROM SIKYATKI

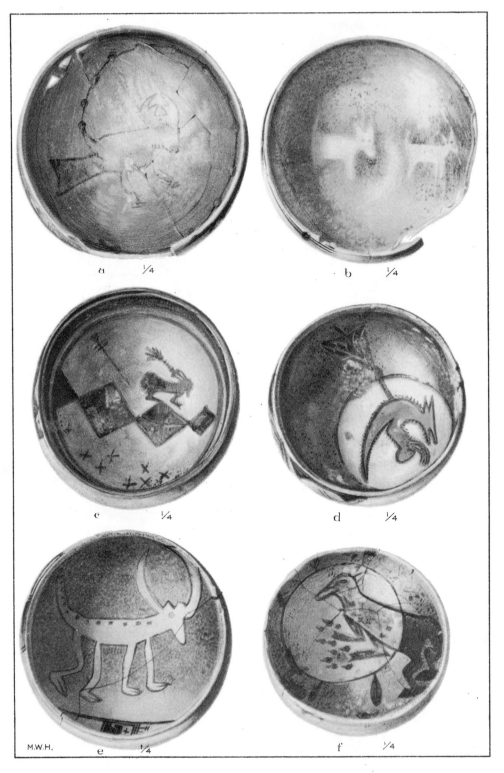

a   ¼   b   ¼

c   ¼   d   ¼

M.W.H.   e   ¼   f   ¼

FOOD BOWLS WITH FIGURES OF QUADRUPEDS FROM SIKYATKI

An enumeration of the pictographic representations of mammalia includes the beautiful food bowl shown in plate CXXX, *e*, which is made of fine clay spattered with brown pigment. This design (reproduced in figure 264) represents probably some ruminant, as the mountain sheep or possibly the antelope, both of which gave names to clans said to have resided at Sikyatki. The hoofs are characteristic, and the markings on the back suggest a fawn or spotted deer. There is a close similarity between the design below this animal and that of the exterior decorations of certain vases and square medicine bowls.

Among the pictures of quadrupedal animals depicted on ancient food bowls there is none more striking than that illustrated in plate CXXX, *f*, which has been identified as the mountain lion. While this identification is more or less problematical, it is highly possible. The claws of the forelegs (figure 265) are evidently those of one of the carnivora of the cat family, of which the mountain lion is the most prominent in Tusayan. The anterior part of the body is spotted; the posterior and the hind legs are black. The snout bears little resemblance to that of the puma.

The entire inner surface of the bowl, save a central circle in which the head, fore-limbs, and anterior part of the body are represented, is decorated by spattering. Within this spattered area there are highly interesting figures, prominent among which is a squatting figure of a man, with the hand raised to the mouth and holding a ceremonial cigarette, as if engaged in smoking. The seven patches in black might well be regarded as either footprints or leaves, four of which appear to be attached to the band-inclosing the central area. In the intervals between three of these there are branched bodies representing plants or bushes.

REPTILES

Snakes and other reptilian forms were represented by the ancient potters in the decoration of food bowls, and it is remarkable how closely some of these correspond in symbolism with conceptions still current in Tusayan. Of all reptilian monsters the worship of which forms a prominent element in Hopi ritual, that of the Great Plumed Snake is perhaps the most important. Effigies of this monster exist in all the larger Hopi villages, and they are used in at least two great rites—the *Soyaluña* in December and the *Palülükonti* in March, as I have already described. The symbolic markings and appendages of the Plumed Snake effigy are distinctive, and are found in all modern representations of this mystic being. While several pictographs of snakes are found on Sikyatki pottery, there is not a single instance in which these modern markings appear; consequently there is considerable doubt in regard to the identification of many of the Sikyatki serpents with modern mythologic representatives.

In questioning the priests in regard to the derivation of the Plumed Serpent cult in Tusayan, I have found that they declare that this cultus was brought into Tusayan from a mythic land in the south, called Palatkwabi, and that the effigies and fetiches pertaining to it were introduced by the Patki or Water-house people.   From good evidence, I suspect that the arrival of this phratry was comparatively late in Tusayan history, and it is possible that Sikyatki was destroyed before their advent, for in all the legends which I have been able to gather no one ascribes to Sikyatki any clan belonging to the phratries which are said to have migrated from the far south.   I believe we must look toward the east, whence the ancestors of the Kokop or

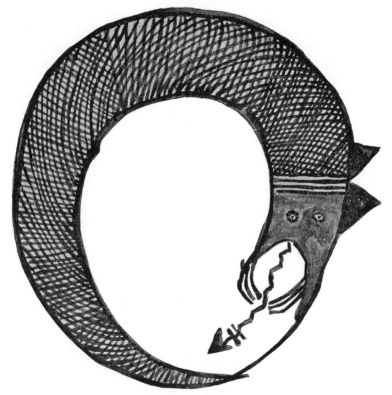

Fig. 266—Plumed serpent

Firewood people are reputed to have come, for the origin of the symbolic markings of the snakes represented on Sikyatki ceramics.   Figures of apodal reptiles, with feathers represented on their heads, occur in Sikyatki pictography, although there is no resemblance in the markings of their bodies to those of modern pictures.   One of the most striking of these occurs on the inside of the food basin shown in plate CXXXII, a.   It represents a serpent with curved body, the tail being connected with the head, like an ancient symbol of eternity.   The body (figure 266) is destitute of any distinctive markings, but is covered with a crosshatching of black lines.   The head bears two triangular markings, which are regarded as feather symbols. The position of the eyes would seem to indicate that the top of the head is represented, but this conclusion is not borne out by comparative studies, for it was often the custom of ancient Tusayan potters, like other primitive artists, to represent both eyes on one side of the head.

The zigzag line occupying the position of the tongue and terminating in a triangle is a lightning symbol, with which the serpent is still associated. While striving not to strain the symbolism of this figure, it is suggested that the three curved marks on the lower and upper jaws represent fangs. It is highly probable that conceptions not greatly unlike those which cluster about the Great Plumed Serpent were associated with this mythic snake, the figure of which is devoid of some of the most essential elements of modern symbolism.

While from the worn character of the middle of the food bowl illustrated in plate CXXXII, b, it is not possible to discover whether the animal was apodal or not from the crosshatching of the body and the resemblance of the appendages of the head to those of the figure last considered, it appears probable that this pictograph likewise was intended to represent a snake of mystic character. Like the previous figure, this also is coiled, with the tail near the head, its body crosshatched, and with two triangular appendages to the head. There is, however, but one eye, and the two jaws are elongated and provided with teeth,[1] as in the case of certain reptiles.

The similarity of the head and its appendages to the snake figure last described would lead me to regard the figure shown in plate CXXXII, c, as representing a like animal, but the latter picture is more elaborately worked out in details, and one of the legs is well represented. I have shown in the discussion of a former figure how the decorator, recognizing the existence of two eyes, represented them both on one side of the head of a profile figure, although only one is visible, and we see in this picture (figure 267) a somewhat similar tendency, which is very common in modern Tusayan figures of animals. The breath line is drawn from the extremity of the snout halfway down the length of the body. In modern pictography a representation of the heart is often depicted at the blind extremity of this line, as if, in fact, there was a connection with this organ and the tubes through which the breath passes. In the Sikyatki pottery, however, I find only this one specimen of drawing in which an attempt to represent internal organs is made.

The tail of this singular picture of a reptile is highly conventionalized, bearing appendages of unknown import, but recalling feathers, while on the back are other appendages which might be compared with wings. Both of these we might expect, considering the association of bird and serpent in the Hopi conception of the Plumed Snake.

---

[1] This form of mouth I have found in pictures of quadrupeds, birds, and insects, and is believed to be conventionalized. Of a somewhat similar structure are the mouths of the *Natacka* monsters which appear in the Walpi *Powamû* ceremony. See the memoir on "Tusayan Katcinas," in the Fifteenth Annual Report.

Exact identifications of these pictures with the animals by which the Hopi are or were surrounded, is, of course, impossible, for they are not realistic representations, but symbolic figures of mythic beings unknown save to the imagination of the primitive mythologist.

A similar reptile is pictured on the food bowl shown in plate CXXXII, *d*, in which design, however, there are important modifications, the most striking of which are: (1) The animal (figure 268) has both fore and hind legs represented; (2) the head is round; (3) the mouth is provided with teeth; and (4) there are four instead of two feather appendages

FIG. 267—Unknown reptile

on the head, two of which are much longer than the others. Were it not that ears are not represented in reptiles, one would be tempted to regard the smaller appendages as representations of these organs. Their similarity to the row of spines on the back and the existence of spines on the head of the "horned toad" suggests this reptile, with which both ancient and modern Hopi are very familiar. On a fragment of a vessel found at Awatobi there is depicted the head of a reptile evidently identical with this, since the drawing is an almost perfect reproduction. There is a like figure, also from Sikyatki, in the col-

ORNAMENTED LADLES FROM SIKYATKI

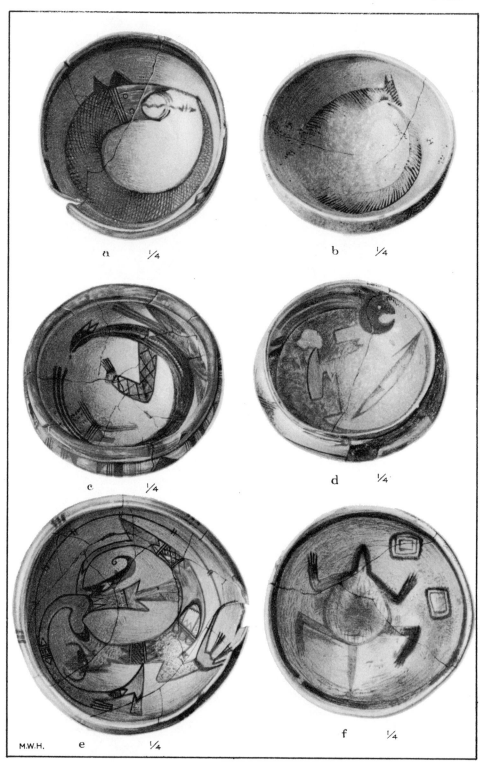

FOOD BOWLS WITH FIGURES OF REPTILES FROM SIKYATKI

lection of pottery made at that ruin by Dr Miller, of Prescott, the
year following my work there.   The most elaborate of all the pictures
of reptiles found on ancient Tusayan pottery is shown in plate CXXXII, *e*,
in which the symbolism is complicated and the details carefully worked
out.   A few of these symbols I am able to decipher; others elude present analysis.   There is no doubt as to the meaning of the appendage
to the head (figure 269), for it well portrays an elaborate feathered
headdress on which the markings that distinguish tail-feathers, three

FIG. 268—Unknown reptile

in number, are prominent.   The extension of the snout is without
homologue elsewhere in Hopi pictography, and, while decorative in
part, is likewise highly conventionalized.   On the body semicircular
rain cloud symbols and markings similar to those of the bodies of certain birds are distinguishable.   The feet likewise are more avian than
reptilian, but of a form quite unusual in structure.   It is interesting to
note the similarity in the curved line with six sets of parallel bars to
the band surrounding the figure of the human hand shown in plate
CXXXVII, *c*.   In attempting to identify the pictograph on the bowl repro-

duced in plate CXXXIV, *a*, there is little to guide me, and the nearest I can come to its significance is to ascribe it to a reptile of some kind. Highly symbolic, greatly conventionalized as this figure is, there is practically nothing on which to base the absolute identification of the figure save the serrated appendage to the body and the leg, which resembles that of the lizard as it is sometimes drawn. The two eyes indicate that the enlargement in which these were placed is the head,

FIG. 269—Unknown reptile

and the extended curved snout a beak. All else is incomprehensible to me, and my identification is therefore provisional and largely speculative.

I wish, however, in leaving the description of this beautiful bowl, to invite attention to the brilliancy and the characteristics of the coloring, which differ from the majority of the decorated ware from Sikyatki.

Among the fragments of pottery found in the Sikyatki graves there was one which, had it been entire, would doubtless have thrown considerable light on ancient pictography. This fragment has depicted

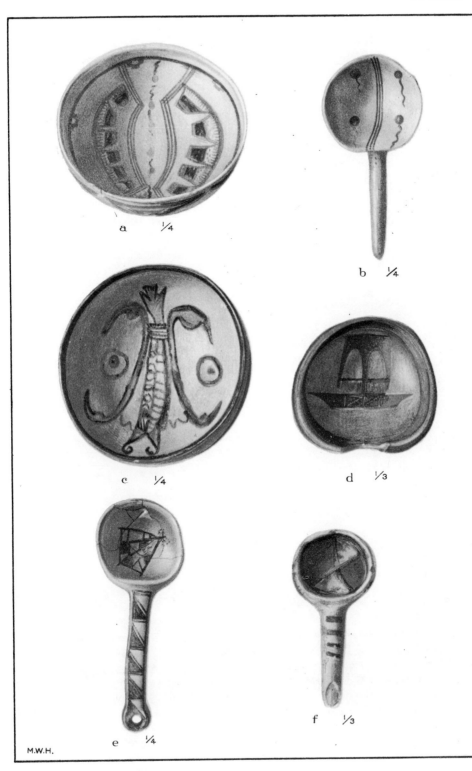

a   1/4

b   1/4

c   1/4

d   1/3

e   1/4

f   1/3

M.W.H.

BOWLS AND DIPPERS WITH FIGURES OF TADPOLES, BIRDS, ETC. FROM SIKYATKI

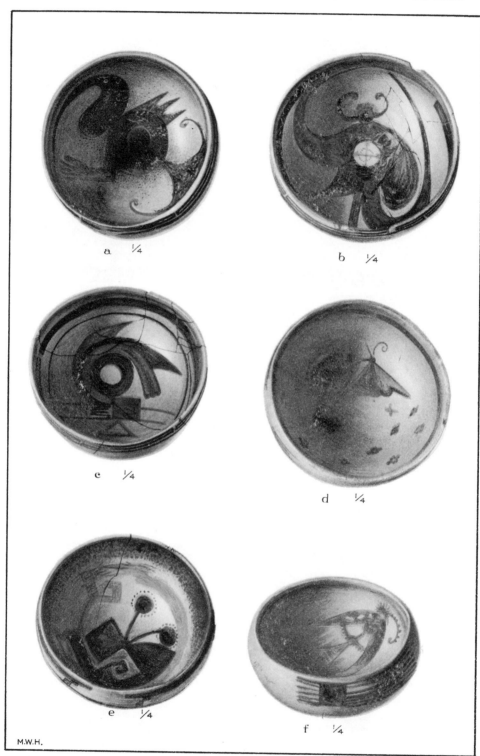

a ¼

b ¼

c ¼

d ¼

e ¼

f ¼

M.W.H.

FOOD BOWLS WITH FIGURES OF SUN, BUTTERFLY, AND FLOWER FROM SIKYATKI

upon it portions of the body and the whole head and neck of a reptilian animal. We find on that part of the body which is represented, three parallel marks which recall those on the modern pictures of the Great Plumed Serpent. On the back there were apparently the representations of wings, a feather of which is shown above the head. The head likewise bears a crest of three feathers, and there are three reptilian like toes. Whether this represents a reptile or a bird it is impossible for me to say, but enough has already been recorded to indicate how close the symbolism of these two groups sometimes is in ancient pictography. It would almost appear as if the profound anatomical discovery of the close kinship of birds and reptiles was unconsciously recognized by a people destitute of the rudiments of the knowledge of morphology.

TADPOLES

Among the inhabitants of an arid region, where rain-making forms a dominant element in their ritual, water animals are eagerly adopted as symbols. Among these the tadpole occupies a foremost position. The figures of this batrachian are very simple, and are among the most common of those used on ceremonial paraphernalia in Tusayan at the present time. In none of these is anything more than a globular head and a zigzag tail represented, and, as in nature, these are colored black. The tadpole appears on several pieces of painted pottery from Sikyatki, one of the best of which is the food bowl illustrated in plate CXXXIII, *a*. The design represents a number of these aquatic animals drawn in line across the diameter of the inner surface of the bowl, while on each side there is a row of rectangular blocks representing rain clouds. These blocks are separated from the tadpole figures by crescentic lines, and above them are short parallel lines recalling the symbol of falling rain.

One of the most beautiful forms of ladles from Sikyatki is figured in plate CXXXIII, *b*, a specimen in which the art of decoration by spattering is effectively displayed. The interior of the bowl of this dipper is divided by parallel lines into two zones, in each of which two tadpoles are represented. The handle is pointed at the end and is decorated. This specimen is considered one of the best from Sikyatki.

The rudely drawn picture on the bowl figured in plate CXXXII, *f*, would be identified as a frog, save for the presence of a tail which would seem to refer it to the lizard kind. But in the evolution of the tadpole into the frog a tailed stage persists in the metamorphosis after the legs develop. In modern pictures[1] of the frog with which I am familiar, this batrachian is always represented dorsally or ventrally with the legs outstretched, while in the lizards, as we have seen, a lateral view is always adopted. As the sole picture found on ancient

---

[1]Figures of the tadpole and frog are often found on modern medicine bowls in Tusayan. The snake, so common on Zuñi ceremonial pottery, has not been seen by me on a single object of earthenware in use in modern Hopi ritual.

pottery where the former method is employed, this fact may be of value in the identification of this rude outline as a frog rather than as a true reptile.

BUTTERFLIES OR MOTHS

One of the most characteristic modern decorations employed by the Hopi, especially as a symbol of fecundity, is the butterfly or moth. It is a constant device on the beautiful white or cotton blankets woven by the men as wedding gifts, where it is embroidered on the margin in the forms of triangles or even in more realistic patterns. This symbol is a simple triangle, which becomes quite realistic when a line is drawn bisecting one of the angles. This double triangle is not only a constant symbol on wedding blankets, but also is found on the dadoes of houses, resembling in design the arrangement of tiles in the Alhambra and other Moorish buildings. This custom of decorating the walls of a building with triangles placed at intervals on

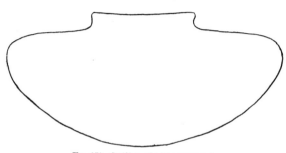

FIG. 270—Outline of plate CXXXV, b

the upper edge of a dado is a feature of cliff-house kivas, as shown in Nordenskiöld's beautiful memoir on the cliff villages of Mesa Verde. While an isosceles triangle represents the simplest form of the butterfly symbol, and is common on ancient pottery, a few vessels from Sikyatki show a much more realistic figure. In plate CXXXIV, f, is shown a moth with extended proboscis and articulated antennæ, and in d of the same plate another form, with the proboscis inserted in a flower, is given. As an associate with summer, the butterfly is regarded as a beneficent being aside from its fecundity, and one of the ancient Hopi clans regarded it as their totem. Perhaps the most striking, and I may say the most inexplicable, use of the symbol of the butterfly is the so-called *Hokona* or Butterfly virgin slab used in the Antelope ceremonies of the Snake dance at Walpi, where it is associated with the tadpole water symbol.

The most beautiful of all the butterfly designs are the six figures on the vase reproduced in plate CXXXV, b. From the number of these pictures it would seem that they bore some relationship to the six world-quarters—north, west, south, east, zenith, and nadir. The vase has a flattened shoulder, and the six butterfly figures are represented as flying toward the orifice. These insect figures closely resemble one another, and are divided into two groups readily distinguished by the symbolism of the heads. Three have each a cross with a single dot in

a   ½

b   ½

M.W.H.

VASES WITH FIGURES OF BUTTERFLIES FROM SIKYATKI

a   ⅓

b   ⅖

M.W.H.   d   ½

VASES WITH FIGURES OF BIRDS AND FEATHERS FROM SIKYATKI

each quadrant, and each of the other three has a dotted head without the cross. These two kinds alternate with each other, and the former probably indicate females, since the same symbols on the heads of the snakes in the sand picture of the Antelope altar in the Snake dance are used to designate the female.[1]

Two antennæ and a double curved proboscis are indicated in all the figures of butterflies on the vase under consideration. The zones above and below are both cut by a "line of life," the opening through which is situated on opposite equatorial poles in the upper and under rim.

FIG. 271—Butterfly design on upper surface of plate CXXXV, *b*

The rectangular figures associated with the butterflies on this elaborately decorated vase are of two patterns alternating with each other. The rectangles forming one of these patterns incloses three vertical feathers, with a triangle on the right side and a crook on the left. The remaining three rectangles also have three feathers, but they are arranged longitudinally on the surface of the vase.

---

[1] *Journal of American Ethnology and Archæology,* vol. IV.

The elaborate decoration of the zone outside the six butterflies is made up of feathers arranged in three clusters of three each, alternating with key patterns, crosshatched crooks, triangles, and frets. The wealth of ornament on this part of the vase is noteworthy, and its interpretation very baffling. This vase may well be considered the most elaborately decorated in the whole collection from Sikyatki.

There are several figures of butterflies, like those shown in plate CXXXI, a, in which the modifications of wings and body have proceeded still further, and the only features which refer them to insects are the jointed antennæ. The passage from this highly conventio alized design into a triangular figure is not very great. There are still others where the head, with attached appendages, arises not from an angle of a triangle, but from the middle of one side. This gives us a very common form of butterfly symbol, which is found, variously modified, on many ancient vessels. In such designs there is commonly a row of dots on each side, which may be represented by a sinuous line, a series of triangles, bars, or parallel bars.

The design reproduced in plate CXXXIV, d, represents a moth or butterfly associated with a flower, and several star symbols. It is evidently similar to that figured in a of the same plate, and has representations of antennæ and extended proboscis, the latter organ placed as if extracting honey from the flower. The conventional flower is likewise shown in e of this plate. The two crescentic designs in plate CXXXV, a, are regarded as butterflies.

The jar illustrated in plate CXLV, b, is ornamented with highly conventionalized figures on four sides, and is the only one taken from the Sikyatki cemeteries in which the designs are limited to the equatorial surface. The most striking figure, which is likewise found on the base of the paint saucer shown in plate CXLVI, f, is a diamond-shape design with a triangle at each corner (figure 276). The pictures drawn on alternating quadrants have very different forms, which are difficult to classify, and I have therefore provisionally associated this beautiful vessel with those bearing the butterfly and the triangle. The form of this vessel closely approaches that of the graceful cooking pots made of coiled and coarse indented ware, but the vessel was evidently not used for cooking purposes, as it bears no marks of soot.[1]

DRAGON-FLIES

Among the most constant designs used in the decoration of Sikyatki pottery are figures of the dragon-fly. These decorations consist of a line, sometimes enlarged into a bulb at one end, with two parallel bars drawn at right angles across the end, below the enlargement. Like the tadpole, the dragon-fly is a symbol of water, and with it are associated many legends connected with the miraculous sprouting of corn in early times. It is a constant symbol on modern ceremonial

---

[1] Although made of beautiful yellow ware, it shows at one point marks of having been overheated in firing, as is often the case with larger vases and jars.

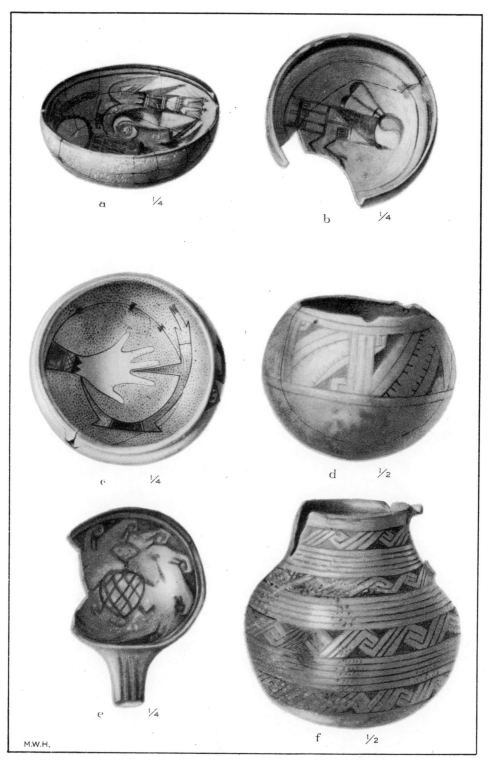

a   ¼

b   ¼

c   ¼

d   ½

e   ¼

f   ½

M.W.H.

VESSELS WITH FIGURES OF HUMAN HAND, BIRDS, TURTLE, ETC. FROM SIKYATKI

paraphernalia, as masks, tablets, and pahos, and it occurs also on several ancient vessels (plates CXL, *b*; CLXIII, *a*), where it always has the same simple linear form, with few essential modifications.

The symbols of four dragon-flies are well shown on the rim of the square box represented in plate CXXVIII, *a*. This box, which was probably for charm liquid, or possibly for feathers used in ceremonials, is unique in form and is one of the most beautiful specimens from the Sikyatki cemeteries. It is elaborately decorated on the four sides with rain-cloud and other symbols, and is painted in colors which retain their original brilliancy. The interior is not decorated.

The four dragon-flies on the rim of this object are placed in such a way as to represent insects flying about the box in a dextral circuit, or with the heads turned to the right. This position indicates a ceremonial circuit, which is exceptional among the Tusayan people, although common in Navaho ceremonies. In the sand picture of the Snake society, for instance, where four snakes are represented in a border surrounding a mountain lion, these reptiles are represented as crawling about the picture from right to left. This sequence is prescribed in Tusayan ceremonials, and has elsewhere been designated by me as the sinistral circuit, or a circuit with the center on the left hand. The circuit used by the decorator of this box is dextral or sunwise.

Several rectangular receptacles of earthenware, some with handles and others without them, were obtained in the excavations at Sikyatki. The variations in their forms may be seen in plates CXXVIII, *a, c*, and CXXV, *f*. These are regarded as medicine bowls, and are supposed to have been used in ancient ceremonials where asperging was performed. In many Tusayan ceremonials square medicine bowls, some of them without handles, are still used,[1] but a more common and evidently more modern variety are round and have handles. The rim of these modern sacred vessels commonly bears, in its four quadrants, terraced elevations representing rain-clouds of the cardinal points, and the outer surface of the bowl is decorated with the same symbols, accompanied with tadpole or dragon-fly designs.

One of the best figures of the dragon-fly is seen on the saucer shown in plate CXX, *f*. The exterior of this vessel is decorated with four rectangular terraced rain-cloud symbols, one in each quadrant, and within each there are three well-drawn figures of the dragon-fly. The curved line below represents a rainbow. The terrace form of rain-cloud symbol is very ancient in Tusayan and antedates the well-known semicircular symbol which was introduced into the country by the Patki people. It is still preserved in the form of tablets[2] worn on

---

[1] One of the best examples of the rectangular or ancient type of medicine bowl is used in the celebration of the Snake dance at Oraibi, where it stands on the rear margin of the altar of the Antelope priesthood of that pueblo.

[2] One of the best of these is that of the Humis-katcina, but good examples occur on the dolls of the Calakomanas. The Lakone maid, however, wears a coronet of circular rain-cloud symbols, which corresponds with traditions which recount that this form was introduced by the southern clans or the Patki people.

the head and in sand paintings and various other decorations on altars and religious paraphernalia.

BIRDS

The bird and the feather far exceed all other motives in the decoration of ancient Tusayan pottery, and the former design was probably the first animal figure employed for that purpose when the art passed out of the stage where simple geometric designs were used exclusively. A somewhat similar predominance is found in the part which the bird and the feather play in the modern Hopi ceremonial system. As one of the oldest elements in the decoration of Tusayan ceramics, figures of birds have in many instances become highly conventionalized; so much so, in fact, that their avian form has been lost, and it is one of the most instructive problems in the study of Hopi decoration to trace the modifications of these designs from the realistic to the more conventionalized. The large series of food bowls from Sikyatki afford abundant material for that purpose, and it may incidentally be said that by this study I have been able to interpret the meaning of certain decorations on Sikyatki bowls of which the best Hopi traditionalists are ignorant.[1] In order to show the method of reasoning in this case I have taken a series illustrating the general form of an unknown bird.

There can be no reasonable doubt that the decoration of the food basin shown in plate CXXXVII, a, represents a bird, and analogy would indicate that it is the picture of some mythologic personage. It has a round head (figure 272), to which is attached a headdress, which we shall later show is a highly modified feather ornament. On each side of the body from the region of the neck there arise organs which are undoubtedly wings, with feathers continued into arrowpoints. The details of these wings are very carefully and, I may add, prescriptively worked out, so that almost every line, curve, or zigzag is important. The tail is composed of three large feathers, which project beyond two triangular extensions, marking the end of the body.

The technic of this figure is exceedingly complicated and the colors very beautiful. Although this bowl was quite badly broken when exhumed, it has been so cleverly mended by Mr Henry Walther that no part of the symbolism is lost.

While it is quite apparent that this figure represents a bird, and while this identification is confirmed by Hopi testimony, it is far from a realistic picture of any known bird with which the ancients could have been familiar. It is highly conventionalized and idealized with significant symbolism, which is highly suggestive.

---

[1] In the evolution of ornament among the Hopi, as among most primitive peoples where new designs have replaced the old, the meaning of the ancient symbols has been lost. Consequently we are forced to adopt comparative methods to decipher them. If, for instance, on a fragment of ancient pottery we find the figure of a bird in which the wing or tail feathers have a certain characteristic symbol form, we are justified, when we find the same symbolic design on another fragment where the rest of the bird is wanting, in considering the figure that of a wing or tail feather. So when the prescribed figure of the feather has been replaced by another form it is not surprising to find it incomprehensible to modern shamans. The comparative ethnologist may in this way learn the meanings of symbols to which the modern Hopi priest can furnish no clue.

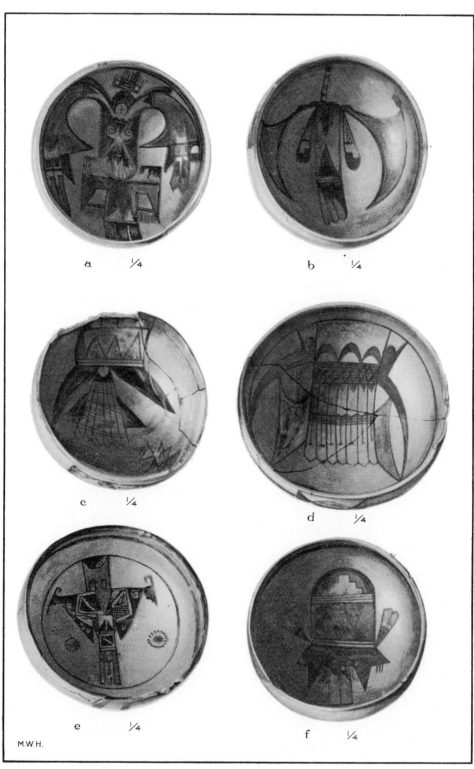

FOOD BOWLS WITH FIGURES OF BIRDS FROM SIKYATKI

Bearing in mind the picture of this bird, we pass to a second form (plate CXXXVIII, *a*), in which we can trace the same parts without difficulty. On a round head is placed a feathered headdress. The different parts of the outstretched wings are readily homologized even in details in the two figures. There are, for instance, two terminal wing feathers in each wing; the appendages to the shoulder exist in both, and the lateral spurs, exteriorly and interiorly, are represented with slight modifications.

FIG. 272—Man-eagle

The body is ornamented in the same way in both figures. It is continued posteriorly on each side into triangular extensions, and the same is true of its anterior, which in one figure has three curved lines, and in the other a simple crook. There are three tail-feathers in each figure. I believe there can be no doubt that both these designs represent the same idea, and that a mythologic bird was intended in each instance.

The step in conventionalism from the last-mentioned figure of a bird to the next (plate CXLVII, *a*) is even greater than in the former. The head in this picture is square or rectangular, and the wings likewise simple, ending in three incurved triangles without appendages. The tail has five feathers instead of three, in which, however, the same symbolic markings which distinguish tail-feathers are indicated.

The conventionalized wings of this figure are repeated again and again in ancient Tusayan pottery decorations, as one may see by an examination of the various birds shown in the plates. In many instances, however, all the other parts of the bird are lost and nothing but the triangular feathers remain; but as these have the same form, whatever organs are missing, the presumption is that their meaning has not changed.

In passing to the figure of the bird shown in plate CXXXVIII, b, we find features homologous with those already considered, but also detect considerable modification. The head is elongated, tipped with three parallel lines, but decorated with markings similar to those of the preceding figure. The outstretched wings have a crescentic form, on the anterior horn of which are round spots with parallel lines arising from them. This is a favorite figure in pottery decoration, and is found very abundantly on the exterior of food bowls; it represents highly conventionalized feathers, and should be so interpreted wherever found. The figure of the body of the bird depicted is simple, and the tail is continued into three tail-feathers, as is ordinarily the case in highly conventionalized bird figures.

The most instructive of all the appendages to the body are the club-shape bodies, one on each side, rising from the point of union of the wings and the breast. These are spatulate in form, with a terraced terminal marking. They, like other appendages, represent feathers, but that peculiar kind which is found under the wing is called the breath feather.[1] This feather is still used in certain ceremonials, and is tied to certain prayer offerings. Its ancient symbolism is very clearly indicated in this picture, and is markedly different from that of either the wing or tail feathers, which have a totally different ceremonial use at the present time.

For convenience of comparison, a number of pictures which undoubtedly refer to different birds in ancient interpretations will be grouped in a single series.

Plate CXXXVIII, d, represents a figure of a bird showing great relative modification of organs when compared with those previously discussed. The head is very much broadened, but the semicircular markings, which occur also on the heads of previously described bird figures, are well drawn. The wings are mere curved appendages, destitute of feather symbols, but are provided with lateral spurs and have knobs at their

---

[1] In an examination of many figures of ancient vessels where this peculiar design occurs it will be found that in all instances they represent feathers, although the remainder of the bird is not to be found. The same may also be said of the design which represents the tail-feathers. This way of representing feathers is not without modern survival, for it may still be seen in many dolls of mystic personages who are reputed to have worn feathered garments.

a   ¼

b   ¼

c   ¼

d   ¼

e   ¼

f   ¼

M.W.H.

FOOD BOWLS WITH FIGURES OF BIRDS FROM SIKYATKI

bases. The body is rectangular; the tail-feathers are numerous, with well-marked symbolism. Perhaps the most striking appendages to the body are the two well-defined extensions of parts of the body itself, which, although represented in other pictures of birds, nowhere reach such relatively large size.

The figure of a bird shown in plate CXXXVIII, c, is similar in many respects to that last described. The semicircular markings on the head of the former are here replaced by triangles, but both are symbolic of rain-clouds. The wings are curved projections, without any suggestion of feathers or basal spurs and knobs. The tail-feathers show nothing exceptional, and the body is bounded posteriorly by triangular extensions, as in figures of birds already described.

The representation of the bird in plate CXXXVIII, e, has a triangular body continued into two points on the posterior end, between which the tail-feathers are situated. The body is covered with terraced and triangular designs, and the head is rectangular in form. On each side of the bird figure there is a symbol of a flower, possibly the sunflower or an aster.

In the figures of birds already considered the relative sizes of the heads and bodies are not overdrawn, but in the picture of a bird on the food bowl shown in plate CXXXVIII, f, the head is very much enlarged. It bears a well-marked terraced rain-cloud symbol above triangles of the same meaning. The wings are represented as diminutive appendages, each consisting of two feathers. The body has a triangular extension on each side, and the tail is composed of two comparatively short rectangular feathers. The figure itself could hardly be identified as a representation of a bird were it not for the correspondence, part for part, with figures which are undoubtedly those of birds or flying animals.

A more highly conventionalized figure of a bird than any thus far described is painted on the food bowl reproduced in plate CXL, b. The head is represented by a terraced figure similar to those which appear as decorations on some of the other vessels; the wings are simply extended crescents, the tips of which are connected by a band which encircles the body and tail; the body is continued at the posterior end into two triangular appendages, between which is a tail, the feathers of which are not differentiated. On each side of the body, in the space inclosed by the band connecting the tips of the wings, a figure of a dragon-fly appears.

The figure on the food bowl illustrated in plate CXXXIX, c, may also be reduced to a conventionalized bird symbol. The two pointed objects on the lower rim represent tail-feathers, and the triangular appendages, one on each side above them, the body, as in the designs which have already been described. Above the triangles is a rectangular figure with terraced rain-cloud emblems, a constant feature on the body and head of the bird, and on each side, near the rim of the bowl, occur the primary feathers of the wings. The cross, so frequently associated with designs representing birds, is replaced by the triple intersecting lines in the remaining area. The resemblance of this figure to those already considered is clearly evident after a little study.

The decoration on the food basin presented in plate CXXXIX, *a*, is interesting in the study of the evolution of bird designs into conventional forms. In this figure those parts which are identified as homologues of the wings extend wholly across the interior of the food bowl, and have the forms of triangles with smaller triangular spurs at their bases. The wings are extended at right angles to the axis of the body, and taper uniformly to the rim of the bowl. The smaller spurs near the union of the wings and body represent the posterior part of the latter, and between them are the tail-feathers, their number being indicated by three triangles.

There is no representation of a head, although the terraced rain-cloud figure is drawn on the anterior of the body between the wings.

The reduction of the triangular wings of the last figure to a simple band drawn diametrically across the inner surface of the bowl is accomplished in the design shown in plate CXXXIX, *b*. At intervals along this line there are arranged groups of blocks, three in each group, representing stars, as will later be shown. The semicircular head has lost all appendages and is reduced to a rain-cloud symbol. The posterior angles of the body are much prolonged, and the tail still bears the markings representing three tail-feathers.

The association of a cross with the bird figure is both appropriate and common; its modified form in this decoration is not exceptional, but why it is appended to the wings is not wholly clear. We shall see its reappearance on other bowls decorated with more highly conventionalized bird figures.

In the peculiar decoration used in the treatment of the food bowl shown in plate CXXXIX, *c*, we have almost a return to geometric figures in a conventional representation of a bird. In this case the semblance to wings is wholly lost in the line drawn diametrically across the interior of the bowl. On one side of it there are many crosses representing stars, and on the other the body and tail of a bird. The posterior triangular extensions of the former are continued to a bounding line of the bowl, and no attempt is made to represent feathers in the tail. The rectangular figure, with serrated lower edge and inclosed terraced figures, finds, however, a homologue in the heads and bodies of most of the representations of birds which have been described.

This gradual reduction in semblance to a bird has gone still further in the figure represented in plate CXXXIX, *d*, where the posterior end of the body is represented by two spurs, and the tail by three feathers, the triangular rain-clouds still persisting in the rectangular body. In fact, it can hardly be seen how a more conventionalized figure of a bird were possible did we not find in *e* of the same plate this reduction still greater. Here the tail is represented by three parallel lines, the

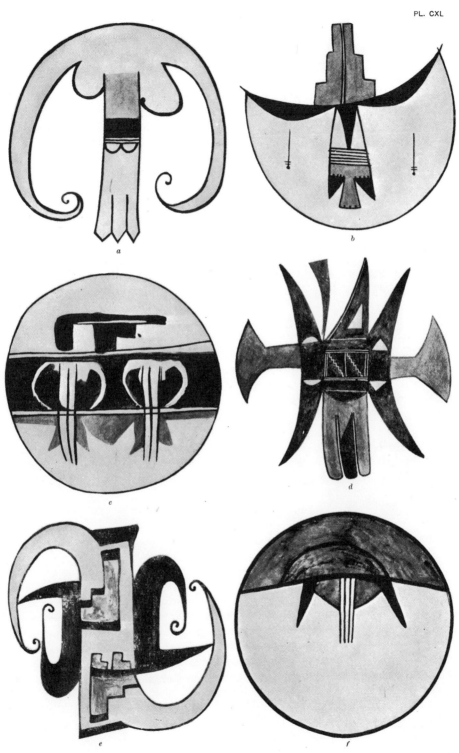

FIGURES OF BIRDS FROM SIKYATKI

posterior of the body by two dentate appendages, and the body itself by a square.

In plate CXL, c, we have a similar conventional bird symbol where two birds, instead of one, are represented. In both these instances it would appear that the diametric band, originally homologous to wings, had lost its former significance.

It must also be pointed out that there is a close likeness between some of these so-called conventionalized figures of birds and those of moths or butterflies. If, for instance, they are compared with the figures of the six designs of the upper surface of the vase shown in plate CXXXV, b, we note especially this resemblance. While, therefore, it can hardly be said there is absolute proof that these highly conventionalized figures always represent birds, we may, I think, be sure that either the bird or the moth or butterfly is generally intended.

There are several modifications of these highly conventionalized figures of birds which may be mentioned, one of the most interesting of which is figured in plate CXXXIX, f. In this representation the two posterior triangular extensions of the body are modified into graceful curves, and the tail-feathers are simply parallel lines. The figure in this instance is little more than a trifid appendage to a broad band across the inner surface of the food bowl. In addition to this highly conventionalized bird figure, however, there are two crosses which represent stars. In this decoration all resemblance to a bird is lost, and it is only by following the reduction of parts that one is able to identify this geometric design with the more elaborate pictures of mythic birds. When questioned in regard to the meaning of this symbol, the best informed Hopi priests had no suggestion to offer.

In all the figures of birds thus far considered, the head, with one or two exceptions, is represented or indicated by symbolic markings. In that which decorates the vessel shown in plate CXL, a, we find a new modification; the wings, instead of being attenuated into a diametric line or band, are in this case curved to form a loose spiral. Between them is the figure of a body and the three tail-feathers, while the triangular extensions which generally indicate the posterior of the body are simply two rounded knobs at the point of union of the wings and tail. There is no indication of a head.

The modifications in the figure of the bird shown in the last mentioned pictograph, and the highly conventionalized forms which the wings and other parts assume, give me confidence to venture an interpretation of a strange figure shown in plate CXLI, a. This picture I regard as a representation of a bird, and I do so for the following resemblances to figures already studied. The head of the bird, as has been shown, is often replaced by a terraced rain-cloud symbol. Such a figure occurs in the pictograph under consideration, where it occupies the position of the head. On either side of what might be regarded as a body we find, at the anterior end, two curved appendages which so closely resemble similarly placed bodies in the pictograph last discussed that they are regarded as representations of wings. These extensions at the posterior end of the body are readily comparable with prolongations in that part on which we have already commented. The tail, although different from that in figures of birds thus far discussed, has many points of resemblance to them. The two circles, one on each side of the bird figure, are important additions which are treated in following pages.[1]

From the study of the conventionalized forms of birds which I have outlined above it is possible to venture the suggestion that the star-shape figure shown in plate CLXVII, *b*, may be referred to the same group, but in this specimen we appear to have duplication, or a representation of the bird symbol repeated in both semicircles of the interior of the bowl. Examining one of these we readily detect the two tail-feathers in the middle, with the triangular end of the body on each side. The lateral appendages duplicated on each side correspond with the band across the middle of the bowl in other specimens, and represent highly conventionalized wings. The middle of this compound figure is decorated with a cross, and in each quadrant there is a row of the same emblems, equidistant from one another.

It would be but a short step from this figure to the ancient sun symbol with which the eagle and other raptorial birds are intimately associated. The figure represented in plate CXXXIII, *c*, is a symbolic bird in which the different parts are directly comparable with the other bird pictographs already described. One may easily detect in it the two wings, the semicircular rain-cloud figures, and the three tail-feathers. As in the picture last considered, we see the two circles, each with a concentric smaller circle, one on each side of the mythic bird represented. Similar circular figures are likewise found in the zone surrounding the centrally placed bird picture.

In the food bowl illustrated in plate CXLI, *b*, we find the two circles shown, and between them a rectangular pictograph the meaning of which is not clear. The only suggestion which I have in regard to the significance of this object is that it is an example of substitution—the substitution of a prayer offering to the mythic bird represented in the other bowls for a figure of the bird itself. This interpretation, however, is highly speculative, and should be accepted only with limitations. I have sometimes thought that the prayer-stick or paho may originally have represented a bird, and the use of it is an instance of the substitution[2] of a symbolic effigy of a bird, a direct survival of the time when a bird was sacrificed to the deity addressed.

At the present time the circle is the totemic signature of the Earth people, representing the horizon, but it has likewise various other meanings. With certain appendages it is the disk of the sun, and there are ceremonial paraphernalia, as amulets, placed on sand pictures or tied to helmets, which may be represented by a simple ring. The meaning of these circles in the bowl referred to above is not clear to me, nor is my series of pictographs sufficiently extensive to enable a discovery of its significance by comparative methods. A ring of meal sometimes drawn on the floor of a kiva is called a "house," and a little imagination would easily identify these with the mythic houses of the sky-bird, but this interpretation is at present only fanciful.

[2] The *paho* is probably a substitution of a sacrifice of corn or meal given as homage to the god addressed.

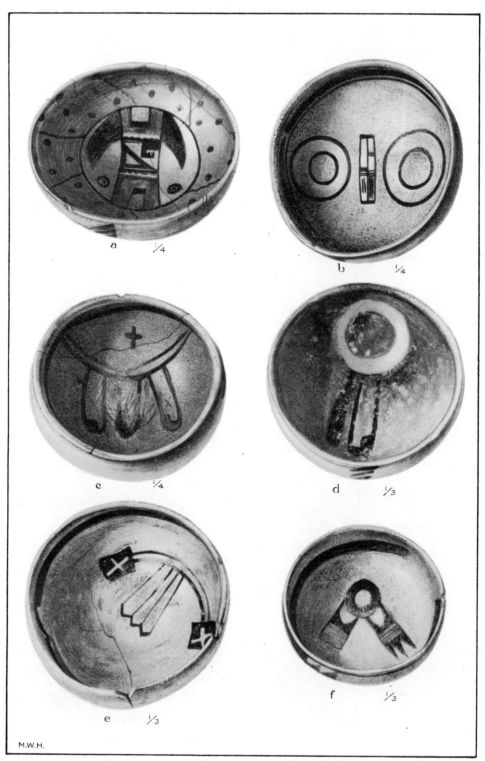

FOOD BOWLS WITH FIGURES OF BIRDS AND FEATHERS FROM SIKYATKI

a

d

e

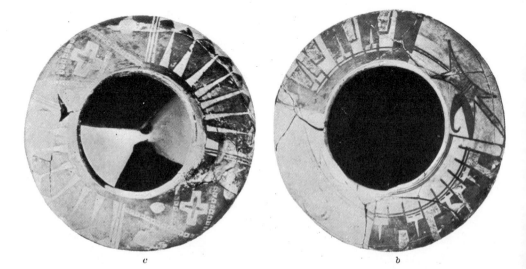

c

b

VASES, BOWL, AND LADLE, WITH FIGURES OF FEATHERS, FROM SIKYATKI

The studies of the conventional bird figures which are developed in the preceding pages make it possible to interpret one of the two pictures on the food bowl represented in plate CLII, while the realistic character of the smaller figure leaves no question that we can rightly identify this also as a bird. In the larger figure the wings are of unequal size and are tipped with appendages of a more or less decorative nature. The posterior part of the body is formed of two triangular extensions, to which feathers are suspended, and the tail is composed of three large pointed feathers. The head bears the terraced rain-cloud designs almost universal in pictographs of birds.

It is hardly necessary for me to indicate the head, body, wings, and legs of the smaller figure, for they are evidently avian, while the character of the beak would indicate that a parrot or raptorial genus was intended. The same beak is found in the decoration of a vase with a bird design, which will later be considered.

From an examination of the various figures of birds on the Sikyatki pottery, and an analysis of the appendages to the wings, body, and legs, it is possible to determine the symbolic markings characteristic of two different kinds of feathers, the large wing or tail feathers and the so-called breath or body feathers. There is therefore no hesitation, when we find an object of pottery ornamented with these symbols, in interpreting them as feathers. Such a bowl is that shown in plate CXLI, c, in which we find a curved line to which are appended three breast feathers. This curved band from which they hang may take the form of a circle with two pendent feathers as in plate CXLI, d.

In the design on the bowl figured in plate CXLI, e, tail-feathers hang from a curved band, at each extremity of which is a square design in which the cross is represented. It has been suggested that this represents the feathered rainbow, a peculiar conception of both the Pueblo and the Navaho Indians. The design appearing on the small food bowl represented in plate CXLI, f, is no doubt connected in some way with that last mentioned, although the likeness between the appendages to the ring and feathers is remote. It is one of those conventionalized pictures, the interpretation of which, with the scanty data at hand, must be largely theoretical.

Figures of feathers are most important features in the decoration of ancient Sikyatki pottery, and their many modifications may readily be seen by an examination of the plates. In modern Tusayan ceremonials the feather is appended to almost all the different objects used in worship; it is essential in the structure of the *tiponi* or badge of the chief, without which no elaborate ceremony can be performed or altar erected; it adorns the images on the altars, decorates the heads of participants, is prescribed for the prayer-sticks, and is always appended to aspergills, rattles, and whistles.

In the performance of certain ceremonials water from sacred springs is used, and this water, sometimes brought from great distances, is

kept in small gourd or clay vases, around the necks of which a string
with attached feathers is tied.   Such a vase is the so-called *patne* which
has been described in a memoir on the Snake ceremonies at Walpi.[1]
The artistic tendency of the ancient people of Sikyatki apparently
exhibited itself in painting these feathers on the outside of similar
small vases.   Plate CXLII, *a*, shows one of these vessels, decorated with
an elaborate design with four breath-feathers suspended from the equator.   (See also figure 273.)   On the vases shown in plate CXLII, *b, c*, are
found figures of tail feathers arranged in two groups on opposite sides
of the rim or orifice.   One of these groups has eight, the other seven,
figures of these feathers, and on the two remaining quadrants are the
star emblems so constantly seen in pottery decorated with bird figures.
The upper surface of the vase (figure 274) shows a similar arrangement, although the feathers here are conventionalized into triangular
dentations, seven on
one side and three on
the other, individual
dentations alternating
with rectangular de-
signs which suggest
rain-clouds. This vase
(plate CXLIII, *a, b*) is
also striking in having
a well-drawn figure of
a bird in profile, the
head, wings, tail, and
legs suggesting a par-
rot. The zone of dec-
oration of this vessel,
which surrounds the

FIG. 273—Pendent feather ornaments on a vase.

rows of feathers, is strikingly complicated, and comprises rain-cloud,
feather, and other designs.

In a discussion of the significance of the design on the food bowl
represented in plate CXXXIX, *a, b*, I have shown ample reason for regarding it a figure of a highly conventionalized bird.   On the upper surface
of the vase (plate CXLIV, *a, b*) are four similar designs, representing
birds of the four cardinal points, one on each quadrant.   The wings are
represented by triangular extensions, destitute of appendages but with
a rounded body at their point of juncture with the trunk.   Each bird
has four tail-feathers and rain-cloud symbols on the anterior end of the
body.   As is the case with the figures on the food basins, there are
crosses representing stars near the extended wings.   A broad band
connects all these birds, and terraced rain-cloud symbols, six in num-

---

[1] *Journal of American Ethnology and Archæology*, vol. IV.   These water gourds figure conspicuously
in many ceremonies of the Tusayan ritual.   The two girls personating the Corn-maids carry them in
the Flute observance, and each of the Antelope priests at Oraibi bears one of these in the Antelope or
Corn dance.

a   ⅓

b   ⅓

M.W.H.

VASE WITH FIGURES OF BIRDS FROM SIKYATKI

a ⁵/₁₈

b ⅓

M.W.H.

VASE WITH FIGURES OF BIRDS FROM SIKYATKI

a 1/2

b 1/2

M.W.H.

VASES WITH FIGURES OF BIRDS FROM SIKYATKI

ber and arranged in pairs, fill the peripheral sections between them. This vase, although broken, is one of the most beautiful and instructive in the rich collection of Sikyatki ceramics.

I have not ventured, in the consideration of the manifold pictures of birds on ancient pottery, to offer an interpretation of their probable generic identification. There is no doubt, however, that they represent mythic conceptions, and are emblematic of birds which figured conspicuously in the ancient Hopi Olympus. The modern legends of Tusayan are replete with references to such bird-like beings which play

Fig. 274—Upper surface of vase with bird decoration

important rôles and which bear evidence of archaic origins. There is, however, one fragment of a food bowl which is adorned with a pictograph so realistic and so true to modern legends of a harpy that I have not hesitated to affix to it the name current in modern Tusayan folklore. This fragment is shown in figure 275.

According to modern folklore there once lived in the sky a winged being called Kwataka, or Man-eagle, who sorely troubled the ancients. He was ultimately slain by their War god, the legends of which have elsewhere been published. There is a pictograph of this monster near

Walpi,[1] and pictures of him, as he exists in modern conceptions, have been drawn for me by the priests. These agree so closely with the picto-graph and with the representation on the potsherd from Sikyatki, that I regard it well-nigh proven that they represent the same personage. The head is round and bears two feathers, while the star emblem appears in the eye. The wing and the stump of a tail are well repre-

FIG. 275—Kwataka eating an animal

sented, while the leg has three talons, which can only be those of this monster. He holds in his grasp some animal form which he is repre-sented as eating. Across the body is a kilt, or ancient blanket, with four diagonal figures which are said to represent flint arrowheads. It is a remarkable fact that these latter symbols are practically the same as those used by Nahuatl people for obsidian arrow- or spear-

---

[1] "A few Tusayan Pictographs;" *American Anthropologist*, Washington, January, 1892.

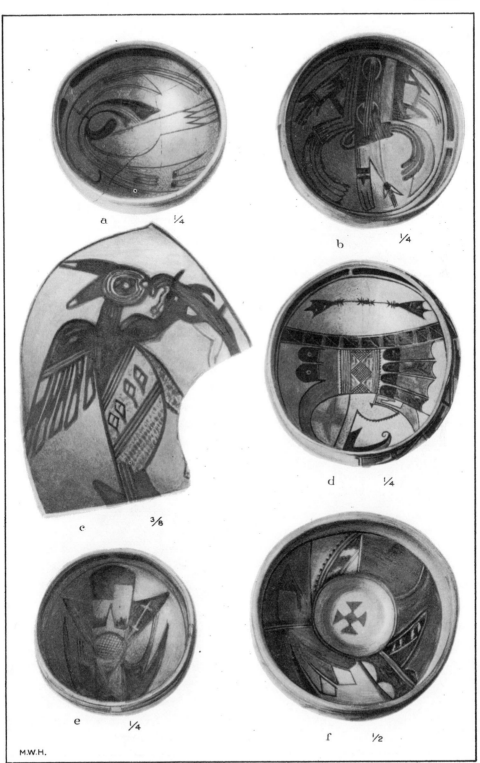

M.W.H.

BOWLS AND POTSHERD WITH FIGURES OF BIRDS, FROM SIKYATKI

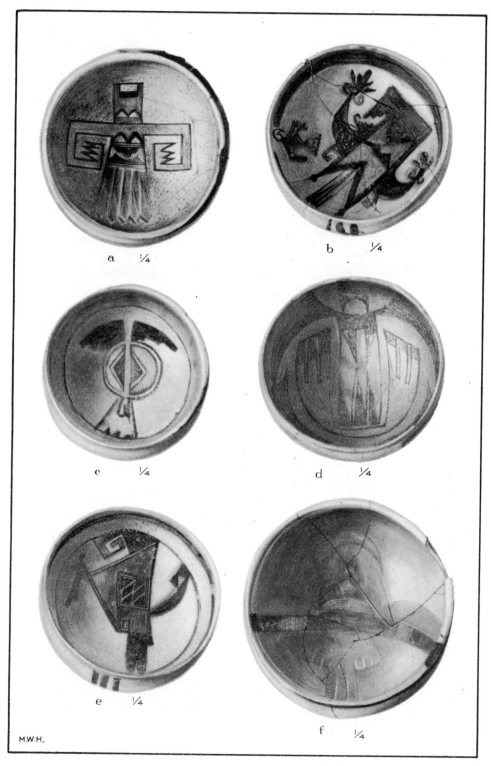

a   ¼

b   ¼

c   ¼

d   ¼

e   ¼

f   ¼

M.W.H.

FOOD BOWLS WITH FIGURES OF BIRDS, FROM SIKYATKI

points. In Hopi lore Kwataka wore a garment of arrowpoints, or, according to some legends, a flint garment, and his wings are said to have been composed of feathers of the same material.

From the pose of the figure and the various details of its symbolism there can be little doubt that the ancient Sikyatki artists intended to represent this monster, of which the modern Hopi rarely speak, and then only in awe. Probably several other bird figures likewise represent Kwataka, but in none of these do the symbols conform so closely to legends of this monster which are still repeated in the Tusayan villages. The home of Kwataka is reputed to be in the sky, and consequently figures of him are commonly associated with star and cloud emblems; he is a god of luck or chance, hence it is not exceptional to find figures of gaming implements[1] in certain elaborate figures of this monster.

By far the most beautiful of the many food bowls from Sikyatki, and, I believe, the finest piece of prehistoric aboriginal pottery from the United States, is that figured in plate CXLVI, d. This remarkable object, found with others in the sands of the necropolis of this pueblo, several feet below the surface, is decorated with a highly conventional figure of a bird in profile, but so modified that it is difficult to determine the different parts. The four appendages to the left represent the tail; the two knobs at the right the head, but the remaining parts are not comprehensible. The delicacy of the detailed crosshatching on the body is astonishing, considering that it was drawn freehand and without pattern. The coloring is bright and the surface glossy.

The curved band from which this strange figure hangs is divided into sections by perpendicular incised lines, which are connected by zigzag diagonals. The signification of the figure in the upper part of the bowl is unknown. While this vessel is unique in the character of its decoration, there are others of equal fineness but less perfect in design. Competent students of ceramics have greatly admired this specimen, and so fresh are the colors that some have found it difficult to believe it of ancient aboriginal manufacture. The specimen itself, now on exhibition in the National Museum, gives a better idea of its excellence than any figure which could be made. This specimen, like all the others, is in exactly the same condition as when exhumed, save that it has been wiped with a moist cloth to clean the traces of food from its inner surface. All the pottery found in the same grave is of the finest character, and although no two specimens are alike in decoration, their general resemblances point to the same maker. This fact has been noticed in several instances, although there were many exceptional cases where the coarsest and most rudely painted vessels were associated with the finest and most elaborately decorated ware.

The ladle illustrated in plate CXLII, e, is one of the most beautiful in the collection. It is decorated with a picture of an unknown animal

---

[1] A beautiful example of this kind was found at Homolobi in the summer of 1896.

with a single feather on the head. The eyes are double and the snout continued into a long stick or tube, on which the animal stands. While the appendage to the head is undoubtedly a feather and the animal recalls a bird, I am in doubt as to its true identification. The star emblems on the handle of the ladle are in harmony with known pictures of birds.

The feather decoration on the broken ladle shown in plate CXXXI, *f*, is of more than usual interest, although it is not wholly comprehensible. The representations include rain-cloud symbols, birds, feathers, and falling rain. The medially placed design, with four parallel lines arising from a round spot, is interpreted as a feather design, and the two triangular figures, one on each side, are believed to represent birds.

The design on the food bowl depicted in plate CXXXI, *e*, is obscure, but in it feather and star symbols predominate. On the inside of the ladle shown in plate CXXXI, *c*, there is a rectangular design with a conventionalized bird at each angle. The reduction of the figure of a bird to head, body, and two or more tail-feathers occurs very constantly in decorations, and in many instances nothing remains save a crook with appended parallel lines representing feathers. Examples of this kind occur on several vessels, of which that shown in plate CXLV, *a*, is an example.

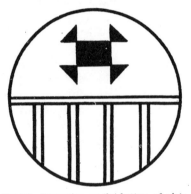

FIG. 276—Decoration on the bottom of plate CXLVI, *f*

There are many pictures of birds and feathers where the design has become so conventionalized that it is very difficult to recognize the intention of the decorator. Plate CXLVII, *f*, shows one of these in which the feather motive is prominent and an approximation to a bird form evident. The wings are shown with a symmetric arrangement on the sides of the tail, while the latter member has the three feathers which form so constant a feature in many bird symbols. In *b* of the same plate there is shown a more elaborated bird figure, also highly modified, yet preserving many of the parts which have been identified in the design last described.

The beautiful design shown in plate CXLVI, *e*, represents a large breath feather with triangular appendages on the sides, recalling the posterior end of the body of the bird figures above discussed.

The interior of the saucer illustrated in plate CLXVI, *f*, is decorated with feather symbols and four triangles. The remaining figures of this plate have already been considered.

The figures on the vessel shown in plate CXLVII are so arranged that there can be little question of their homologies, and from comparisons it is clear that they should all be regarded as representations of birds.

a   ¼

b   ¼

c   ¼

d   ¼

e   ¼

f   ¼

M.W.H.

FOOD BOWLS WITH SYMBOLS OF FEATHERS FROM SIKYATKI

a   ¼

b   ¼

c   ¼

d   ¼

e   ¼

f   ¼

M.W.H.

FOOD BOWLS WITH SYMBOLS OF FEATHERS FROM SIKYATKI

There appears no necessity of discussing figures *a* and *b* of the plate in this interpretation. In figure *c* the center of the design becomes circular, recalling certain sun symbols, and the tail-feathers are readily recognized on one side. I am by no means sure, however, that the lateral terraced appendages at the opposite pole are representations of wings, but such an interpretation can not be regarded as a forced one. Figure *d* shows the three tail-feathers, lateral appendages suggestive of wings, and a square body with the usual decorations of the body and head of a bird. The design shown in figure *f* suggests in many ways a sun-bird, and is comparable with those previously studied and illustrated. There is no question of the homologues of tail, head, and wings. The meridional band across the bowl is similar to those already discussed, and its relationship to the head and tail of the bird identical. This design is interpreted as that of one of the numerous birds associated with the sun. The crescentic extension above what is apparently the head occurs in many bird figures and may represent a beak.

Many food bowls from Sikyatki are ornamented on their interior with highly conventionalized figures, generally of curved form, in which the feather is predominant. Many of these are shown in plates CXLVIII to CLVII, inclusive, and in studying them I have found it very difficult to interpret the symbolism, although the figures of feathers are easy to find in many of them. While my attempt at decipherment is not regarded as final, it is hoped that it may at least reveal the important place which the feather plays in Tusayan ceramic decoration.

Plate CXLVIII, *a*, shows the spiral ornament worn down to its lowest terms, with no hint of the feather appendage, but its likeness in outline to those designs where the feather occurs leads me to introduce it in connection with those in which the feather is more prominent. Figure *b* of the same plate represents a spiral figure with a bird form at the inner end, and a bundle of tail-feathers at the outer extremity. On this design there is likewise a figure of the dragon-fly and several unknown emblems. Figure *c* has at one extremity a trifid appendage, recalling a feather ornament on the head of a bird shown in plate CXXXVIII, *a*. Figure *d* has no conventionalized feather decoration, but the curved line terminates with a triangle. Its signification is unknown to me. For several reasons the design in *e* reminds me of a bird; it is accompanied by three crosses, which are almost invariably found in connection with bird figures, and at the inner end there is attached a breath feather. This end of the figure is supposed to be the head, as will appear by later comparative studies. The bird form is masked in *f*, but the feather designs are prominent. This bowl is exceptional in having an encircling band broken at two points, one of the components of which is red, the other black.

Feather designs are conspicuous in plate CXLIX, *a*, *b*, in the former of which curved incised lines are successfully used. In *c*, however, is found the best example of the use of incised work as an aid in pottery decoration, for in this specimen there are semicircles, and rings with four triangles, straight lines, and circles. The symbolism of the whole figure has eluded analysis. Figure *d* has no feather symbols, but *e* may later be reduced to a circle with feathers. The only symbols in the design shown in *f* which are at all recognizable are the two zigzag figures which may have been intended to represent snakes, lightning, or tadpoles.

When the design in plate CL, *a*, is compared with the beautiful bowl shown in plate CXLVI, *d*, a treatment of somewhat similar nature is found. It is believed that both represent birds drawn in profile; the four bands (*a*) are tail-feathers, while the rectangle represents the body and the curved appendage a part of the head. From a similarity to modern figures of a turkey feather, it is possible that the triangle at the end of the curved appendage is the feather of this bird. An examination of *b* leads to the conclusion that the inner end of the spiral represents a bird's head. Two eyes are represented therein, and from it feathers are appended. The parallel marks on the body are suggestive of similar decorations on the figure of the Plumed Snake painted on the kilts of the Snake priests of Walpi. The star emblems are constant accompaniments of bird designs. Figure *c* has, in addition to the spiral, the star symbols and what appears to be a flower. The design shown in *d* is so exceptional that it is here represented with the circular forms. It will be seen that there are well-marked feathers in its composition. Figure *f* is made up of several bird forms, feathers, rectangles, and triangles, combined in a complicated design, the parts of which may readily be interpreted in the light of what has already been recorded.

The significance of the spiral in the design on plate CLI, *a*, is unknown. It is found in several pictures, in some of which it appears to have avian relationship. Figure *b* of the same plate is a square terraced design appended to the median line, on which symbolic stars are depicted. As in many bird figures, a star is found on the opposite semicircle. There is a remote likeness between this figure and that of the head of the bird shown in plate CXLV, *d*. Plate CLI, *c*, is a compound figure, with four feathers arranged in two pairs at right angles to a median band. The triangular figure associated with them is sometimes found in symbols of the sun. Figure *d* is undoubtedly a bird symbol, as may be seen by a comparison of it with the bird figures shown in plate CXXXVIII, *a–f*. There are two tail-feathers, two outstretched wings, and a head which is rectangular, with terraced designs. The cross is triple, and occupies the opposite segment, which is finely spattered with pigment. This trifid cross represents a game played by the Hopi with reeds and is depicted on many objects of pottery. As representations of it sometimes accompany those of birds I am led to interpret the figure (plate CLVII, *c*) as that of a bird, which it somewhat resem-

FIGURES OF BIRDS AND FEATHERS FROM SIKYATKI

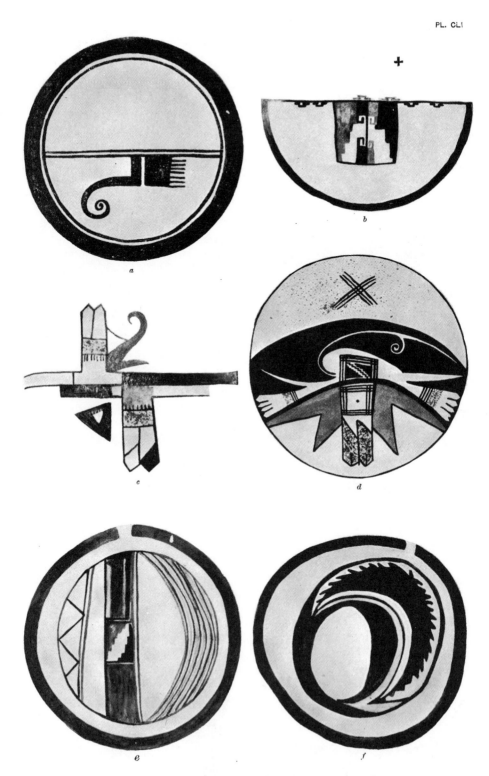

FIGURES OF BIRDS AND FEATHERS FROM SIKYATKI

bles. The two designs shown in plate CLI, *e, f,* are believed to be decorative, or, if symbolic, they have been so worn by the constant use of the vessel that it is impossible to determine their meaning by comparative methods. Both of these figures show the "line of life" in a somewhat better way than any yet considered.

In plate CLII, *a,* is shown a compound figure of doubtful significance, made up of a series of crescents, triangles, and spirals, which, in *c,* are more compactly joined together, and accompanied by three parallel lines crossing three other lines. The curved figure shown in *b* represents three feathers; a large one on each side, inclosing a medially smaller member. In *d* is shown the spiral bird form with appended feathers, triangles, and terraced figures. Figure *f* of this plate is decorated with a design which bears many resemblances to a flower, the peripheral appendages resembling bracts of a sunflower. A somewhat similar design is painted on the side of the helmets of some *katcina* dancers, where the bracts or petals are colored in sequence, with the pigments corresponding to the six directions—north, west, south, east, above, and below. In the decoration on the ancient Sikyatki bowl we find seven peripheral bracts, one of which is speckled. The six groups of stamens(?) are represented between the triangular bracts.

The designs shown in plates CLIII to CLV, inclusive, still preserve the spiral form with attached feathers, some of them being greatly conventionalized or differentiated. In the first of these plates (figure *b*) is represented a bird form with triangular head with four feathers arranged in fan shape. These feathers are different from any which I have been able to find attached to the bodies of birds, and are thus identified from morphological rather than from other reasons.

The body of the conventionalized bird is decorated with terraced figures, spirals, flowers, and other designs arranged in a highly complicated manner. From a bar connecting the spiral with the encircling line there arises a tuft of feathers. Figure *a* of the same plate is characterized by a medially placed triangle and a graceful pendant from which hangs seven feathers. In this instance these structures take the form of triangles and pairs of lines. The relation of these structures to feathers would appear highly speculative, but they have been so interpreted for the following reason: If we compare them with the appendages represented in the design on the vase shown in CXLIII, *b,* we find them the same in number, form, and arrangement; the triangles in the design on this vase are directly comparable with the figures in plate CXLIII, *b,* in the same position, which are undoubtedly feathers, as has been shown in the discussion of this figure. Consequently, although the triangles on the pendant in plate CLIII, *a,* appear at first glance to have no relation to the prescribed feather symbol, morphology shows their true interpretation. The reduction of the wing feather to a simple triangular figure is likewise shown in several other pictures on food vessels, notably in the figure, undoubtedly of a bird, represented in plate CXLVI, *a*.

In the two figures forming plate CLIV are found simple bird symbols and feather designs very much conventionalized. The same is true of the two figures given in plate CLV.

The vessels illustrated in plate CLVI, *a*, *b*, are decorated with designs of unknown meaning, save that the latter recalls the modification of the feather into long triangular forms. On the outer surface this bowl has a row of tadpoles encircling it in a sinistral direction, or with the center of the bowl on the left. The design of figure *c* shows a bird's head in profile, with a crest of feathers and with the two eyes on one side of the head and a necklace. The triangular figure bears the symbolism of the turkey feather, as at present designated in Tusayan altar paraphernalia. As with other bird figures, there is a representation in red of the triple star.

Figure *d* is the only specimen of a vessel in the conventional form of a bird which was found at Sikyatki; it evidently formerly had a handle. The vessel itself is globular, and the form of the bird is intensified by the designs on its surface. The bird's head is turned to the observer, and the row of triangles represent wing feathers. The signification of the designs on *e* and *f* is unknown to me.

Figures *e* and *f* of plate CLVI are avian decorations, reduced in the case of the former to geometric forms. The triangular figure is a marked feature in the latter design.

The designs represented in plate CLVII are aberrant bird forms. Of these *a* and *b* are the simplest and *c* one of the most complicated. Figure *d* is interpreted as a double bird, or twins with a common head and tails pointing in opposite directions. Figure *e* shows a bird in profile with one wing, furnished with triangular feathers, extended. There is some doubt about the identification of *f* as a bird, but there is no question that the wing, tail, and breath feathers are represented in it. Of the last mentioned there are three, shown by the notch, colored black at their extremities.

VEGETAL DESIGNS

Inasmuch as they so readily lend themselves as a motive of decoration, it is remarkable that the ancient Hopi seem to have used plants and their various organs so sparingly in their pottery painting. Elsewhere, especially among modern Pueblos, this is not the case, and while plants, flowers, and leaves are not among the common designs on modern Tusayan ware, they are often employed. It would appear that the corn plant or fruit would be found among other designs, especially as corn plays a highly symbolic part in mythic conceptions, but we fail to find it used as a decoration on any ancient vessel.

In a figure previously described, a flower, evidently an aster or sunflower, appears with a butterfly, and in the bowl shown in plate

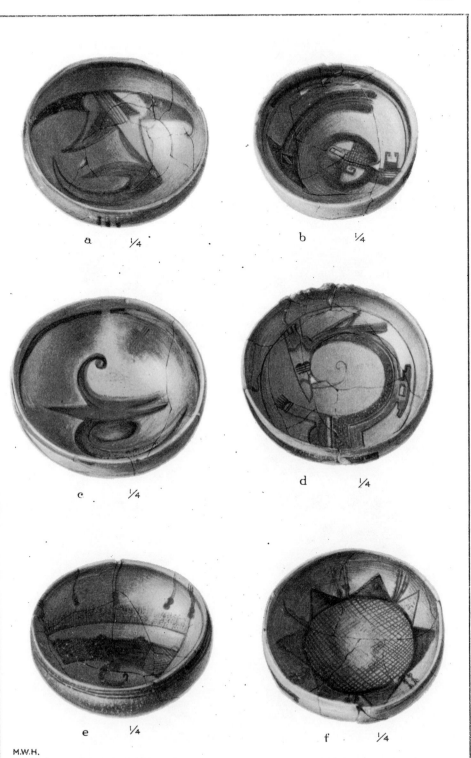

a   ¼

b   ¼

c   ¼

d   ¼

e   ¼

f   ¼

M.W.H.

FOOD BOWLS WITH BIRD, FEATHER, AND FLOWER SYMBOLS FROM SIKYATKI

a   ½

M.W.H.

b   ½

FOOD BOWLS WITH FIGURES OF BIRDS AND FEATHERS FROM SIKYATKI

CXXXIV, *e*, we have a similar design. This figure evidently represents the sunflower, the seeds of which were ground and eaten in ancient times. The plant apparently is represented as growing from the earth and is surrounded by a broad band of red in rudely circular form. The totem of the earth today among the Hopi is a circle; possibly it was the same among the ancients, in which case the horizon may have been represented by the red encircling band, which is accompanied by the crook and the emblem of rain. The petals are represented by a row of dots and no leaves are shown. From the kinship of the ancient accolents of Sikyatki with the Flute people, it is to be expected that in their designs figures of asters or sunflowers would appear, for these plants play a not inconspicuous rôle in the ritual of this society which has survived to modern times.

THE SUN

Sun worship plays a most important part in modern Tusayan ritual, and the symbol of the sun in modern pictography can not be mistaken for any other. It is a circle with radiating feathers on the periphery and ordinarily with four lines arranged in quaternary groups. The face of the sun is indicated by triangles on the forehead, two slits for eyes, and a double triangle for the mouth. This symbol, however, is not always used as that of the sun, for in the Oraibi *Powalawû* there is an altar in which a sand picture of the sun has the form of a four-pointed star. The former of these sun symbols is not found on Sikyatki pottery, but there is one picture which closely resembles the latter. This occurs on the bowl illustrated in plate CLXI, *c*. The main design is a four-pointed star, alternating with crosses and surrounded by a zone in which are rectangular blocks. While the identification may be fanciful, its resemblances are highly suggestive. The existence of a double triangle adjacent to this figure on the same bowl, and its likeness to the modern mouth-design of sun pictures, appears to be more than a coincidence, and is so regarded in this identification.

In the design shown in plate CLVIII, *a*, one of the elaborate ancient sun figures is represented. As in modern symbols, the tail-feathers of the periphery of the disk are arranged in the four quadrants, and in addition there are appended to the same points curved figures which recall the objects, identified as stringed feathers, attached to the blanket of the maid (plate CXXIX, *a*). The design on the disk is different from that of any sun emblem known to me, and escapes my interpretation. I have used the distribution of the feathers on the four quadrants as an indication that this figure is a sun symbol, although it must be confessed this evidence is not so strong as might be wished. The triangles at the sides of two feathers indicate that a tail-feather is intended, and for the correlated facts supporting this conclusion the reader is referred to the description of the vessels shown in plate CXXXVIII.

It would appear that there is even more probability that the picture on the bowl illustrated in plate CLVIII, *b*, is a sun symbol. It represents a disk with tail and wing feathers arranged on the periphery in four groups. This recalls the sun emblems used in Tusayan at the present time, although the face of the sun is not represented on this specimen. There is a still closer approximation to the modern symbol of the sun on a bowl in a private collection from Sikyatki.

In plate CLVIII, *c*, the sun's disk is represented with the four clusters of feathers replaced by the extremities of the bodies of four birds, the tail-feathers, for some unknown reason, being omitted. The design on the disk is highly symbolic, and the only modern sun symbol found in it are the triangles, which form the mouth of the face of the sun in modern Hopi symbolism.

One of the most aberrant pictures of the sun, which I think can be identified with probability, is shown in the design on the specimen illustrated in plate CXXXIV, *b*. The reasons which have led me to this identification may briefly be stated as follows:

Among the many supernaturals with which modern Hopi mythology is replete is one called Calako taka, or the male Calako. In legends he is the husband of the two Corn-maids of like name. The ceremonials connected with this being occur in Sichomovi in July, when four giant personifications enter the village as have been described in a former memoir. The heads of these giants are provided with two curved horns, between which is a crest of eagle tail-feathers.

Two of these giants, under another name, but with the same symbolism, are depicted on the altars of the *katcinas* at Walpi and Mishoñinovi, where they represent the sun. A chief personifying the same supernatural flogs children when they are initiated into the knowledge of the *katcinas*.

The figure on the bowl under discussion has many points of resemblance to the symbolism of this personage as depicted on the altars mentioned. The head has two horns, one on each side, with a crest, apparently of feathers, between them. The eyes and mouth are represented, and on the body there is a four-pointed cross. The meaning of the remaining appendages is unknown, but the likenesses to Calako-taka [1] symbolism are noteworthy and important. The figure on the food bowl illustrated in plate CXXXIV, *c*, is likewise regarded as a sun emblem. The disk is represented by a ring in the center, to which feathers are appended. The triangle, which is still a sun symbol, is shown below a band across the bowl. This band is decorated with highly conventionalized feathers.

---

[1] In this connection the reader is referred to the story, already told in former pages of this memoir, concerning the flogging of the youth by the husband of the two women who brought the Hopi the seeds of corn. It may be mentioned as corroboratory evidence that Calako-taka represents a supernatural sun-bird, that the Tataukyamû priests carry a shield with Tunwup (Calako-taka) upon it in the *Soyaluña*. These priests, as shown by the etymology of their name, are associated with the sun. In the Sun drama, or Calako ceremony, in July, Calako-takas are personated, and at Zuñi the Shalako is a great winter sun ceremony.

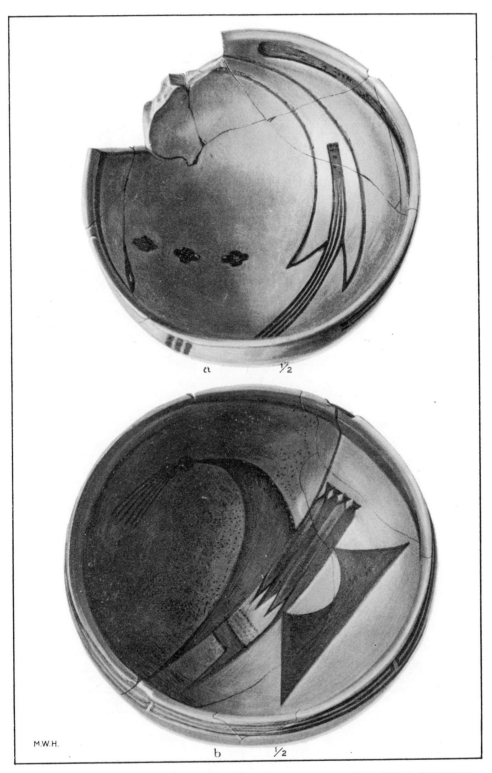

M.W.H.

a   ½

b   ½

FOOD BOWLS WITH FIGURES OF BIRDS AND FEATHERS FROM SIKYATKI

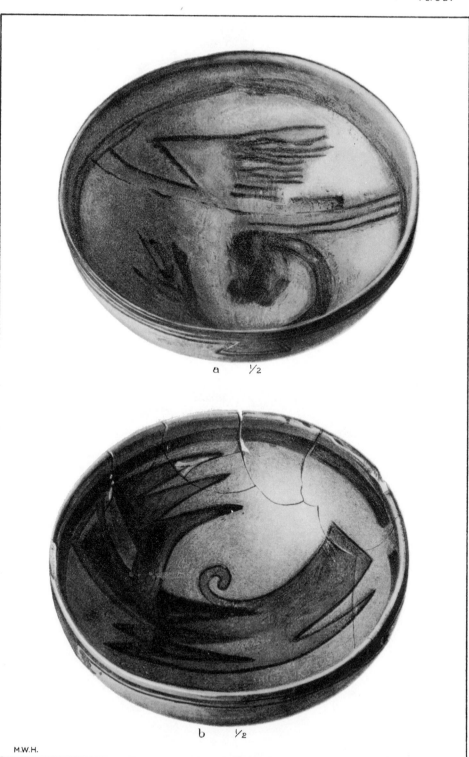

a ½

b ½

M.W.H.

FOOD BOWLS WITH FIGURES OF BIRDS AND FEATHERS FROM SIKYATKI

It may be added that in this figure we have probably the most aberrant sun-symbol yet recognized, and on that account there is a possibility that the validity of my identification is more or less doubtful.

The three designs shown in plate CLVIII, *c, d, e,* evidently belong in association with sun or star symbols, but it is hardly legitimate to definitely declare that such an interpretation can be demonstrated. The modern Tusayan Indians declare that the equal-arm cross is a symbol of the "Heart of the Sky" god, which, from my studies of the effigies of this personage on various altars, I have good reason to identify with the lightning.

GEOMETRIC FIGURES

INTERPRETATION OF THE FIGURES

Most of the pottery from Sikyatki is ornamented with geometric designs and linear figures, the import of many of which are unknown.

Two extreme views are current in regard to the significance of these designs. To one school everything is symbolic of something or some religious conception; to the other the majority are meaningless save as decorations. I find the middle path the more conservative, and while regarding many of the designs as highly conventionalized symbols, believe that there are also many where the decorator had no thought of symbolism. I have ventured an explanation of a few of the former.

Terraced figures are among the most common rectangular elements in Pueblo ceramic decorations. These designs bear so close a likeness to the modern rain cloud symbol that they probably may all be referred to this category. Their arrangement on a bowl or jar is often of such a nature as to impart very different patterns. Thus terraced figures placed in opposition to each other may leave zigzag spaces suggesting lightning, but such forms can hardly be regarded as designed for symbols.

Rectangular patterns (plates CLXII–CLXV) are more ancient in the evolution of designs on Tusayan pottery than curved geometric figures, and far outnumber them in the most ancient specimens; but there has been no epoch in the development reaching to modern times when they have been superseded. While there are many specimens of Sikyatki pottery of the type decorated with geometric figures, which bear ornamentations of simple and complex terraced forms, the majority placed in this type are not reducible to stepped or terraced designs, but are modified straight lines, bars, crosshatching, and the like. In older Pueblo pottery the relative proportion of terraced figures is even less, which would appear to indicate that basket-ware patterns were secondary rather than primary decorative forms.

By far the largest element in ancient Tusayan pottery decoration must be regarded as simple geometric lines, triangles, spirals, curves, crosshatching, and the like, some of which are no doubt symbolic, others purely decorative (plate CLXVI). In the evolution of design I am inclined to believe that this was the simplest form, and I find it the most constant in the oldest ware. Rectangular figures are regarded as older than circular figures, and they possibly preceded the latter in evolution, but in many instances both are forms of reversion, highly conventionalized representations of more elaborate figures. Circles and crosses are sometimes combined, the former modified into a wavy line surrounding the latter, as in plate CLIX, c, d, where there is a suggestion (d) of a sun emblem.

CROSSES

A large number of food bowls are decorated with simple or elaborate crosses, stars, and like patterns. Simple crosses with arms of equal length appear on the vessels shown in plate CLIX, c, d. There are many similar crosses, subordinate to the main design, in various bowls, especially those decorated with figures of birds and sky deities.

Plate CLX, a, exhibits a cruciform design, to the extremities of three arms of which bird figures are attached. In this design there are likewise two sunflower symbols. The modified cross figure in b of the same plate, like that just mentioned, suggests a swastica, but fails to be one, and unless the complicated design in figure c may be so interpreted, no swastica was found at Sikyatki or Awatobi. Plate CLX, d, shows another form of cross, two arms of which are modified into triangles.

On the opening of the great ceremony called *Powamû* or "Bean-planting," which occurs in February in the modern Tusayan villages, there occurs a ceremony about a sand picture of the sun which is called *Powalawû*. The object of this rite is the fructification of all seeds known to the Hopi. The sand picture of the sun which is made at that time is in its essentials identical with the design on the food bowl illustrated in plate CLXI, c; consequently it is possible that this star emblem represents the sun, and the occurrence of the eight triangles in the rim, replaced in the modern altar by four concentric bands of differently colored sands, adds weight to this conclusion. The twin triangles outside the main figure are identical with those in the mouth of modern sun emblems. These same twin triangles are arranged in lines which cross at right angles in plate CLXI, d, but from their resemblance to figure b they possibly have a different meaning.

The most complicated of all the star-shape figures, like the simplest, takes us to sun emblems, and it seems probable that there is a relationship between the two. Plate CLXI, f, represents four bundles of feathers arranged in quadrants about a rectangular center. These feathers vary in form and arrangement, and the angles between them are occupied by horn-shape bodies, two of which have highly complicated extremities recalling conventionalized birds.

A large number of crosses are respresented in plate CLXII, d, in which the remaining semicircle is filled with a tessellated pattern. A spiral

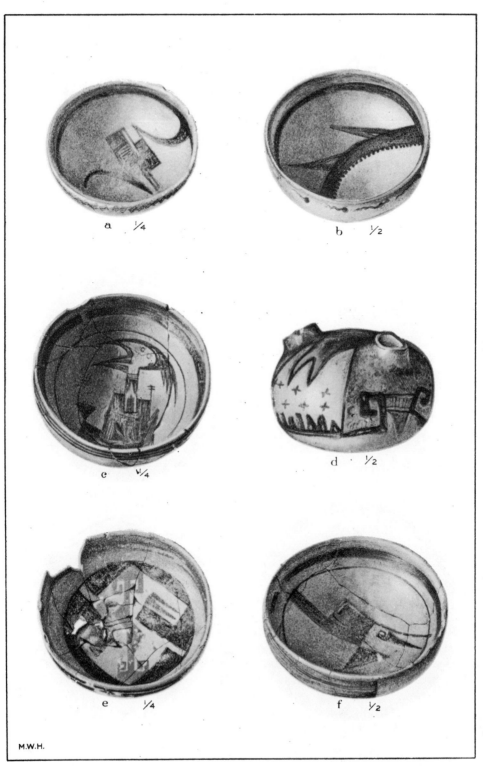

a ¼

b ½

c ¼

d · ½

e ¼

f ½

M.W.H.

FOOD BOWLS WITH FIGURES OF BIRDS AND FEATHERS FROM SIKYATKI

FIGURES OF BIRDS AND FEATHERS FROM SIKYATKI

line with round spots at intervals adorns the specimen shown in plate CLXI, *a*. Parallel lines with similar spots appear on the vessel illustrated in plate CLXII, *e*, and a network of the same is shown in *f* of the same plate. Plate CLXVII, *b*, represents a compound star.

While simple swasticas are not found on any of the Sikyatki pottery, modified and compound forms are well represented. There are several specimens of figures of the Maltese cross, and one closely approximating the Saint Andrew's cross. It is scarcely necessary to say that the presence of the various kinds of crosses do not necessarily indicate the influence of Semitic or Aryan races, for I have already shown[1] that even cross-shape prayer-sticks were in use among the Pueblos when Coronado first visited them.

TERRACED FIGURES

Among the most common of all geometric designs on ancient Tusayan pottery none excel in variety or number those which I place in the above group. They form the major part of all decoration, and there is hardly a score of ornamented vessels in which they can not be detected. In a typical form they appear as stepped designs, rectangular figures with diagonals continuous, or as triangular designs with steps represented along their sides.

While it is probable that in some instances these figures are simply decorative, with no attempt at symbolism, in other cases without doubt they symbolize rain-clouds, and the same figures are still used with similar intent in modern ceremonial paraphernalia—altars, mask-tablets, and the like. Decorative modifications of this figure were no doubt adopted by artistic potters, thus giving varieties where the essential meaning has been much obscured or lost.

THE CROOK

Among the forms of geometric designs on ancient Tusayan pottery there are many jars, bowls, and other objects on which a crook, variously modified, is the essential type. This figure is so constant that it must have had a symbolic as well as a decorative meaning. The crook plays an important part in the modern ritual, and is prominent on many Tusayan altars. Around the sand picture of the rain-cloud, for example, we find a row of wooden rods with curved ends, and in the public Snake dance these are carried by participants called the Antelopes. A crook in the form of a staff to which an ear of corn and several feathers are attached is borne by *katcinas* or masked participants in certain rain dances. It is held in the hand by a personage who flogs the children when they are initiated into certain religious societies. Many other instances might be mentioned in which this crozier-like

---

[1] *American Anthropologist*, April, 1895, p. 133. As these cross-shape pahos which are now made in Tusayan are attributed to the Kawaika or Keres group of Indians, and as they were seen at the Keresan pueblo of Acoma in 1540, it is probable that they are derivative among the Hopi; but simple cross decorations on ancient pottery were probably autochthonous.

object is carried by important personages. While it is not entirely clear to me that in all instances this crook is a badge of authority, in some cases it undoubtedly represents the standing of the bearer. There are, likewise, prayer offerings in the form of crooks, and even common forms of prayer-sticks have miniature curved sticks attached to them.

Some of the warrior societies are said to make offerings in the form of a crook, and a stick of similar form is associated with the gods of war. There is little doubt that some of the crook-form decorations on ancient vessels may have been used as symbols with the same intent as the sticks referred to above. The majority of the figures of this shape elude interpretation. Many of them have probably no definite meaning, but are simply an effective motive of decoration.

In some instances the figure of the crook on old pottery is a symbol of a prayer offering of a warrior society, made in the form of an ancient weapon, allied to a bow.

THE GERMINATIVE SYMBOL

The ordinary symbol of germination, a median projection with lateral extensions at the base (plate CXLIX, e), occurs among the figures on this ancient pottery. In its simplest form, a median line with a triangle on each side attached to one end, it is a phallic emblem. When this median line becomes oval, and the triangles elongated and curved at the ends, it represents the ordinary squash symbol,[1] also used as an emblem of fertility.

The triangle is also an emblem of germination and of fecundity—the female, as the previously mentioned principle represents the male. The geometric designs on the ancient Sikyatki ware abundantly illustrate both these forms.

BROKEN LINES

In examining the simple encircling bands of many of the food bowls, jars, and other ceramic objects, it will be noticed that they are not continuous, but that there is a break at one point, and this break is usually limited to one point in all the specimens. Various explanations of the meaning of this failure to complete the band have been suggested, and it is a remarkable fact that it is one of the most widely extended characteristics of ancient pottery decoration in the whole Pueblo area, including the Salado and Gila basins. While in the specimens from Sikyatki the break is simple and confined to one point, in those from other regions we find two or three similar failures in the continuity of encircling lines, and in some instances the lines at the point of separation are modified into spirals, terraces, and other forms of geometric figures. In the more complex figures we find the

---

[1] In dolls of the Corn-maids this germinative symbol is often found made of wood and mounted on an elaborate tablet representing rain-clouds.

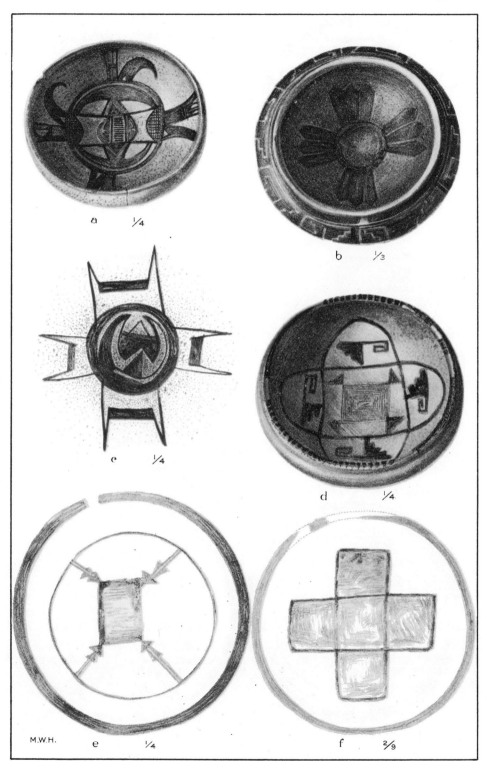

a 1/4

b 1/3

c 1/4

d 1/4

M.W.H. e 1/4

f 2/9

FOOD BOWLS WITH FIGURES OF SUN AND RELATED SYMBOLS
FROM SIKYATKI

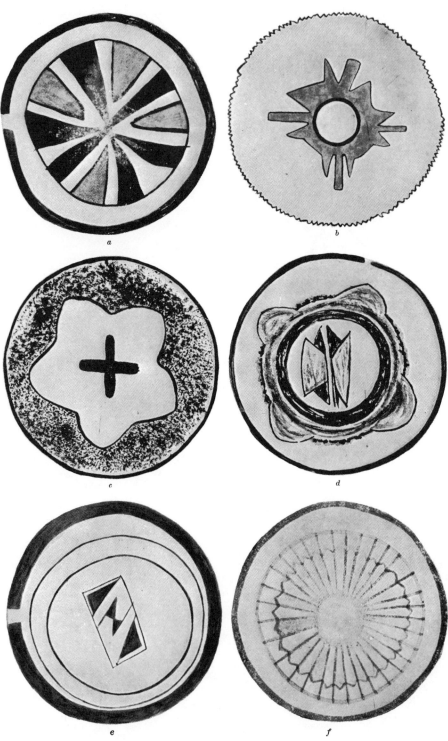

CROSS AND RELATED DESIGNS FROM SIKYATKI

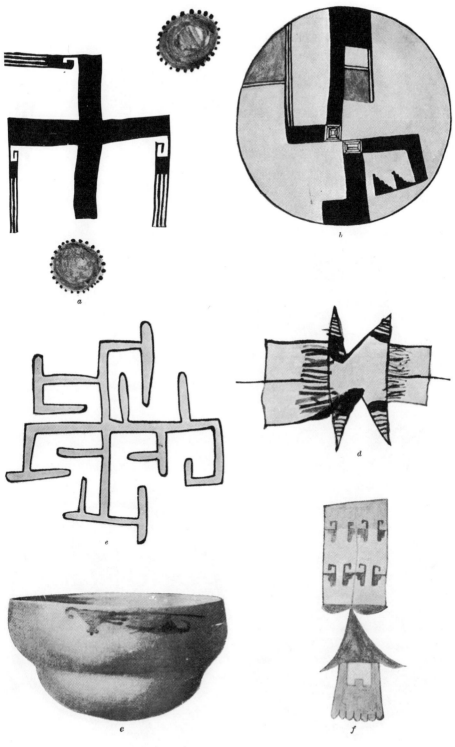

CROSS AND OTHER SYMBOLS FROM SIKYATKI

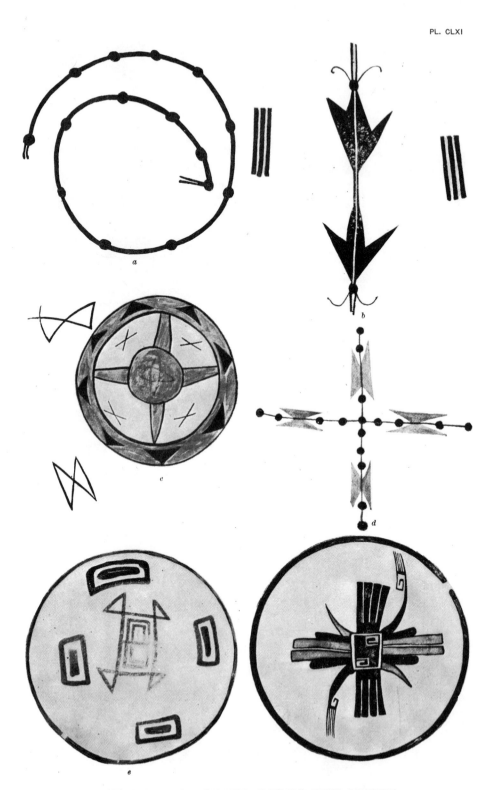

STAR, SUN, AND RELATED SYMBOLS FROM SIKYATKI

most intricate variations, which depart so widely from the simple forms that their resemblances are somewhat difficult to follow. A brief consideration of these modifications may aid toward an understanding of the character of certain geometric ornamental motives.

If any of the interlocking spirals on bowls or vases are traced, it is found that they do not join at the center of the figure. The same is true when these spirals become frets. There is always a break in the network which they form. This break is comparable with the hiatus on encircling bands and probably admits of the same interpretation. In a simple form this motive appears as two crescents or two key patterns with the ends overlapping. This simple ornament, called the friendship sign, is commonly used in the decoration of the bodies of *katcinas*, and has been likened to the interlocking of fingers or hands of the participants in certain dances, the fingers half retracted with inner surfaces approximated, the palms of the hands facing in opposite directions and the wrists at opposite points. If the points be extended into an elaborate key pattern or curved into extended spirals, a complicated figure is produced in which the separation is less conspicuous although always present.

The same points may be modified into terraced figures, the separation then appearing as a zigzag line drawn across the figure, or they may have interlocking dentate or serrate prolongations imparting a variety of forms to the interval between them.[1] In order to trace out these modifications it would be necessary to specify each individual case, but I think that is unnecessary. In other words, the broken line appears to be a characteristic not only of simple encircling bands, but also of all geometric figures in which highly complicated designs extend about the periphery of a utensil.

DECORATIONS ON THE EXTERIOR OF FOOD BOWLS

The decorations on the exterior of the ancient food bowls are in most instances very characteristic and sometimes artistic. Generally they reproduce patterns which are found on the outside of vases and jars and sometimes have a distant relationship to the designs in the interior of the bowl upon which they occur. Usually these external decorations are found only on one side, and in that respect they differ from the modern food bowls, in which nothing similar to them appears.

The characteristics of the external decorations of food bowls are symbolic, mostly geometric, square or rectangular, triangular or stepped

---

[1] Many similarities might be mentioned between the terraced figures used in decoration in Old Mexico and in ancient Tusayan pottery, but I will refer to but a single instance, that of the stuccoed walls of Mitla, Oaxaca, and Teotitlan del Valle. Many designs from these ruins are gathered together for comparative purposes by that eminent Mexicanist, Dr E. Seler, in his beautiful memoir on Mitla (*Wandmalereien von Mitla*, plate x). In this plate exact counterparts of many geometric patterns on Sikyatki pottery appear, and even the broken spiral is beautifully represented. There are key patterns and terraced figures in stucco on monuments of Central America identical with the figures on pottery from Sikyatki.

figures; curved lines and spirals rarely if ever occur, and human or animal figures are unknown in this position in Sityatki pottery; the geometric figures can be reduced to a few patterns of marked simplicity.

It is apparent that I can best discuss the variety of geometric designs by considering these external decorations of food vessels at length.

From the fact that they are limited to one side, the design is less complicated by repetition and seems practically the same as the more typical forms. It is rarely that two of these designs are found to be exactly the same, and as there appears to be no duplication a classification of them is difficult. Each potter seems to have decorated her ware without regard to the work of her contemporaries, using simple designs but combining them in original ways. Hence the great variety found even in the grave of the same woman, whose handiwork was buried with her. As, however, the art of the potter degenerated, as it has in later times, the patterns became more alike, so that modern Tusayan decorated earthenware has little variety in ornamentation and no originality in design. Every potter uses the same figures.

FIG. 277—Oblique parallel line decoration

FIG. 278—Parallel lines fused at one point

The simplest form of decoration on the exterior of a food bowl is a band encircling it. This line may be complete or it may be broken at one point. The next more complicated geometric decoration is a double or multiple band, which, however, does not occur in any of the specimens from Sikyatki. The breaking up of this multiple band into parallel bars is shown in figure 277. These bars generally have a quadruple

FIG. 279—Parallel lines with zigzag arrangement

arrangement, and are horizontal, vertical, or, as in the illustration, inclined at an angle. They are often found on the lips of the bowls and in a similar position on jars, dippers, and vases. The parallel lines shown in figure 278 are seven in number, and do not encircle the bowl. They are joined by a broad connecting band near one extremity. The number of parallel bands in this decoration is highly suggestive.

GEOMETRIC ORNAMENTATION FROM SIKYATKI

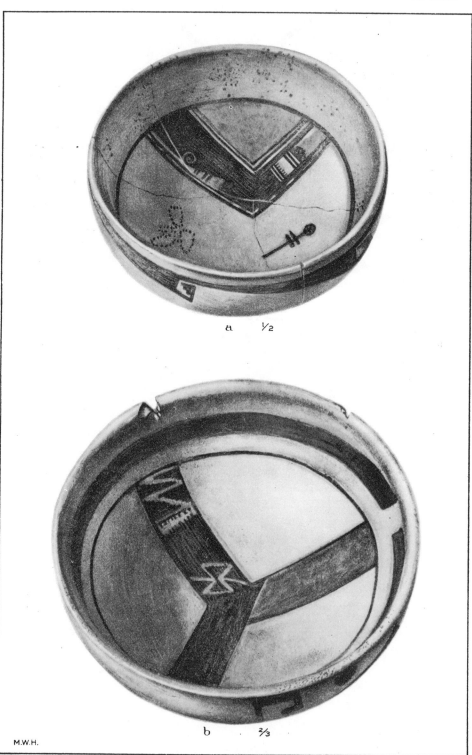

a ½

b ⅔

M.W.H.

FOOD BOWLS WITH GEOMETRIC ORNAMENTATION FROM SIKYATKI

Four parallel bands encircle the bowl shown in figure 279, but they are so modified in their course as to form a number of trapezoidal figures placed with alternating sides parallel. This interesting pattern is found only on one vessel.

The use of simple parallel bars, arranged at equal intervals on the outside of food bowls, is not confined to these vessels, for they occur on the margin of vases, cups, and dippers. They likewise occur on ladle handles, where they are arranged in alternate transverse and longitudinal clusters.

FIG. 280—Parallel lines connected by middle bar

The combination of two vertical bands connected by a horizontal band, forming the letter H, is an ornamental design frequently occurring on the finest Hopi ware. Figure 280 shows such an H form, which is ordinarily repeated four times about the bowl.

The interval between the parallel bands around the vessel may be

FIG. 281—Parallel lines of different width; serrate margin

very much reduced in size, and some of the bands may be of different width or otherwise modified. Such a deviation is seen in figure 281, which has three bands, one of which is broad with straight edges, the other with serrate margin and hook-like appendages.

FIG. 282—Parallel lines of different width; median serrate

In figure 282 eight bands are shown, the marginal broad with edges entire, and the median pair serrated, the long teeth fitting each other in such a way as to impart a zigzag effect to the space which separates them. The remaining four lines, two on each side, appear as black

FIG.283—Parallel lines of different width; marginal serrate

bands on a white ground. It will be noticed that an attempt was made to relieve the monotony of the middle band of figure 282 by the introduction of a white line in zigzag form. A similar result was accomplished in the design shown in figure 283 by rectangles and dots.

The modification of the multiple bands in figure 283 has produced a very different decorative form. This design is composed of five bands, the marginal on each side serrate, and the middle band relatively very broad, with diagonals, each containing four round dots regularly

FIG. 284—Parallel lines and triangles

arranged. In figure 284 there are many parallel, noncontinuous bands of different breadth, arranged in groups separated by triangles with sides parallel, and the whole united by bounding lines. This is the most complicated form of design where straight lines only are used.

FIG. 285—Line with alternate triangles

We nave thus far considered modifications brought about by fusion and other changes in simple parallel lines. They may be confined to one side of the food bowl, may repeat each other at intervals, or surround the whole vessel. Ordinarily, however, they are confined to one side of the bowls from Sikyatki.

FIG. 286—Single line with alternate spurs

Returning to the single encircling band, it is found, in figure 285, broken up into alternating equilateral triangles, each pair united at their right angles. This modification is carried still further in figure 286, where the triangles on each side of the single line are prolonged

FIG. 287—Single line with hourglass figures

into oblique spurs, the pairs separated a short distance from each other. In figure 287 there is shown still another arrangement of these triangular decorations, the pairs forming hourglass-shape figures connected by an encircling line passing through their points of junction.

In figure 288 the double triangles, one on each side of the encircling band, are so placed that their line of separation is lost, and a single triangle replaces the pair.   These are connected by the line surrounding

FIG. 288—Single lines with triangles

the bowl and there is a dot at the smallest angle.   In figure 289 there is a similar design, except that alternating with each triangle, which bears more decoration than that shown in figure 288, there are hour-

FIG. 289—Single line with alternate triangles and ovals

glass figures composed of ovals and triangles.   The dots at the apex of that design are replaced by short parallel lines of varying width. The triangles and ovals last considered are arranged symmetrically in

FIG. 290—Triangles and quadrilaterals

relation to a simple band.   By a reduction in the intervening spaces these triangles may be brought together and the line disappears.   I have found no specimen of design illustrating the simplest form of the

FIG. 291—Triangle with spurs

resultant motive, but that shown in figure 290 is a new combination comparable with it.

The simple triangular decorative design reaches a high degree of

FIG. 292—Rectangle with single line

complication in figure 290, where a connecting line is absent, and two triangles having their smallest angles facing each other are separated

by a lozenge shape figure made up of many parallel lines placed obliquely to the axis of the design. The central part is composed of seven
parallel lines, the marginal of which, on two opposite sides, is minutely
dentate. The median band is very broad and is relieved by two wavy
white lines. The axis of the design on each side is continued into two
triangular spurs, rising from a rectangle in the middle of each triangle.

FIG. 293—Double triangle; multiple lines

This complicated design is the highest development reached by the use
of simple triangles. In figure 291, however, we have a simpler form of
triangular decoration, in which no element other than the rectangle is
employed. In the chaste decoration seen in figure 292 the use of the
rectangle is shown combined with the triangle on a simple encircling

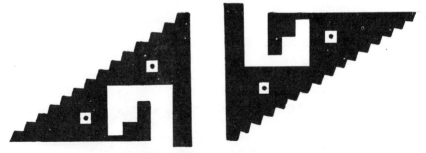

FIG. 294—Double triangle; terraced edges

band. This design is reducible to that shown in figure 290, but is simpler,
yet not less effective. In figure 293 there is an aberrant form of design
in which the triangle is used in combination with parallel and oblique
bands. This form, while one of the simplest in its elements, is effective
and characteristic. The triangle predominates in figure 294, but the

FIG. 295—Single line; closed fret

details are worked out in rectangular patterns, producing the terraced
designs so common in all Pueblo decorations. Rectangular figures
are more commonly used than the triangular in the decoration of the
exterior of the bowls, and their many combinations are often very
perplexing to analyze.

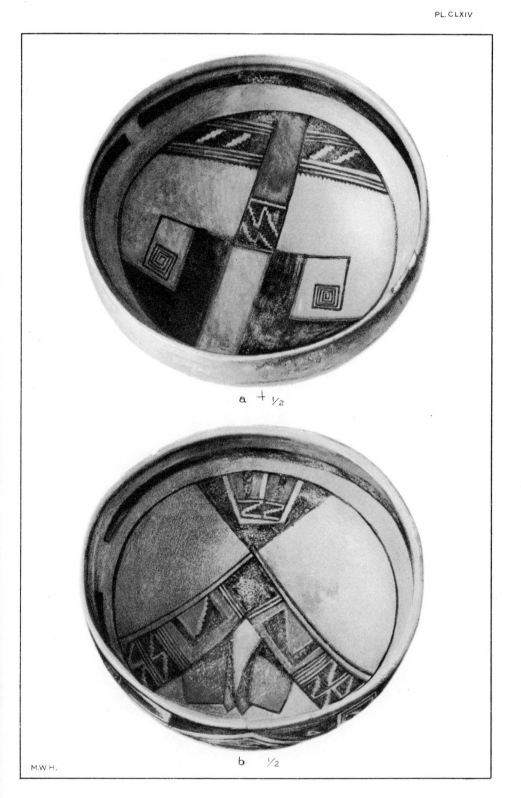

a $+$ ½

b ½

M.W.H.

FOOD BOWLS WITH GEOMETRIC ORNAMENTATION FROM SIKYATKI.

In figure 295, starting with the simple encircling band, it is found
divided into alternating rectangles. The line is continuous, and hence
one side of each rectangle is not complete. Both this design and its

FIG. 296—Single line; open fret

modification in figure 296 consist of an unbroken line of equal breadth
throughout. In the latter figure, however, the openings in the sides
are larger or the approach to a straight line closer. The forms are

FIG. 297—Single line; broken fret

strictly rectangular, with no additional elements. Figure 297 intro-
duces an important modification of the rectangular motive, consisting

FIG. 298—Single line; parts displaced

of a succession of lines broken at intervals, but when joined are always
arranged at right angles.

Possibly the least complex form of rectangular ornamentation, next

FIG. 299—Open fret; attachment displaced

to a simple bar or square, is the combination shown in figure 298, a type
in which many changes are made in interior as well as in exterior decorations of Pueblo ware. One of these is shown in figure 299, where the

FIG. 300—Simple rectangular design

figure about the vessel is continuous. An analysis of the elements in
figure 300 shows squares united at their angles, like the last, but that
in addition to parallel bands connecting adjacent figures there are two

marginal lines uniting the series. Each of the inner parallel lines is bound to a marginal on the opposite side by a band at right angles to it. The marginal lines are unbroken through the length of the figure.

Fig. 301—Rectangular reversed S-form

Like the last, this motive also may be regarded as developed from a single line.

Figures 301 and 302 are even simpler than the design shown in figure

Fig. 302—Rectangular S-form with crooks

300, with appended square key patterns, all preserving rectangular forms and destitute of all others. They are of S-form, and differ more especially in the character of their appendages.

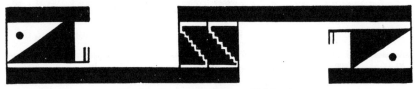

Fig. 303—Rectangular S-form with triangles

While the same rectangular idea predominates in figure 303, it is worked out with the introduction of triangles and quadrilateral designs. This fairly compound pattern, however, is still classified among rectangular forms. A combination of rectangular and triangular geometric

Fig. 304—Rectangular S-form with terraced triangles

designs, in which, however, the former predominate, is shown in figure 304, which can readily be reduced to certain of those forms already mentioned. The triangles appear to be subordinated to the rectangles, and even they are fringed on their longer sides with terraced forms. It may be said that there are but two elements involved, the rectangle and the triangle.

The decoration in figure 305 consists of rectangular and triangular figures, the latter so closely approximated as to leave zigzag lines in

Fig. 305—S-form with interdigitating spurs

white. These lines are simply highly modified breaks in bands which join in other designs, and lead by comparison to the so-called "line of life" which many of these figures illustrate.

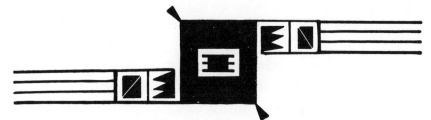

Fig. 306—Square with rectangles and parallel lines

The distinctive feature of figure 306 is the square, with rectangular designs appended to diagonally opposite angles and small triangles at intermediate corners. These designs have a distant resemblance to

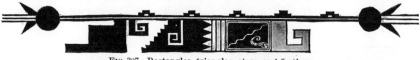

Fig. 307—Rectangles, triangles, stars, and feathers

figures later referred to as highly conventionalized birds, although they may be merely simple geometrical patterns which have lost their symbolic meaning.

Fig. 308—Crook, feathers, and parallel lines

Figure 307 shows a complicated design, introducing at least two elements in addition to rectangles and triangles. One of these is a curved crook etched on a black ground. In no other exterior decoration have curved lines been found except in the form of circles, and it is worthy of note how large a proportion of the figures are drawn in straight lines. The circular figures with three parallel lines extending from them are found so constantly in exterior decorations, and are so strikingly like some of the figures elsewhere discussed, that I have ventured a suggestion in regard to their meaning. I believe they represent

FIG. 309—Crooks and feathers

feathers, because the tail-feathers of certain birds are symbolized in that manner, and their number corresponds with those generally depicted in the highly conventionalized tails of birds. With this thought in mind, it may be interesting to compare the two projections, one on each side of the three tail-feathers of this figure, with the extremity of the body of a bird shown in plate CXLI, e. On the supposi-

FIG. 310—Rectangle, triangles, and feathers

tion that a bird figure was intended in this design, it is interesting also to note the rectangular decorations of the body and the association with stars made of three blocks in several bird figures, as already described. It is instructive also to note the fact that the figure of a maid represented in plate CXXIX, a, has two of the round designs with appended parallel lines hanging to her garment, and four parallel marks drawn

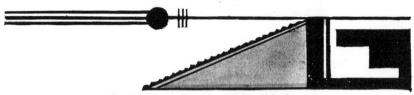

FIG. 311—Terraced crook, triangle, and feathers

from her blanket. It is still customary in Hopi ceremonials to tie feathers to the garments of those who personate certain mythic beings, and it is possible that such was also the custom at Sikyatki. If so, it affords additional evidence that the parallel lines are representations of feathers.

In figure 308 a number of these parallel lines are represented, and the general character of the design is rectangular. In figure 309 is

a   ½

b   ½

FOOD BOWLS WITH GEOMETRIC ORNAMENTATION FROM SIKYATKI

shown a combination of rectangular and triangular figures with three tapering points and circles with lines at their tips radiating instead of parallel.   Another modification is shown in figure 310 in which the

FIG. 312—Double key

triangle predominates, and figure 311 evidently represents one-half of a similar device with modifications.

One of the most common designs on ancient pottery is the stepped

FIG. 313—Triangular terrace

figure, a rectangular ornamentation, modifications of which are shown in figures 312–314.   This is a very common design on the interior of food vessels, where it is commonly interpreted as a rain-cloud symbol.

Of all patterns on ancient Tusayan ware, that of the terrace figures

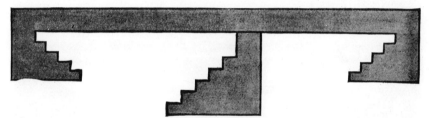

FIG. 314—Crook, serrate end

most closely resemble the geometrical ornamentation of cliff-house pottery, and there seems every reason to suppose that this form of design admits of a like interpretation.   The evolution of this pattern from plaited basketry has been ably discussed by Holmes and Nordenskiöld, whose works have already been quoted in this memoir. The terraced forms from the exterior of food bowls here considered are highly aberrent; they may be forms of survivals, motives of decoration which have persisted from very early times. Whatever the origin of the stepped figure in Pueblo art was, it is well to remember, as shown by

FIG. 315—Key pattern; rectangle and triangles

Holmes, that it is "impossible to show that any particular design of the highly constituted kind was desired through a certain identifiable series of progressive steps."

For some unknown reason the majority of the simple designs on the

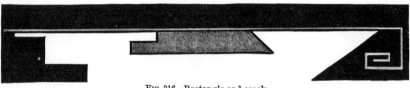

FIG. 316—Rectangle and crook

exterior of food bowls from Tusayan are rectangular, triangular, or linear in their character. Many can be reduced to simple or multiple lines. Others were suggested by plaited ware.

In figure 312 is found one of the simplest of rectangular designs, a

FIG. 317—Crook and tail feathers

simple band, key pattern in form, at one end, with a reentrant square depression at the opposite extremity. In figure 313 is an equally simple terrace pattern with stepped figures at the ends and in the middle. These forms are common decorative elements on the exterior of jars and vases, where they occur in many combinations, all of which are reducible to these types. The simplest form of the key pattern is shown in figure 314, and in figure 315 there is a second modification of the same design a little more complicated. This becomes somewhat changed in figure 316, not only by the modifications of the two extremities, but also by the addition of a median geometric figure.

FIG. 318—Rectangle, triangle, and serrate spurs

The design in figure 317 is rectangular, showing a key pattern at one end, with two long feathers at the opposite extremity. The five bodies on the same end of the figure are unique and comparable with conventionalized star emblems. The series of designs in the upper left-hand end of this figure are unlike any which have yet been found on the

FIG. 319—W-pattern; terminal crooks

exterior of food bowls, but are similar to designs which have elsewhere been interpreted as feathers. On the hypothesis that these two parts of the figure are tail-feathers, we find in the crook the analogue of the head of a bird. Thus the designs on the equator of the vase (plate CXLV, a), which are birds, have the same crook for the head, and two

FIG. 320—W-pattern; terminal rectangles

simple tail-feathers, rudely drawn but comparable with the two in figure 317. The five dentate bodies on the lower left-hand end of the figure also tell in favor of the avian character of the design, for the following reason: These bodies are often found accompanying figures of conventionalized birds (plates CXLIV, CLIV, and others). They are regarded as modified crosses of equal arms, which are all but universally present in combinations with birds and feathers (plates CXLIV, a, b; CLIV, a), from the fact that in a line of crosses depicted on a bowl one of the crosses is replaced by a design of similar character. The arms of the cross are represented; their intersection is left in white. The interpretation of figure 317 as a highly conventionalized bird design is also in accord with the same interpretation of a number of similar, although less complicated, figures which appear with crosses. Thus the three arms of plate CLX, *a*, have highly conventionalized bird symbols attached to their extremities. In the cross figure shown in plate CLVIII, *d*, we find four bird figures with short, stumpy tail-feathers. These highly con-

Fig. 321—W-pattern; terminal terraces and crooks.

ventionalized birds, with the head in the form of a crook and the tail-feathers as parallel lines, are illustrated on many pottery objects, nowhere better, however, than in those shown in plates CXXVI, *a*, and CLX, *e*. Figure 318 may be compared with figure 317.

Numerous modifications of a key pattern, often assuming a double triangular form, but with rectangular elements, are found on the exterior of many food bowls. These are variations of a pattern the simplest form of which is shown in figure 319. Resolving this figure into

Fig. 322—W pattern; terminal spurs

two parts by drawing a median line, we find the arrangement is bilaterally symmetrical, the two sides exactly corresponding. Each side consists of a simple key pattern with the shank inclined to the rim of the bowl and a bird emblem at its junction with the other member.

In figure 320 there is a greater development of this pattern by an elaboration of the key, which is continued in a line resembling a square spiral. There are also dentations on a section of the edge of the lines.

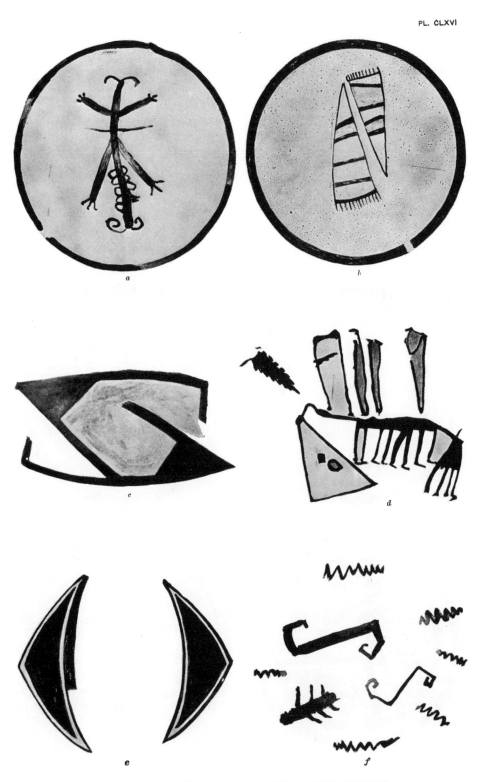

LINEAR FIGURES ON FOOD BOWLS FROM SIKYATKI

GEOMETRIC ORNAMENTATION FROM AWATOBI

In figure 321 there is a still further development of the same design and a lack of symmetry on the two sides. The square spirals are replaced on the left by three stepped figures, and white spaces with parallel lines are introduced in the arms of a W-shape figure.

In figure 322 the same design is again somewhat changed by modification of the spirals into three triangles rimmed on one side with a

FIG. 323—W-pattern; bird form

row of dots, which are also found on the outer lines surrounding the lower part of the design.

In figure 323 the same W shape design is preserved, but the space in the lower reentrant angle is occupied by a symmetrical figure resembling two tail-feathers and the extremity of the body of a bird. When this figure is compared with the design on plate CXLVI, *a*, resemblances are found in the two lateral appendages or wings. The star emblem is also present in the design. The median figure in that design which I have compared to the tail of a bird is replaced in figure 324 by

FIG. 324—W-pattern; median triangle

a triangular ornament. The two wings are not symmetrical, but no new decorative element is introduced. It, however, will be noticed that there is a want of symmetry on the two sides of a vertical line in the figure last mentioned. The right hand upper side is continued into five pointed projections, which fail on the left-hand side. There is likewise a difference in the arrangement of the terraced figures in the two parts. The sides of the median triangles are formed of alternating black and white blocks, and the quadrate figure which it incloses is etched with a diagonal and cross.

The decoration in figure 325 consists of two triangles side by side,

FIG. 325—Double triangle; two breath feathers

each having marginal serrations, and a median square key pattern. One side of these triangles is continued into a line from which hang two breath feathers, while the other end of the same line ends in a

FIG. 326—Double triangle; median trapezoid

round dot with four radiating, straight lines. The triangles recall the butterfly symbol, the key pattern representing the head.

In figure 326 there is a still more aberrant form of the W-shape

FIG. 327—Double triangle; median rectangle

design. The wings are folded, ending in triangles, and prolonged at their angles into projections to which are appended round dots with three parallel lines. The median portion, or that in the reentrant

FIG. 328—Double compound triangle; median rectangle

angle of the W, is a four-sided figure in which the triangle predominates with notched edges. Figure 327 shows the same design with the median portion replaced by a rectangle, and in which the key pattern has wholly disappeared from the wings. In figure 328 there are still greater modifications, but the symmetry about a median axis remains. The ends of the wings instead of being folded are expanded,

FIG. 329—Double triangle; median triangle

and the three triangles formerly inclosed are now free and extended. The simple median rectangle is ornamented with a terrace pattern on its lower angles.

FIG. 330—Double compound triangle

Figure 329 shows a design in which the extended triangles are even more regular and simple, with triangular terraced figures on their inner edge. The median figure is a triangle instead of a rectangle.

FIG. 331—Double rectangle; median rectangle

Figure 330 shows the same design with modification in the position of the median figure, and a slight curvature in two of its sides.

Somewhat similar designs, readily reduced to the same type as the

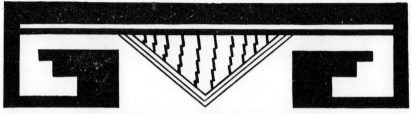

FIG. 332—Double rectangle; median triangle

last three or four which have been mentioned, are shown in figures 331 and 332. The resemblances are so close that I need not refer to them in detail. The W form is wholly lost, and there is no resemblance to a bird, even in its most highly conventionalized forms. The median design in figure 331 consists of a rectangle and two triangles so arranged as to leave a rectangular white space between them. In figure 332 the median triangle is crossed by parallel and vertical zigzag lines.

FIG. 333—Double triangle with crooks

In the design represented in figure 333 there are two triangular figures, one on each side of a median line, in relation to which they are symmetrical. Each triangle has a simple key pattern in the middle, and the line from which they appear to hang is blocked off with alter-

FIG. 334—W shape figure; single line with feathers

nating black and white rectangles. At either extremity of this line there is a circular dot from which extend four parallel lines.

A somewhat simpler form of the same design is found in figure 334, showing a straight line above terminating with dots, from which extend

FIG. 335—Compound rectangle, triangles, and feathers

parallel lines, and two triangular figures below, symmetrically placed in reference to an hypothetical upright line between them.

Figure 335 bears a similarity to the last mentioned only so far as the lower half of the design is concerned. The upper part is not symmet-

FIG. 336—Double triangle

rical, but no new decorative element is introduced. Triangles, frets, and terraced figures are inserted between two parallel lines which terminate in round dots with parallel lines.

The design in figure 336 is likewise unsymmetrical, but it has two lateral triangles with incurved terrace and dentate patterns. The

same general form is exhibited in figure 337, with the introduction of
two pointed appendages facing the hypothetical middle line. From
the general form of these pointed designs, each of which is double,
they have been interpreted as feathers. They closely resemble the tail-

FIG. 337—Double triangle and feathers

feathers of bird figures on several bowls in the collection, as will be seen
in several of the illustrations.

Figure 338 is composed of two triangular designs fused at the greatest

FIG. 338—Twin triangles

angles. The regularity of these triangles is broken by a square space
at the fusion. At each of the acute angles of the two triangles there
are circular designs with radiating lines, a common motive on the

FIG. 339—Triangle with terraced appendages

exterior of food bowls. Although no new elements appear in figure
338, with the exception of bracket marks, one on each side of a circle,
the arrangement of the two parts symmetrically about a line parallel

FIG. 340—Mosaic pattern

with the rim of the bowl imparts to the design a unique form. The
motive in figure 339 is reducible to triangular and rectangular forms,
and while exceptional as to their arrangement, no new decorative feature is introduced.

The specimen represented in figure 340 has as its decorative elements, rectangles, triangles, parallel lines, and birds' tails, to which may be added star and crosshatch motives. It is therefore the most complicated of all the exterior decorations which have thus far been considered. There is no symmetry in the arrangement of figures about a central axis, but rather a repetition of similar designs.

The use of crosshatching is very common on the most ancient Pueblo ware, and is very common in designs on cliff-house pottery. This style

FIG. 341—Rectangles, stars, crooks, and parallel lines

of decoration is only sparingly used on Sikyatki ware. The crosshatching is provisionally interpreted as a mosaic pattern, and reminds one of those beautiful forms of turquois mosaic on shell, bone, or wood found in ancient pueblos, and best known in modern times in the square ear pendants of Hopi women. Figure 340 is one of the few designs having terraced figures with short parallel lines depending from them. These figures vividly recall the rain-cloud symbol with falling rain rep-

FIG. 342—Continuous crooks

resented by the parallel lines. Figure 341 is a perfectly symmetrical design with figures of stars, rectangles, and parallel lines. It may be compared with that shown in figure 340 in order to demonstrate how wide the difference in design may become by the absence of symmetrical relationship. It has been shown in some of the previous motives that the crook sometimes represents a bird's head, and parallel lines appended to it the tail-feathers. Possibly the same interpretation may

FIG. 343—Rectangular terrace pattern

be given to these designs in the following figures, and the presence of stars adjacent to them lends weight to this hypothesis.

An indefinite repetition of the same pattern of rectangular design is shown in figure 342. This highly decorative motive may be varied indefinitely by extension or concentration, and while it is modified in that manner in many of the decorations of vases, it is not so changed on the exterior of food bowls.

There are a number of forms which I am unable to classify with the foregoing, none of which show any new decorative design. All possible changes have been made in them without abandoning the elemental ornamental motives already considered. The tendency to step or terrace patterns predominates, as exemplified in simple form in figure

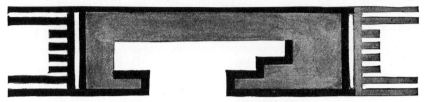

Fig. 344—Terrace pattern with parallel lines

343. In figure 344 there is a different arrangement of the same terrace pattern, and the design is helped out with parallel bands of different length at the ends of a rectangular figure. A variation in the depth of color of these lines adds to the effectiveness of the design. This style of ornamentation is successfully used in the designs represented

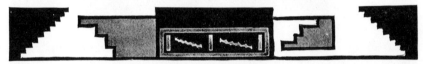

Fig. 345—Terrace pattern

in figures 345 and 346, in the body of which a crescentic figure in the black serves to add variety to a design otherwise monotonous. The two appendages to the right of figure 346 are interpreted as feathers, although their depart forms widely from that usually assumed by these designs. The terraced patterns are replaced by dentate margins in

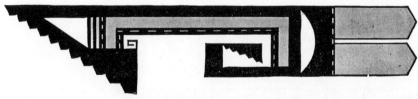

Fig. 346—Triangular pattern with feathers

this figure, and there is a successful use of most of the rectangular and triangular designs.

In the specimens represented in figures 347 and 348 marginal dentations are used. I have called the design referred to an S-form, which, however, owing to its elongation is somewhat masked. The oblique bar in the middle of the figure represents the body of the letter, the two extremities taking the forms of triangles.

So far as decorative elements are concerned the design in figure 349 can be compared with some of those preceding, but it differs from them in combination. The motive in figure 350 is not unlike the ornamentation of certain oriental vases, except from the presence of the terraced

FIG. 347—S-pattern

figures. In figure 351 there are two designs separated by an inclined break the edge of which is dentate. This figure is introduced to show the method of treatment of alternating triangles of varying depth of color and the breaks in the marginal bands or "lines of life." One of

FIG. 348—Triangular and terrace figures

the simplest combinations of triangular and rectangular figures is shown in figure 353, proving how effectually the original design may be obscured by concentration.

In the foregoing descriptions I have endeavored to demonstrate that,

FIG. 349—Crook, terrace, and parallel lines

notwithstanding the great variety of designs considered, the types used are very limited in number. The geometrical forms are rarely curved lines, and it may be said that spirals, which appear so constantly on pottery from other (and possibly equally ancient or older) pueblos

FIG. 350—Triangles, squares, and terraces

than Sikyatki, are absent in the external decorations of specimens found in the ruins of the latter village.

Every student of ancient and modern Pueblo pottery has been impressed by the predominance of terraced figures in its ornamentation, and the meaning of these terraces has elsewhere been spoken of at some length. It would, I believe, be going too far to say that these step designs always represent clouds, as in some instances they are produced by such an arrangement of rectangular figures that no other forms could result.

The material at hand adds nothing new to the theory of the evolution of the terraced ornament from basketry or textile productions, so

FIG. 351—Bifurcated rectangular design

ably discussed by Holmes, Nordenskiöld, and others. When the Sikyatki potters decorated their ware the ornamentation of pottery had reached a high development, and figures both simple and complicated were used contemporaneously. While, therefore, we can so arrange

FIG. 352—Lines of life and triangles

them as to make a series, tracing modifications from simple to complex designs, thus forming a supposed line of evolution, it is evident that there is no proof that the simplest figures are the oldest. The great number of terraced figures and their use in the representation of

FIG. 353—Infolded triangles

animals seem to me to indicate that they antedate all others, and I see no reason why they should not have been derived from basketry patterns. We must, however, look to pottery with decorations less highly developed for evidence bearing on this point. The Sikyatki artists had advanced beyond simple geometric figures, and had so highly modified these that it is impossible to determine the primitive form.

As I have shown elsewhere, the human hand is used as a decorative element in the ornamentation of the interior of several food bowls. It is likewise in one instance chosen to adorn the exterior. It is the only part of the human limbs thus used. Figure 354 shows the hand with marks on the palm probably intended to represent the lines which are

Fig. 354—Human hand

used in the measurement of the length of pahos or prayer-sticks. From between the index and the middle finger rises a line which recalls that spoken of in the account of the hand on the interior of the food bowl shown in plate CXXXVII.

Fig. 355—Animal paw, limb, and triangle

The limb of an animal with a paw, or possibly a human arm and hand, appears as a decoration on the outside of another food bowl, where it is combined with the ever-constant stepped figure, as shown in figure 355.

DESIGNS ON PREHISTORIC HOPI POTTERY

BY

JESSE WALTER FEWKES

CONTENTS

Page

Introduction.. 215
  Chronology of Hopi pottery symbols....................................... 215
The ruin, Sikyatki.. 218
  Sikyatki epoch... 219
  Human figures.. 220
  Quadruped figures.. 223
  Reptilian figures.. 225
  Winged figures... 227
    Dorsal views of birds.. 228
    Lateral views of birds... 233
    Feather designs.. 236
      Feathers suspended from strings...................................... 241
  Sky-band... 242
    Vertical attachment to sky-band.. 243
    Birds attached longitudinally to sky-band.............................. 246
      Decorations on exteriors of food bowls............................... 248
      Curved figure with attached feathers................................. 251
  Spider and insects... 252
  Butterfly and moth... 252
  Geometrical designs.. 255
  Rain clouds.. 256
  Stars.. 257
  Sun emblems.. 258
  Rectangular figures representing shrines................................. 262
  Symbols introduced from San Juan River settlements....................... 264
  Symbols introduced by the Snake people................................... 265
Tanoan epoch... 266
  Symbols introduced from the Little Colorado.............................. 267
  Symbols introduced by the Badger and Kachina clans....................... 273
  Symbols introduced from Awatobi.. 275
  Shalako mana... 275
  Symbols of Hano clans.. 279
Conclusion... 281
Authorities cited.. 284

ILLUSTRATIONS

PLATES

		Page
76.	Various forms of conventionalized feathers	238
77.	Conventionalized tail feathers	240
78.	Conventionalized feathers attached to strings (nakwakwoci)	240
79.	Sky-bands	242
80.	Geometrical figures on outside of bowls	250
81.	Geometrical figures on outside of bowls	250
82.	Geometrical figures on outside of bowls	250
83.	Geometrical figures on outside of bowls	250
84.	Geometrical figures on outside of bowls	250
85.	Conventionalized bird designs	250
86.	Conventionalized bird designs	250
87.	Bird, sun, and spider and sun symbols	258
88.	Conventionalized bird figures	258
89.	Shalako mana, Corn Maid (from tablet dance)	276
90.	Top of butterfly vase	276

TEXT FIGURES

12.	Human head with hair in characteristic whorls	221
13.	Woman with serpent-like animal	221
14.	Kneeling woman, showing hair in characteristic whorls	222
15.	Three human figures	223
16.	a, Deer; b, rabbit	224
17.	Quadruped	224
18.	Antelope or mountain sheep	224
19.	Mountain lion	225
20.	Problematical reptile	225
21.	Reptile	225
22.	Reptile	225
23.	Reptile	226
24.	Reptile	227
25.	Turtle	227
26.	Clouds and tadpoles	228
27.	Tadpoles	228
28.	Dorsal view of a bird	229
29.	Bird figure, two halves restored to natural position	229
30.	Dorsal view of bird	230
31.	Bird figure	230
32.	Bird figure	231
33.	Bird figure	231
34.	Bird figure	231
35.	Bird figure (Thunderbird)	231
36.	Bird figure	232
37.	Highly conventionalized figure of bird from dorsal side	232
38.	Conventional figure of a bird	233

Page

39. Conventional figure of a bird... 233
40. Conventional figure of a bird... 233
41. Conventional figure of a bird... 233
42. Conventional figure of a bird... 234
43. Triangular form of bird... 234
44. Triangular form of bird... 234
45. Simple form of bird with terraced body..................................... 234
46. Lateral view of triangular bird with two tail feathers...................... 234
47. Lateral view of bird with three tail feathers............................... 234
48. Problematical bird figure... 234
49. Bird with two tail feathers... 234
50. Highly conventionalized bird figure... 234
51. Lateral view of bird.. 235
52. Profile of bird... 235
53. Lateral view of bird with outspread wing.................................... 235
54. Lateral view of bird with twisted tail and wing feathers.................... 235
55. Lateral view of conventionalized bird....................................... 236
56. Lateral view of conventionalized bird....................................... 236
57. Feather symbol with black notch... 237
58. Feather symbol with black notch... 237
59. Feathers.. 241
60. Curved feathers... 241
61. Conventional feathers... 241
62. Parallel lines representing feathers.. 241
63. Conventionalized bird form hanging from sky-band, top view.................. 244
64. Conventionalized bird form hanging from sky-band, top view.................. 244
65. Conventionalized bird form hanging from sky-band, top view.................. 244
66. Conventionalized bird form hanging from sky-band, top view.................. 244
67. Conventionalized bird form hanging from sky-band, top view.................. 245
68. Conventionalized bird form hanging from sky-band, top view.................. 245
69. Conventionalized bird form hanging from sky-band, top view.................. 245
70. Conventionalized bird form hanging from sky-band, top view.................. 246
71. Conventionalized bird form hanging from sky-band, top view.................. 246
72. Conventionalized bird form hanging from sky-band, top view.................. 247
73. Conventionalized bird form hanging from sky-band, top view.................. 247
74. Lateral view of bird hanging from sky-band.................................. 247
75. Lateral view of bird hanging from sky-band.................................. 248
76. Lateral view of bird with extended wing..................................... 248
77. Lateral view of bird hanging from sky-band.................................. 249
78. Lateral view of bird hanging from sky-band.................................. 249
79. Butterfly and flower.. 252
80. Butterfly with extended proboscis... 253
81. Highly conventionalized butterfly... 253
82. Moth.. 254
83. Moth.. 254
84. Moth of geometrical form.. 255
85. Geometrical form of moth.. 255
86. Highly conventionalized butterfly... 255
87. Geometrical form of moth.. 255
88. Circle with triangles... 255
89. Rain cloud.. 257
90. Rain cloud.. 257
91. Ring with appended feathers... 258

                                                                    Page
 92. Two circles with figure..   259
 93. Sun with feathers...   259
 94. Sun symbol..   259
 95. Ring with appended feathers.......................................   260
 96. Ring figure with legs and appended feathers.......................   260
 97. Sun emblem with appended feathers.................................   260
 98. Sun symbol..   261
 99. Sun symbol..   261
100. Horned snake with conventionalized shrine.........................   263
101. Shrine..   263
102. Shrine..   264
103. Conventionalized winged bird with shrine..........................   264
104. Lateral view of bird with double eyes.............................   269
105. Lateral view of bird with double eyes.............................   270
106. Bird with double eyes..   271
107. Two birds with rain clouds.......................................   272
108. Head of Shalako mana, or Corn maid...............................   276
109. Head of Kokle, or Earth woman....................................   280
110. Head of Hahaiwugti, or Earth woman...............................   280
111. Ladle with clown carved on handle and Earth woman on bowl...........   281
112. Püükon hoya, little War god......................................   281

DESIGNS ON PREHISTORIC HOPI POTTERY

By Jesse Walter Fewkes

INTRODUCTION

In the following pages the author has endeavored to draw attention to some of the most important symbols on Hopi pottery, especially those of prehistoric times.

Consideration of this subject has led to a discussion of the character of pottery designs at different epochs and the interpretation, by study of survivals, of ancient designs in modern times. This chronological treatment has necessitated an examination of ceramic material from ruins of different ages and an ethnological study of ancient symbols still surviving in ceremonials now practiced. It has also led to sociological researches on the composition of the tribe, the sequence in the arrival of clans at Walpi, and their culture in distant homes from which they migrated. It will thus appear that the subject is a very complicated one, and that the data upon which conclusions are based are sociological as well as archeological. There are many ruins from which material might have been obtained, but only a few have been adequately investigated. The small number of ruins in the Hopi country which have thus far been excavated necessarily makes our knowledge not only provisional but also imperfect. It is hoped, however, that this article may serve to stimulate others to renewed field work and so add desired data to the little we have bearing on the subject.

Chronology of Hopi Pottery Symbols

At least three well-marked epochs can be distinguished in the history of Hopi ceramic symbolism. Each of these is intimately associated with certain clans that have from time to time joined the Hopi and whose descendants compose the present population. Although these epochs follow each other in direct sequence, each was not evolved from its predecessor or modified by it, except to a very limited extent. Each epoch has left to the succeeding one a heritage of symbols, survivals which are somewhat difficult to differentiate from exotic symbols introduced by incoming clans. So that while each epoch grades almost imperceptibly into the one directly following it, an abrupt change is sometimes evident in the passage.

In order to appreciate the relations between ceramic decoration and history let me sketch in brief outline what I regard as the historical development of the Hopi living near or on the East Mesa. We know little of the group of people who first settled here except that they belonged to the Bear clan, which is traditionally referred to the eastern pueblo region. At about the time they entered Hopiland there was a settlement called Sikyatki composed of Jemez colonists, situated about 3 miles from the southern point of East Mesa, and other towns or pueblos on Awatobi Mesa and in Antelope Valley, 10 miles away.

The first great additions to this original population were Snake clans, who came from the San Juan, followed by Flute clans from the same direction but originally of southern origin. Having become well established at the point of the East Mesa, the combined settlement overthrew Sikyatki and appropriated its clans.

Then came the strenuous days of Spanish invasion and the destruction of Awatobi in 1700. The Little Colorado clans had already begun to seek refuge in the Hopi mountains and their number was greatly augmented by those from Zuñi, a Rio Grande settlement called Tewadi, and elsewhere, each addition bringing new forms of culture and settling new pueblos on or near the East Mesa, as has been shown in previous publications. Traditions point out their former settlements and it remains for the archeologist to excavate those settlements, now in ruins, and verify these traditions. This can be done by a study of artifacts found in them.

As a rule archeologists have relied on technique, form, and especially color, in the classification of Pueblo pottery, leading, on the technical side, to the groups known as (a) rough, coiled ware, and (b) smooth, polished ware; and on that of form, to bowls, vases, jars, dippers, etc. When color is used as the basis of classification the divisions black and white, red, yellow, orange, and polychrome are readily differentiated. Classifications based on these data are useful, as they indicate cultural as well as geographical differences in Pueblo ceramics; but these divisions can be used only with limitations in a study of stages of culture growth. The fact that they are not emphasized in the present article is not because their importance is overlooked, but rather for the purpose of supplementing them with a classification that is independent of and in some particulars more reliable for indicating chronology and culture distinctions.

The life-forms on ancient Sikyatki and other Hopi pottery are painted on what is known as yellow ware, which is regarded by some authors as characteristic of the Hopi area; but pottery of the same color, yet with radically different symbolic life-forms, occurs also in other areas. It thus appears that while a classification of Pueblo pottery by color is convenient, differences of color are not so much indications of diversity in culture as of geologic environment. Designs on pottery are more comprehensive and more definite in culture studies than color, and are so regarded in these pages.

As there exists a general similarity in the form of prehistoric pottery throughout the Southwest, shape alone is also inadequate for a determination of Pueblo culture centers. The great multiplicity and localization of symbols on Pueblo pottery furnishes adequate material for classification by means of the designs depicted on vases, bowls, and other pottery objects. Sikyatki pottery is especially suited to a classification on such a basis, for it is recognized as the most beautiful and the most elaborately decorated prehistoric pottery found in the Southwest. Life-forms are abundant and their symbolism is sufficiently characteristic to be regarded as typical of a well-defined ceramic area. There can, of course, be no question regarding the ancient character of the designs on Sikyatki pottery, nor were they introduced or modified by white men, but are purely aboriginal and prehistoric.

Pottery from the Sikyatki ruin is chosen as a type of the most highly developed or golden epoch in Hopi ceramics. Several other ruins were inhabited when Sikyatki was in its prime and pottery from these belongs to the same epoch, and would probably be equally good to illustrate its character. Fortunately, specimens are available from many of these, as Awatobi, and the ruins in Antelope Valley, old Shumopavi, and other Middle Mesa ruins. The date of the origin of this epoch, or the highest development of Hopi ceramics, is not known, but there is evidence that it lasted until the fall of Awatobi, in 1700. The destruction of Sikyatki occurred before 1540, but Sikyatki has given the name to the epoch and is taken as the type, not only because of the abundance of ceramic material available from that ruin, but also because there can be no doubt of the prehistoric nature of material from it.

There is abundant evidence that the culture of Sikyatki was never influenced by white man. After the overthrow of Awatobi there developed on the East Mesa of the Hopi country a third ceramic epoch which was largely influenced by the influx of Tanoan (Tewa) clans. They came either directly from the Rio Grande or by way of Zuñi and other pueblos. Among other arrivals about 1710 were those clans which settled Hano, a Tewa pueblo on the East Mesa. The Hano and other symbols introduced in this epoch are best known in the present generation by the earlier productions of Nampeo, an expert modern potter.

The pottery of this epoch differs from that of the second in form, color, and technique, but mainly in its symbolism, which is radically different from that of the epochs that preceded it. The symbolism of this phase is easily determined from large collections now in museums. This epoch was succeeded in 1895 by a fourth, in which there was a renaissance of old Sikyatki patterns, under the lead of Nampeo. In that year Nampeo visited the excavations at Sikyatki and made pencil copies of the designs on mortuary bowls. From that time all pottery manufactured by her was decorated with modified Sikyatki symbols, largely to meet the demand for this beautiful ancient ware. The extent of her work, for which there was a large demand, may be judged by the great numbers of Hopi bowls displayed in every Harvey store from New Mexico to California. This modified Sikyatki ware, often sold by unscrupulous traders as ancient, is the fourth, or present, epoch of Hopi ceramics. These clever imitations, however, are not as fine as the productions of the second epoch. There is danger that in a few years some of Nampeo's imitations will be regarded as ancient Hopi ware of the second epoch, and more or less confusion introduced by the difficulty in distinguishing her work from that obtained in the ruins.

THE RUIN, SIKYATKI

The ruins of the ancient pueblo of Sikyatki, consisting of mounds and a few outcropping walls, are situated on rocky elevations rising from the sand hills at the eastern or sunny base of the East Mesa, about 3 miles from the modern Hopi pueblo of Walpi in northeastern Arizona. The founders of Sikyatki are said, in very circumstantial migration legends, to have belonged to a [Keres?] clan called the Kokop, or Firewood, which previously lived in a pueblo near Jemez, New Mexico. Preliminary excavations were made at Sikyatki, under the author's direction, by the Smithsonian Institution in 1895, when there was obtained, chiefly from its cemeteries, a valuable collection of pottery, most of which is now installed in the National Museum.[1]

Little is known of the history of Sikyatki save through tradition, but enough has been discovered to show that it was abandoned before 1540, the year of the visit to Tusayan of Pedro Tovar, an officer of the Coronado expedition. It was probably settled much earlier, perhaps about the time the Bear clans, also said to have come from the Jemez region, built the first houses of Walpi near the point of the terrace at the west or cold side of the East Mesa, below the present settlement.[2] Both of these prehistoric pueblos occupied sites exposed

---

[1] A report on the field work at Sikyatki will be found in the *Seventeenth Ann. Rept. Bur. Amer. Ethn.,* part 2.

[2] Traces of the ancient village of Walpi at this point are still to be seen, and certain ancestral ceremonies are still performed here, in the New-fire rites, as elsewhere described.

to attack by enemies and were not built on mesa tops, hence it may be assumed that there were no enemies to fear in Tusayan at the time of their establishment. But later, when the Snake clans from the north joined the Bear settlement at Walpi, trouble seems to have commenced. As above mentioned, the Bear clans came from the same region as the Kokop and were presumably friendly, probably kin of the Sikyatkians; but the Snake clans came from Tokonabi, in the north, and were no doubt of foreign stock, implying a hostility that may have been the indirect cause of the overthrow of Sikyatki and Awatobi by the other Hopi.

The two epochs in Hopi ceramic development that can be distinguished with certainty are (1) the Sikyatki epoch and (2) the Tanoan or historic epoch. The third, or renaissance, of the Sikyatki dates back to 1895, and may be called the modern epoch. The Sikyatki epoch gave way to the Tanoan about the beginning of the eighteenth century. It did not develop from any group preexisting in the neighborhood of the present Hopi pueblos but was derived from the east and it ceased suddenly, being replaced by a totally different group introduced by radically different clans.[1]

SIKYATKI EPOCH

The most characteristic Hopi pottery bearing symbols of the Sikyatki epoch occurs in a few ruins near the Hopi mesas, but from lack of exploration it is impossible to determine the boundaries of the area in which it is found.

Several museums contain collections of Hopi ware of this epoch, among which may be mentioned the National Museum at Washington, the Field Columbian Museum of Natural History at Chicago, the Museum of the University of Pennsylvania, the Peabody Museum at Cambridge, and the Museum für Volkerkünde at Berlin, Germany. Many bowls of this epoch are likewise found in the American Museum of Natural History, New York, and in the Museum of the Brooklyn Institute. Several private collections in Europe and the United States likewise contain specimens of Sikyatki ware, among them being that gathered by the late Dr. Miller, now at Phoenix, Arizona. The collection of prehistoric Hopi pottery in the National Museum is particularly rich, containing many specimens gathered by the Stevenson expeditions, by the author, and by Dr. Hough, of the U. S. National Museum.

The symbols on the ancient pottery from the Middle Mesa of the Hopi are almost identical with those of Sikyatki, indicating a similarity of culture, a common geographical origin, and a synchronous

---

[1] Pottery making is a woman's industry, and as among the Pueblo the woman determines the clan, so she determines the symbolism of the pottery. Consequently symbolism of pottery is related to that of the clan.

culture. From the character of the symbols on the ancient pottery from the ancient Middle Mesa pueblos it is probable that the clans who founded them came, like the colonists who settled Sikyatki, from the Jemez plateau in New Mexico. Although the Field collection is very rich in old Walpi ware, nothing of importance has been published on the symbols of this collection; it contains some of the most instructive examples of the Sikyatki epoch. A large and probably the most valuable portion of this collection was gathered by Dr. George A. Dorsey and Mr. Charles L. Owen, while many pieces were purchased from Mr. Frank Wattron, of Holbrook, and from the late Mr. T. V. Keam, of Keams Canyon, Arizona. The source of many of the Wattron specimens is unknown, but it is evident from their decoration that some of them are ancient Hopi and probably belong to the Sikyatki epoch and came from Shongopovi, Awatobi, or Sikyatki.

Shortly before his death Mr. T. V. Keam sold to the Museum für Volkerkünde at Berlin, Germany, a rich collection of pottery obtained mainly from Awatobi and Sikyatki, containing several specimens of the Sikyatki epoch which are highly instructive. Some of the designs on the pottery of this collection are unique, and their publication would be a great aid to a study of the most important epoch of Hopi ceramics.

A large proportion of life-forms used in the decoration of Sikyatki pottery are mythological subjects, showing the predominance of supernatural beings and their magic power in the minds of the makers. Like a child, the primitive artist is fond of complexity of detail, and figures in which motion is indicated appealed more to his fancy than those objects that do not move. It needs but a glance at the ancient Sikyatki life-figures to show a tendency to represent detail and to convince one of the superiority of the Sikyatki potters in this respect over those of modern times. There has been a gradual deterioration, not only less care being now devoted to the technique of the pottery but also to the drawing of the figures. This lack in itself is significant, for while modern ware reflects in its hasty crudeness the domination of commercialism, the ancient pottery shows no indication of such influence. Pottery is now made to please the purchaser; in ancient times another motive influenced the maker, for then it was a product worthy of the highest use to which it could be put, since it often formed a part of sacred paraphernalia in religious ceremonies.

HUMAN FIGURES

Sikyatki pictures of human beings depict men and women, singly or in company, and are few in number and crude in execution. Or-

gans of the body—hands, feet, arms, and legs—are often represented
separately. The hand is portrayed on two vessels, and the foot,
elaborately drawn, appears on an-
other; as a general thing when parts
of the body are represented they
are greatly conventionalized. The
few human figures on Sikyatki pottery are crude representations as
compared with those of animals,
and especially of birds. Several of
the figures are represented wearing
ancient costumes and ornaments,
and one or two have their hair done
up in unusual styles; others have
the body or face tattooed or
painted; but as a whole these decorations are rare and shed little light

FIG. 12. — Human head with hair in
characteristic whorls.

on prehistoric customs. There is nothing that can be identified
as a time count, calendric, hieroglyphic, or phonetic signs, or any
record of historical events.

None of the human figures are represented with masks or head-

FIG. 13.—Woman with serpent-like animal.

dresses to indicate the impersona-
tion of kachinas, nor are there
double figures or animal heads depicted on human bodies. The absence of animal or kachina heads
shows one of the marked differences between Sikyatki pictures
and the designs so common on some
other pottery, where a relatively
large number of the heads of the
latter occur. The best representation of a human head is shown in
figure 12,[1] in which a characteristic
coiffure is shown. Fig 13 is identified as a figure of a maiden whose
hair is dressed in two whorls, one above each ear, like a modern
Hopi maid.[2] Opposite this maid is a reptile or similar animal with

---

[1] Many of the illustrations appearing in this paper are taken from the author's memoir
on the results of the Sikyatki excavations in the *17th Ann. Rep. Bur. Amer. Ethnol.,* part 2.

[2] Hopi maidens dress their hair in two whorls, one above each ear, which on marriage
are taken down and braided in two coils. There are differences in the style of putting up
the hair, as appear in different ceremonial personages, but the custom of wearing it in
whorls was probably general among ancient Pueblo maidens and is still followed in certain
ceremonial dances in which women are personated by men. For the difference in the style
of the whorls, see the author's series of pictures of Hopi kachimas in the *Twenty-first
Ann. Rept. Bur. Amer. Ethn.*

head decorated with two eyes on one side and a single foreleg. These two figures probably refer to some episode or Indian legend connecting a Sikyatki maiden with some monster.

The maiden depicted in figure 14 is evidently kneeling, her knees being brought together below, and separated by four median parallel lines that are supposed to indicate feathers; the curved objects at the lower corners of the rectangular blanket probably are also feathers. One hand of the maiden is raised to her head, while the other holds an unknown object, possibly an ear of corn. The woman with an ear of corn recalls a figure on the elaborately painted wooden slab carried by women in the Hopi Marau dance or that on the wooden slab, or *monkohu*, carried by the priests representing Alosaka, Eototo, and other ceremonial personages. These painted slabs do not always

Fig. 14.—Kneeling woman, showing hair in characteristic whorls.

bear pictures of corn ears, for those of the priests known as the Aaltu have, instead of pictures of corn, the corn itself tied to them; in the New-fire ceremony at Walpi members of the Tataukyamû priesthood, at Walpi, also hold ears of corn with or without wooden slabs, while those borne by the warrior Kwakwantû are carved in the form of the sacred plumed serpent, which is their patron.[1]

Different styles of hairdressing are exhibited in figures 13 and 14, that of figure 14 being similar to the modern Hopi. The group of three figures (fig. 15) possibly illustrates some ancient ceremony. The middle figure of this group is represented as carrying a branched stick, or cornstalk, in his mouth.[2] The accompanying figure, or that to the right, has in his hand one of the strange frames used as rattles [3] in historic times by clans (Asa or Honani) of Jemez or of Tewa descent who had settled at the East Mesa. The author is inclined to identify the object held by this figure as one of these ceremonial frames and the man as a Yaya priest.

---

[1] The best idol of this god known to the author appears on one of the Flute altars at Oraibi. It has a single horn (representing the serpent horn) on the head, two wings, and two legs with lightning symbols their whole length. The horned plumed Lightning god of the Kwakwantû at Walpi is represented by plumed serpent effigies in the March ceremony or dramatization elsewhere described.

[2] In the Antelope dance at Walpi, a stalk of corn instead of a snake is carried in the mouth on the day before the Snake dance. (Fewkes, Snake Ceremonials at Walpi, pp. 73–74.)

[3] For descriptions of similar objects see Fewkes, Hopi Ceremonial Frames from Cañon de Chelly, Arizona, pp. 664–670; Fewkes, The Lesser New-fire Ceremony at Walpi, p. 438, pl. XI; also *Twenty-first Ann. Rept. Bur. Amer. Ethn.*, pls. XXXIV, XXXV.

Another interpretation of the central figure of the group, figure 15, is that he is performing the celebrated stick-swallowing act which was practiced at Walpi until a few years ago. The last explanation suggested implies that the human figures represent Snake and Antelope priests, a doubtful interpretation, since, according to legends, these priests were never represented at Sikyatki.[1]

The character shown in another figure, not copied, may represent the supernatural being, called the God of the Dead (Masauû) whose body, according to legend, is spotted and girt by bands. The Little Fire god (Shulewitse), when personated in modern ceremonies of the Tewa at Hano, is represented by a man daubed with pigments of several colors. He is personated likewise in the Hopi (Tewa) village of Sichomovi.[2]

FIG. 15.—Three human figures.

Several Zuñi ceremonies show evidence of derivation from eastern New Mexican pueblos,[3] but a critical examination of the origin and migration of Zuñi clan relations of societies still awaits the student of this interesting pueblo. It is probable that Zuñi sociology is in some respects like that of Walpi and that the present population is composite, having descended from clans which have drifted together from different directions, each bringing characteristic ceremonies and mythological conceptions, while certain rites have been incorporated from time to time from other Pueblo people.

QUADRUPED FIGURES

Representations of quadrupeds are almost as rare as human figures in Sikyatki pottery decorations. The deer (fig. 16, *a*), antelope, mountain sheep, mountain lion, rabbit, and one or two other animals are recognizable, but pictures of these are neither so common nor so highly conventionalized as those of birds,

---

[1] As a matter of history, the Snake people of Walpi may have been hostile to the Kokop of Sikyatki on account of linguistic or tribal differences which culminated in the destruction of the latter pueblo in prehistoric times.

[2] The pueblo of Sichomovi, called by the Hopi Sioki, or Zuñi pueblo, was settled by Asa clans, who were apparently of exotic origin but who went to Sichomovi from Zuñi, in which pueblo the Asa people are known as Aiyahokwe. The Sichomovi people still preserve Zuñi ceremonies and Zuñi kachinas, although they now speak the Hopi language— an example of a pueblo in which alien ceremonies and personations have survived or been incorporated, although its language has been superseded by another.

[3] Thus the Heyamashikwe may be supposed to have originally come from Jemez. The Zuñi Sumaikoli, like that of the Hopi, is practically Tewa in origin.

Figure 17 shows one of two mammalian figures on a bowl, the surrounding surface consisting of spatterwork, an uncommon but effective mode of treatment.

The outline of the animal shown in figure 18 is intensified by spattering, as in the case of the animal last mentioned. The black spots

along the back and tail are absent in other figures. The design below the figure suggests, in some particulars, that of a highly conventionalized shrine, but its true meaning is unknown.

FIG. 16.—*a,* Deer; *b,* rabbit.

The design in figure 19 has been regarded as representing a mountain lion, but there is some doubt of the validity of this identification. Although the feet are like those of a carnivorous animal, the head is not. The two projections from the head, which may represent horns, are not unlike those associated with the two figures next described, which have been regarded as feathers.

FIG 17.—Quadruped.

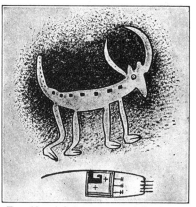

FIG. 18.—Antelope or mountain sheep.

The creature shown in figure 20 is also problematical. The appendages to the head are prolonged, terminating in feathers that bend backward and touch the body. The anterior body appendage has two crescentic prolongations between which are parallel lines of unequal length. The posterior limb is jointed, the lower half extending backward and terminating in two claws, one long, the other short. Between these extensions are two groups of slightly radiating lines that may be regarded as feathers. The body has feathers like those of a highly conventionalized bird, while the limbs resemble those of a lizard. The body is serpentine, and tail feathers are wanting; both legs have talons like those of birds, and the appendage to the head suggests a feather headdress; the line connecting the head appendage and one claw of the posterior limbs recalls a sky-band, commonly found in representations of sky gods.

The animal depicted in figure 21, which resembles figure 19 in the

Fig. 19.—Mountain lion.

Fig. 20.—Problematical reptile.

form of the appendages to the head and mouth, is suspended inside of a circle in the one case and is half within a circle in the other.

Reptilian Figures

Several figures of reptiles and serpents occur in the Sikyatki collection. Figure 22 represents an animal like a reptile; only two legs

Fig. 21.—Reptile.

Fig. 22.—Reptile.

are shown in the design and the form of the tail recalls that of a bird. The head of this figure bears two horns resembling feathers in some respects; the legs terminate in four claws. From a projection at the posterior end of the body there arises a curved line dotted at intervals and terminating in feathers. The dorsal appendage resembles the carapace of a turtle, from beneath which feathers project.

Figure 22 depicts a reptile from the head of which project horns and two long feathers. Its back bears a row of feathers, but it has only two legs.

The legless creature, figure 23, has two triangular earlike feathers rising from the head, and two eyes; a wide-open mouth, in which are six long, curved teeth, three in each jaw. The tongue terminates in an arrow-shaped figure, recalling a conventional symbol of lightning, or the death-dealing power of the serpent. The meaning of the narrow line connecting the upper jaw with the tail is not known. The curved shape of the body of the reptile is necessitated by the shape of the bowl on which it is drawn. This figure may represent the monster feathered serpent of Sikyatki, or a flying reptile, one of the most mysterious of the elemental gods. It is interesting to note that while the effigies of the feathered serpent used in Hopi (Walpi) and Zuñi religious practices has a single horn on the head, the one here described is different from both, for it is provided with two appendages resembling conventionalized feathers. The Hopi feathered serpent was derived from the same source as the Zuñi, namely, clans which originally came to the Little Colorado from Gila Valley.[1]

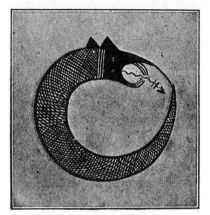

FIG. 23.—Reptile.

The Hopi (Walpi) figure is in a measure comparable with that shown in figure 23—each has two hornlike feathers on the head, and the bodies are curved in the same direction—that is, with the center (?) on the right (dextral circuit), the reverse of modern Hopi pictures, which are placed as if the figures were moving in a sinistral circuit.[2]

The form shown in figure 24 reminds one of a frog or a turtle. The body and feet are turtlelike. As in several pictures of reptiles, it is provided with an anterior appendage, evidently the front leg, which has characteristic claws. The row of white dots extending from the mouth through the neck represents the esophagus or windpipe. The author is unable to offer any interpretation of the append-

---

[1] See Fewkes, The Butterfly in Hopi Myth and Ritual, pp. 576–594.

[2] The clay images representing the Tewa plumed serpent on the Winter Solstice altar at Hano have rows of feathers inserted along their backs (as in the case of the reptile shown in figure 22) as well as rudimentary horns, teeth made of corn kernels, and necklaces of the same. (Fewkes, Winter solstice altars at Hano pueblo, pp. 269–270.) A mosaic of corn kernels on a clay base (*kaetukwi*) is known in ceremonies derived from Sikyatki and Awatobi.

ages to the tail, but suggests that they may have been intended for feathers. Figure 25 *a, b*, is identified as a turtle.

Figure 26 was evidently designed to represent several tadpoles swimming across a bowl between rows of rain clouds, the whole inclosed in a circle to which are attached five stars at approximately equal intervals. The form of the rain clouds reminds one of conventional tail feathers. There are six of these rain-cloud figures on one side of the field of decoration and five on the other. The tadpoles shown in figure 27 occur on the inside of the ladle.

FIG. 24.—Reptile.

WINGED FIGURES

The term "winged figures" is here employed to designate all flying creatures, as birds, insects, and bats, even though they belong zoologically to different groups of animals. Among the prehistoric Hopi, insects and birds were designated by similar symbols and when highly conventionalized sometimes merge into one another. It was the custom of Sikyatki potters to give more attention to specific than generic characters of flying creatures, distinguishing different kinds of birds by the form of their feathers. The symbol of a turkey, an eagle, or a hawk feather was distinct from that of an owl, and each kind of a bird had its own special symbolic marking, especially indicated in the different kinds of feathers. Thus it occurs that Sikyatki bird designs, instead of being realistically represented, are often so highly conventionalized that the genus can not be identified.

a   *b*

FIG. 25.—Turtle.

The flight of birds, like the movement of serpents, is regarded as mysterious, and anything mysterious or uncanny has always profoundly affected the mind of primitive man. The chief visible characteristics connected with the flight of a bird are wings and feathers, and the kind of feathers of a particular bird led to their association with the supposed magic power of the bird itself among both the ancient and modern Hopi. Different kinds of feathers have different powers; thus the feathers of the turkey, for example, among the modern Hopi, are potent in inducing rain; those of the eagle or the hawk pertain especially to the power of the sun; a breast feather of

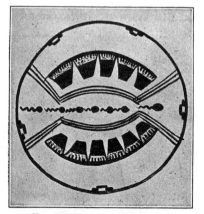

FIG. 26.—Clouds and tadpoles.

an eagle is chosen as an individual prayer bearer. The feathers of an owl, like the owl itself,[1] are generally regarded as having a sinister influence; but sometimes the feather of this bird is beneficial, it is believed, in making peach trees yield abundantly. From the variety of feather designs and the frequency with which they occur in modern Hopi ceremonies[2] it is evident that the Sikyatki people, like their descendants, attributed special magic power to different kinds of these objects.

In their simplest forms bird symbols are little more than triangles, the tail feathers being represented by appended parallel lines, which are mere suggestions of birds and may be designated as cursive forms. Such simple pictures of birds sometimes have, in addition to the appended parallel lines referred to, an angular or a curved line or hook extending from one of the angles of the triangle to represent a beak. Such triangular bird figures may be free or attached; in the latter case they are suspended from other figures or rise from the corners of a rectangular design when one of the triangles may be without tail or beak appendages, another may have parallel lines, while a third may take a form readily recognizable as that of a bird. The form of the beak and the claws of bird figures also varies, the claws often appearing

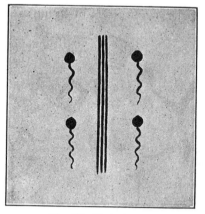

FIG. 27.—Tadpoles.

as simple crosses or crescents. The beak is sometimes toothed, often hooked like that of a raptorial bird. The bird is designated by the combination of the beak, claws, and body, as well as the feathers.

DORSAL VIEWS OF BIRDS

Among the conventional pictures of birds on Sikyatki pottery some are shown as seen from above, or dorsally, others from below, or

[1] The hoot of the owl portends disaster among the Hopi, as among the ancient Greeks.
[2] Every priest has a box in which his feathers are preserved until needed.

ventrally, and still others laterally. These pictures sometimes become so conventionalized that it is difficult to identify the parts represented, as will appear from illustrations to follow.

Figure 28 represents a bird design in which three parallel bands representing tail feathers of a well-marked type hang between two curved extensions that occupy the relative position of wings. In the angles near the attachment of these tail feathers there are two globular enlargements which occur also in other pictures. The extremity of each winglike crescent is spirally curved inward. Two semicircular figures representing rain clouds are surmounted by two parallel lines and a heavy, solid band, appearing at the proximal end of the tail in the position where the body should end, as in other figures where the rain-cloud symbols are much more complex.

FIG. 28.—Dorsal view of a bird.

The two drawings shown in figure 29 are the two halves of a single figure cut along its medial line. One of these halves is reversed in such a way that corresponding parts are found on the same side. Viewing these two parts in this position, we can readily identify various organs of a highly conventionalized bird whose wings are represented by a curved body terminating in a spiral, the body decorated with rain-cloud figures and the bowl with conventionalized figures. This is the only figure showing the distortions and reversions of the two halves of the bird's body and appendages.

FIG. 29.—Bird figure, two halves restored to natural position.

Homologous parts are recognizable also in the bird design shown in figure 30, but in this picture the size of the wings is. greatly reduced, each consisting merely of two feathers. The rectangular body bears a single large terraced or rectangular rain-cloud symbol, three semicircular figures, and two triangles. Two tail feathers and two posterior extensions of the body, one on each side, are shown. There are three parallel lines on each side of these posterior extensions. In a bird design, figure 31, the body is decorated with four triangular rain clouds and the wings are extended. The tail has six feathers with a lateral extension on each side. The two detached figures asso-

FIG. 30.—Dorsal view of a bird.

ciated with this bird design possibly were intended to represent the shrines of these birds.

The curved appendages are spreading in figure 32, and at their point of junction with the body arises a typical feather symbol. The body has four solid semicircular figures, possibly representing rain clouds, and a single feather on the top of the head. Organs corresponding to wings, body, and tail are traceable, but they are somewhat modified in comparison with the forms already considered. This design is partly surrounded by a band to which two star designs are attached.

We find all the parts or organs associated with the bird designs already described represented in figure 33, but the details of the symbolism are more elaborated than in any of the preceding. Here the wings are bent inward, while the feathers have taken

more angular forms. The head is rectangular, bearing representations of two rain clouds just above the wings, while two others appear below. These have the same form as the cloud symbols shown in figure 20. Although this drawing is far from being a realistic representation of a bird, the presence of symbols characteristic of certain avian features leaves no doubt that a bird was intended.

In figure 34 is shown a Sikyatki bird figure still further conventionalized, but the parts are depicted in such manner as to make the

FIG. 31.—Bird figure.

identification as a bird practically certain. Head, body, wings, and tail are elaborately represented. The head is semicircular and surmounted by a headdress with three vertical feathers. The wings are large, each terminating in two symbols representing the feathers,[1] with pointed distal extremities. The tail feathers have rounded ex-

---

[1] Compare with feathers, pl. 90, d.

tremities and are three in number. On each side of the feathers of
the headdress, wings, and tail hang figures of unknown meaning.
This is one of the most instructive bird figures in the collection from
Sikyatki.

Figure 35 represents a very elaborate figure of a bird, readily
comparable with the last mentioned, from which it differs in certain

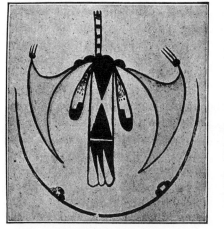

FIG. 32.—Bird figure.

FIG. 33.—Bird figure.

particulars. This bird design is replete with symbolism and may
be regarded as one of the most instructive pictures that has come to
us from the ancient Hopi. The view is from the back, the legs being

FIG. 34.—Bird figure.

FIG. 35.—Bird figure. (Thunderbird.)

much reduced in size, the claws alone being represented at each upper
corner of the body directly under the attachment of the wings. The
beak is invisible, but an elaborate headdress,[1] in which tail feathers

---

[1] Probably the serrated circle to which the headdress is attached was not designed as the
outline of the head, but the headband turned out of perspective.

are conspicuous, is a prominent feature. The form of the tail and wing feathers of this bird is practically the same as the last, except that they are more elaborately drawn. Each wing has two feathers, and three others form the tail. The arrow points projecting from beneath the extremities of the wing feathers are possibly lightning symbols. Each is crossed by two bars in the same manner as the tongue projecting from the mouth of the serpent shown in figure 23, which is also a lightning symbol.

The design illustrated in figure 36 represents a bird, as seen from the back, with outstretched wings, recalling the lateral view of a bird shown in figure 54 in having smaller bird figures attached to the tips of the wings. The place of attachment of the wings to the body is embellished with crosshatched lines and stepped figures, recalling the rain-cloud symbols. The head is rectangular, destitute of a beak, inclosing two square figures with short parallel lines, representing falling rain, projecting from the upper side. On one side of the head is a semicircular design. The tail has three feathers, the two on the sides being broader than the one in the middle. These feathers are without markings, but the end of the body from which they depend is ornamented with stepped figures surmounted by two horizontal parallel lines and two triangles. In the background, at each side of the body, there are dotted circles, suggesting flowers, a feature often accompanying designs representing butterflies or moths.

FIG. 36.—Bird figure.

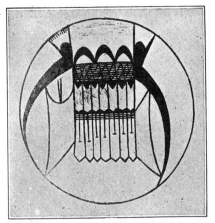

FIG. 37.—Highly conventionalized figure of bird from dorsal side.

In figure 37 is shown a highly conventionalized dorsal view of a bird, with sickle-formed wings slightly extended, seven pointed tail feathers with lateral appendages, and a rectangular head with three semicircular rain-cloud figures. The globular enlargement at the base of the wings in one instance is accompanied by a fan-shaped figure.

The design shown in figure 38 is regarded as a highly conventionalized bird symbol, each wing being represented by a curved pendant,
to the extremities of which feathers
are attached. The body is rectangular and decorated with a median
horizontal white band continued
above and below into black lateral
triangles which possibly may represent feathers, and flanked triangular white areas on each side.

FIG. 38.—Conventional figure of a bird.

In figure 39 the
design has been
so greatly con-
ventionalized
that almost all
resemblance to a bird has been lost. The wings
are represented by simple terraces, the body by a
rectangular figure, and the head terminates in
three points. It is possible that the limit of bird
conventionalization has been reached in this variant, and the difficulty of identification of organs is
correspondingly great.

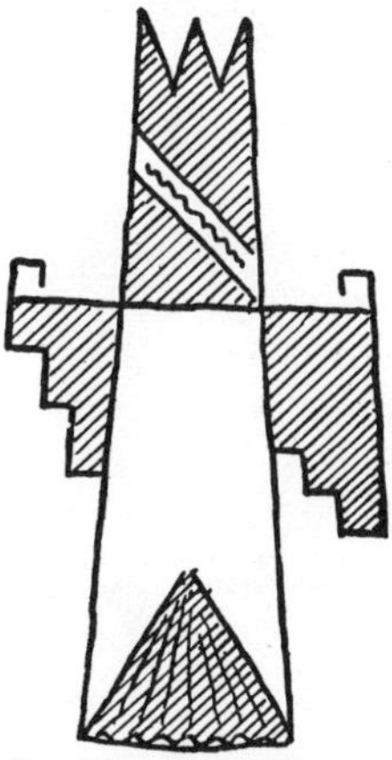

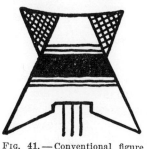

FIG. 39.—Conventional
figure of a bird.

The design shown in figure 40 would perhaps
more logically fall within the series of circular
figures, identified as sun em-
blems, elsewhere considered, ex-
cept for the extensions representing wings and tail.
This is mentioned as one of the instances where
organs of birds are combined with a circle to represent the Sun god.

Figure 41 resembles
figure 40 in some essential
points and may also be
considered in connection
with sun emblems. On
account of the presence of feathers it is
here included among the bird designs.

FIG. 40.—Conven-
tional figure of a
bird.

Figure 42 exhibits an exceptional bird
form as viewed from the rear.[1] Wings,
body, tail, and possibly the head, are recognized after some study.

FIG. 41.—Conventional figure
of a bird.

LATERAL VIEWS OF BIRDS

Drawings representing side views of birds are usually highly conventionalized, often taking the forms of simple geometric figures,

[1] See *Seventeenth Ann. Rept. Bur. Amer. Ethn.*, pt. 2, pl. CXLI, *a*. A circle is here drawn
on each side of the bird.

as shown in figures 43–45. The simplest representation of a bird viewed from the side is a triangle, but another, slightly elaborated and a little more complicated (fig. 43), consists of a triangular body with curved lines representing a head and beak, extending from one of the angles, and with two short lines indicating a feathered head crest. The head of the bird shown in figure 44 resembles a section of a Greek fret, which in figure 45 has become still further simplified. Figure 46 represents a bird with triangular body and key-shaped head. Figure 47 shows a similar design, except that the body is partly rectangular, with breast slightly concave. The body in figure 48 is simply an outline of a terrace and the tail is indicated by five parallel lines.

Fig. 42.—Conventional figure of a bird.

Fig. 43.—Triangular form of bird.

The bird design shown in profile in figure 49 is realistic, all the parts being clearly recognizable. This figure is one of four, each attached to a corner of a rectangle.

Fig. 44.—Triangular form of bird.

Fig. 45.—Simple form of bird with terraced body.

Fig. 46.—Lateral view of triangular bird with two tail feathers.

Another figure which may be a lateral view of a bird is represented in figure 50, in which the part representing the head is curved, the body square, and two obliquely twisted feathers represent the tail.

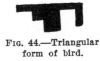

Fig. 47.—Lateral view of bird with three tail feathers.

Fig. 48.—Problematical bird figure.

Fig. 49.—Bird with two tail feathers.

This figure exhibits avian features more obscurely than those already considered, but the head and the tail feathers are quite birdlike.

In figure 51 is shown a lateral view of a bird, seemingly in flight, the head and beak of which are birdlike. The wings, feet, head, and body are not difficult to recognize. Two legs and one wing are shown, and the well-drawn tail, terminating in white-tipped feathers, suggests the turkey, which bird is regarded by the modern Hopi as so efficacious in bringing rain that its feathers are employed in almost all rain ceremonies. The author has seen a similar drawing on altar

Fig. 50.—Highly conventionalized bird figure.

and other ceremonial paraphernalia among the Hopi priests of the present day. The white tips which characterize the tail feathers of the turkey originated, according to a Hopi legend, at the time when this bird dragged the end of its tail in the mud after a flood had subsided.

The bird shown in figure 52 has a curved, elongated

FIG. 51.—Lateral view of bird.

beak, a more or less angular body, two legs, and two small wings. The tail consists of three feathers [1] with characteristic projections.

FIG. 52.—Profile of bird.

One of the best bird pictures on Sikyatki pottery is shown in figure 53. The body is somewhat triangular in shape and the wing is spread out, here shown above the back; the tail is provided with three feathers placed vertically instead of horizontally, and bent over at their ends into triangles, evidently owing to the lack of available space. The beak is characteristically curved; the single eye is provided with a pupil. The long

FIG. 53.—Lateral view of bird with outspread wing.

FIG. 54.—Lateral view of bird with twisted tail and wing feathers.

claws, single on each foot, suggest an eagle, hawk, or other raptorial bird. The spiral appendage to the under rim of the tail is of unknown meaning.

The design shown in figure 54 is one of the most complex bird drawings found on Sikyatki pottery. The head is triangular, with an eye situated in the center, and the beak continued into a very large, elaborate fret. The body is rhomboidal in shape, the upper portion being occupied by a patterned square. Rising above the

---

[1] It is, of course, only a coincidence that so many of the Sikyatki bird designs have three tail feathers like Egyptian representations

body is a conventionalized wing, while depending from its lowermost angle is a diminutive figure resembling feathers. The tail consists of two elongate feathers, rounded at their outer ends and fused at the point of union with the body.

Having seen how prone the ancient Hopi were to represent birds on their pottery and the extent to which conventionalization of these figures prevailed, one finds many designs so closely related to known bird figures that the tendency is to include with them many the identification of which is doubtful. Certain simple geometrical forms originally derived from bird designs were copied by these early potters, presumably without intending to represent birds, but rather merely as decorative motives. Two of these problematic designs are shown in figures 55 and 56.

FIG. 55.—Lateral view of conventionalized bird.

FEATHER DESIGNS

A large number of conventional figures representing feathers have been identified, but there are many others which yet remain to be interpreted, and the particular genus of birds to which each should be referred is likewise problematical. There is no doubt, from a study of the uses of different kinds of feathers in modern Hopi ceremonials, that each form depicted on pottery represents a feather which played an important rôle in ancient Hopi rituals.

Many unquestionable feather designs pictured on Sikyatki pottery are found

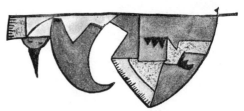

FIG. 56.—Lateral view of conventionalized bird.

depicted on serpents, or are attached to inanimate objects, such as rainbows, clouds, and lightning.

It is probable that the majority of feather designs on ancient Hopi earthenware are included in the following types, to which no doubt

other forms of feather designs will be added later. These types
are abundant in vessels of the Sikyatki epoch.

From the above pictures of birds and many others it may be seen
that feather symbols assume a variety of forms in sikyatki pottery
decoration. There are probably more than 50 different designs,
each representing a different kind of feather, and implying for each
a distinct use or ceremonial efficacy, as among the modern Hopi.
Our knowledge of ancient Hopi symbolism is not yet sufficient to
enable us to identify all the different birds to which
these various forms of feathers belong, nor do we
know the uses to which all these feathers were put.[1]

FIG. 57. — Feather
symbol with black
notch.

Several wooden slabs and idols on Hopi altars
have features drawn upon them, and many cere-
monial sand-pictures contain designs representing feathers. In rare
instances, as in the altar of the Powamû,[2] typical Sikyatki symbols
of feathers are still used, but feather symbols of a form not found
on Sikyatki pottery far outnumber those from that ruin. The existence of one type of Sikyatki feathers on the figure of Pokema in
kachina altars may point to the derivation of this feather symbol from Sikyatki, but some of these types are widespread.[3]

The forms assumed by feathers on Sikyatki pottery may best be
presented by considering a few examples of the more common types.

Figure 57 represents an unusual type of feather
symbol, readily distinguished from others by the
notch at the end, the edge of which is commonly
rounded. There are two subdivisions of this type,
one with a dotted shaft (fig. 58), the other plain.

FIG. 58. — Feather
symbol with black
notch.

This form of feather design is found in most unexpected associations,
occurring on the heads of serpents or attached to various parts of the
body and under the wings of birds. It also hangs from diametrical
bands drawn across the inside of food bowls and from other objects
constituting the decoration of vessels. In a few instances this type
of feather is enlarged and constitutes the essential part of the design, with other symbols attached.

---

[1] Feathers are among the most important objects employed in Pueblo ceremonies, and
among the modern Hopi feathers of different birds are regarded as efficacious for different
specific purposes. Thus the turkey feather symbol is efficacious to bring rain, and the
hawk and eagle feathers are potent in war. The specific feather used ceremonially by
modern Hopi priests is regarded by them as of great importance, and the same doubtless
was true of the priests of ancient Sikyatki and Awatobi. Belief in a difference in the
magic power of certain feathers was deeply rooted in the primitive mind, and was regarded as of great importance by the ancient as well as the modern Hopi.

[2] Compare the sand-mosaic of the sun associated with the Powalawû altar of Oraibi, and
the sun emblem shown in fig. 98.

[3] Mallery (*Fourth Ann. Rept. Bur. Ethn.*, p. 47, fig. 12) illustrates two clusters of
characteristic Hopi feathers copied by Mr. G. K. Gilbert from petroglyphs at Oakley
Springs, Arizona. The first cluster belongs to the type shown in our fig. 57 as eagle tails,
the second to that illustrated in fig. 31. They were identified by the Oraibi chief, Tuba,
and so far as known have not been subsequently figured.

This type of feather sometimes forms a part of a bird's tail, but it does not occur in the wings, although, as above stated, it occurs under a wing or on the body or the head of a bird, a localization that leads to the belief that the device was designed to represent a breast feather, such as the Hopi now use in their prayers. In ancient Hopi symbolism it is often attached to circles representing the sun and represents a tail feather.

In plate 76, *a*, three feathers are represented with pointed tips and without interior markings. It is one of the simplest drawings of the type mentioned.

This figure illustrates a well-known type of feather symbol. It has many variations, all clearly differentiated from the form last described, from which it differs in its elongate form and pointed tip. What may be regarded as a subtype of this is marked with diagonal bands drawn either at right angles at one edge or extending across the figure and terminating at right angles to the opposite edge. Feather symbols of this type, which have not been identified with any particular bird, are constantly found in birds' tails and wings.

The next design (pl. 76, *b*) is similar in outline, but the three feathers are painted solid black and are separated by spaces. This conventional form of feather is common on wings and tails of birds.

The group of symbols shown in plate 76, *c*, has pointed tips, like the others described, but part of the shaft is painted, while the other is plain, the line of demarcation between which is drawn diagonally. This form occurs on the tails rather than on the wings of birds.

The tips of the feathers in plate 76, *d*, are connected by a black band and are divided by short vertical lines. A distinguishing feature of this symbol is the oblique marking of each feather on the right side, by which the feathers are narrowed at the base. A solid semicircular figure with a double notch ornaments the upper edge. The few known examples of this type of feather symbol are from the tails of unknown birds.

The next form of feather, shown in *e*, differs from the last in that the shaft is spotted and the proximal end is cut diagonally in a somewhat different way.[1] The tips are slit as in the figure last described.

The width of the feathers shown in *f* is uniform throughout. The distal ends are tipped with black; the proximal ends are each ornamented with a black triangle. Midway of the length of the feathers are four continuous parallel horizontal lines.

The two feathers shown in *g* have in one instance a black and in the other a white tip separated from the rest of the shaft by an oblique line. The essential difference between this form of pointed

---

[1] Compare feathers, pl. 90, *wf*.

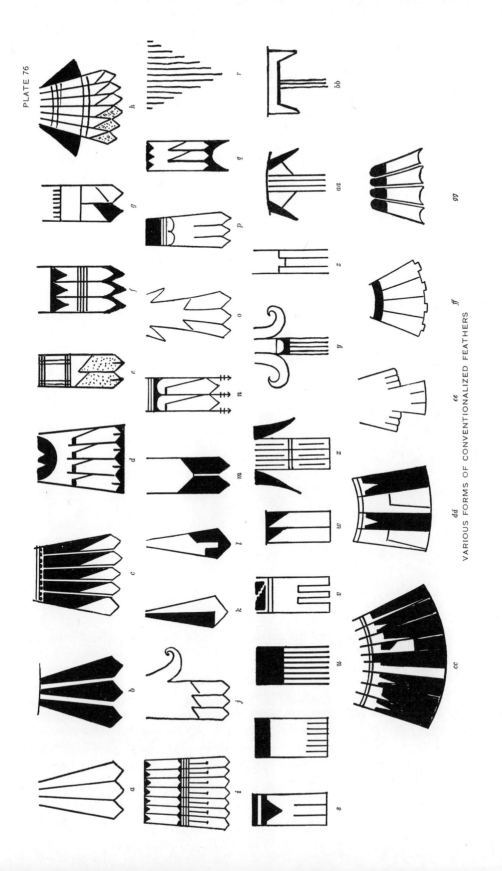

PLATE 76

VARIOUS FORMS OF CONVENTIONALIZED FEATHERS

feather and those previously considered is that the diagonal line marking the tip is drawn at a greater angle.

The six feathers shown in *h* resemble the last, but the terminal portions of three are spotted instead of solid black. Like some of the others described, this form tapers slightly from its distal end to its base.

In *i* the feathers are likewise pointed at their tips, but are of almost uniform breadth. Each is intersected by a series of triangles and parallel lines, and suspended from the latter, one in each feather, are several vertical lines, each with terminal dots.

The symbol shown in *j* is not unlike that already illustrated, but it has in addition to the structure enumerated a lateral hornlike appendage common in the tails of birds (see pl. 90, *i, tf*).

The form of feather design shown in *k* is somewhat different from those already considered. The distal end is broad and pointed; the proximal narrows almost to a point. The left half of the body of the feather is black; the remainder, including the point, is plain. The design *l* has the same general form as *k*, but its tip is marked in a different manner.

The double-pointed symbol represented in *m* was evidently designed as a feather (possibly two feathers), with parallel sides, and pointed tips painted black. The symbol *n* is similar to *d* in outline, but it lacks the terminal slit and black bands. There project, however, from the angles formed by the tips of the feathers three vertical lines, each with an arrow point at the extremity and two short crosslines, as in one of the bird designs previously described (fig. 35). The present design represents wing feathers; the complete bird figure (fig. 35), where they also occur, represents a thunderbird.

The three tail feathers shown in *o* are in no respect peculiar. The two-pointed appendages seen above are an almost constant feature of the drawings of birds as seen from the back. The feathers represented in *p* are unlike others in their mode of attachment and in the ornamentation at the base.

Thus far we have considered a type of feathers with pointed tips (pl. 76, *a–p*) imparting to the whole tail a serrate appearance. While in the next figure, *q*, the tail feathers still terminate in points, a black band connecting their extremities is prolonged at each side, recalling the tail of certain swallows.

Feathers are often represented on Sikyatki pottery as elsewhere in the Southwest by parallel straight lines. The feathers represented in *r* are exceptional in that their length varies considerably, the median feather here being the longest.

While undoubtedly the series of designs shown in *s* to *bb*, inclusive, in each instance representing the feathers in the tail of a bird, are all highly conventionalized, in one or two instances, as u and bb, the relation to feathers can be recognized only by comparative studies.

The design illustrated in cc, taken from the neck of a vase, represents several peculiar feathers of a type not yet described but highly characteristic. Comparison of this with that of dd shows the similarity of the two and suggests that they pertain to the same kind of bird. The tails represented in v, aa, and bb are characteristic; the last represents tail feathers hanging from the band later described.

The series of feathers (possibly tail feathers) shown in several figures have rounded tips, and as a rule are of uniform size and without ornamentation. In plate 77, a, the three feathers composing the tail are painted black and are slightly separated, while those of b are half black and half plain, the solid area being separated from the plain by a diagonal line extending from the proximal to the distal extremity.

The four feathers in c are separated by slight intervals and lightly shaded; otherwise they are similar to those in a. The two outside feathers of d are much broader than the middle feather, which is reduced to a narrow line. In e the three feathers are broader at the tips, in which respect they differ from c.

In the tail shown in f, the feathers are indicated by shallow notches from which short parallel lines extend inward. They are without superficial markings. Figure g belongs to the notched type represented above.

The four feather symbols shown in the drawing of the bird's tail illustrated in h differ from all others in the shape of their distal ends, which are alternately black and plain, and are without superficial ornamentation. Evidently this feather design, which is represented on a single vessel from Sikyatki, is of a distinct type.

There is some doubt whether i represents a bird's tail, the head and body from which the design was taken being more like those of a moth or a butterfly. The meaning of the design in j is also doubtful. Figure k represents a single "breath" feather like that shown in figure 57.

There is a general resemblance between the tail feathers of the bird designed in e and l; the latter represents the tail of a bird, hanging between two triangles under a star design.

Figure m represents a bird's tail with three tail feathers and lateral extensions, while in n, where we also have a figure of the tail of a bird, each feather is marked by a rectangular pattern. The four pairs of parallel lines extending from these feathers may be regarded as parts of these structures.

Figures o to q, while suggesting bird and feather designs, are still more or less problematical. In the same category belong the designs

PLATE 77

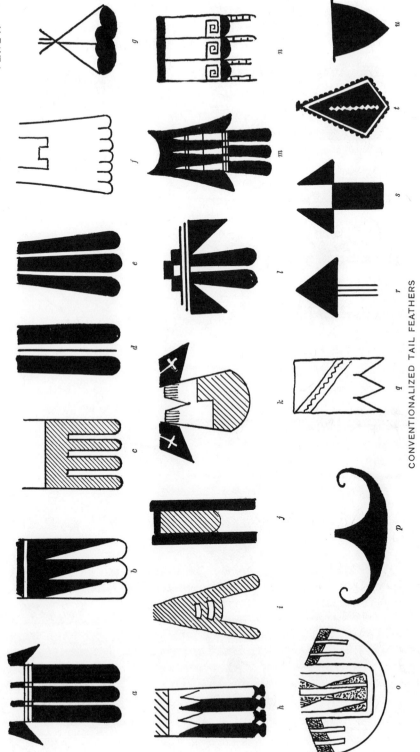

CONVENTIONALIZED TAIL FEATHERS

PLATE 78

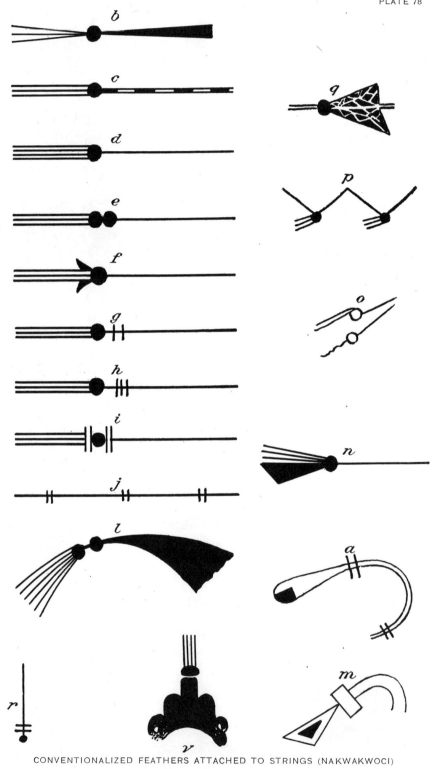

CONVENTIONALIZED FEATHERS ATTACHED TO STRINGS (NAKWAKWOCI)

illustrated in figures *r* to *u*. There is reason to believe that of these *o–r* represent feathers, but a definite identification can not yet be made of figures *s–u*.

Two triangular designs, one above another, are believed to represent feathers, but are rarely found on ancient Hopi pottery. They appear on the heads of birds in Acoma, Laguna, and other pottery designs, which are the nearest modern representatives of ancient Hopi decorations.

Fig. 59.—Feathers.

Fig. 60.—Curved feathers.

A unique feather symbol from Sikyatki is characterized by a cigar-shaped body outlined at the distal end, which is plain (fig. 59).

There often occurs on Sikyatki pottery a combination of feather designs, generally three, with other symbols. One form of these (fig. 60) has four curved tail feathers. Other feathers of aberrant shape are shown in figure 61, *a–e*.

FEATHERS SUSPENDED FROM STRINGS

In their ceremonies the modern Hopi priests use in great numbers a kind of prayer offering called *nakwakwoci*, consisting of breast feathers tied in a prescribed way to the ends of strings. The same type of prayer offerings is one of the most common designs on Sikyatki pottery. Various modifications of it are shown in the accompanying illustration (fig. 62).

This use of the feather string as a decorative device is seemingly peculiar to prehistoric Hopi pottery, not having been found in the pictography of the people formerly inhabiting the valleys of San Juan and Little Colorado Rivers. This restriction in its use indicates its local

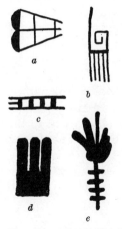

Fig. 61. — Conventional feathers.

origin and application, although descendants of clans from both the San Juan and the Little Colorado are represented among the Hopi.

Fig. 62.—Parallel lines representing feathers.

In one of the simplest forms of the stringed-feather designs is a line (pl. 78, *b*, *c*, *d*) sometimes taking the form of an elongate triangle, terminating in a ball from which spring three or more diverging or parallel lines. This enlargement on stringed-feather designs may represent a knot, as will appear from certain variations in the form of the feathered string to which attention will be given later.

In some cases (*e, l*) two knots appear between the string and the attached feathers, while in another instance (*f*) one of the knots or balls is replaced by two triangles.

Other representations of stringed-feather or *nakwakwoci* designs show modifications in each of the three elements mentioned, the line (string), the enlargement (knot), and the terminal projections (feathers). The occurrence of crossbars near the dot (*g, h, i*) vary in number from one to four, and are always parallel, but usually are placed on one side of the knot, although in some cases (*i*) they appear on both sides. In one example (*j*) no ball or knot is provided, the *nakwakwoci* consisting merely of the string intersected by pairs of equidistant crosslines. A special modification of the dot with crosslines is shown in the figure with the leaflike attachment (*q*).

One of the most significant of the stringed-feather designs is shown in *a*, where a feather of the first type is attached to the string intersected by crosslines. As a terminal element in corresponding designs is a typical feather symbol, this figure is also identical. The figure of a string with enlargements and a pair of lines (*g*) probably represents that form of stringed feather called by the Hopi a *purhu*, " road," an offering laid by the Hopi on the trails approaching the pueblo to indicate that ceremonies are being performed, or on altars to show the pathway of blessings.

In another stringed-feather design (*n*) appears a triangular symbol attached to the enlargement, the string terminating in radiating lines. The feather sometimes preserves its triangular form (*m*). These variations in the drawings of stringed feathers and the modifications of the knot, string, and terminal attachments, are constantly repeated in Sikyatki pottery decoration.

SKY-BAND

Many food bowls from Sikyatki have a band from which is suspended the figure of a nondescript animal passing diametrically across it. Representations of a similar band with like appendage girt the necks of small pottery objects and are, so far as is known, characteristic of prehistoric Hopi pottery.

Lines identified as sky-bands shown in plate 79 vary from single (*a*) or double (*b*) to a broad undecorated band (*c*). In its simplest form the sky-band extends entirely across the inside of the bowl, but in the more complicated examples it surrounds the vessel parallel with the rim surrounding the design on the inside of the bowl. Appendages of several kinds as dots (*d*) or as stars (*f*), made up of oblong figures in terrace form placed at intervals, are attached

PLATE 79

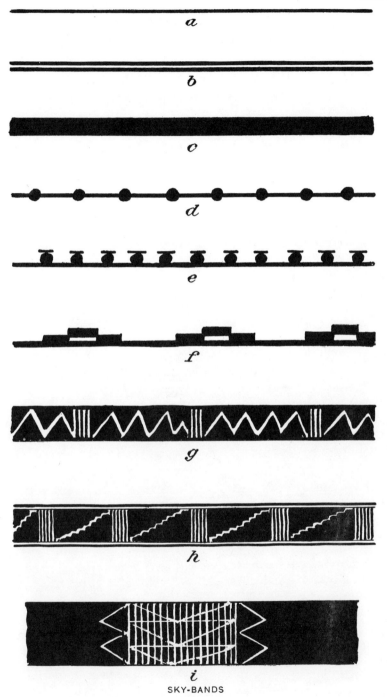

SKY-BANDS

to this band. The sky-band itself varies in width, being broad or narrow, crossed by series of vertical parallel, zigzag, or other lines arranged at intervals, or alternating with geometrical figures (*g*, *h*). In a single example (*i*) the decoration is etched into the burnt clay, although in most instances the decorations are painted.

Various explanations of the meaning of this band have been suggested, it being regarded by some of the priests as the Milky Way, by others as the path of the sun through the sky, but so far as known this ancient design is rare on modern Hopi ware.[1] According to Harrington the Tewa recognize a "backbone" of the sky.

In several Hopi legends there are allusions to a monster bird that had been killed and hung in the sky by a cultus hero; and the general character of this decorative band in Sikyatki pottery decoration renders it probable that it was intended to represent some supernatural being, as the Sky god.

The chief interest of the Sikyatki sky-band lies in the figure or figures attached to it, or suspended from it, and regarded as the conventionalized representation of a bird. Sometimes the creature is placed longitudinally, sometimes vertically. In some instances it is elaborately drawn, in others it is a simple geometric figure bearing so little resemblance to a life form as to make it one of the most highly conventionalized of all ancient Hopi designs.

Like other bird designs, these suspended figures may be considered under two heads: (1) Those attached to the band in such a way as to be seen from above (the dorsal side) or from below (the ventral side); and (2) those suspended lengthwise of the band, showing one side in which the tail and other parts are twisted into a plane at right angles. The structure and relations of the hanging figure can best be seen by holding the bowl in such manner that the sky-band is horizontal, bringing the body of the suspended animal into the lower semicircle.

VERTICAL ATTACHMENT TO SKY-BAND

Several Sikyatki pottery designs showing the sky-band with the bird figure hanging vertically from it are shown in the accompanying illustrations. In order that the modifications in form may be readily followed, those parts of the bird figures regarded as homologous are indicated by the same letters.

---

[1] The only design in modern Hopi symbolism comparable with the sky-band occurs on a wooden slab on the altar of the Owakulti, a society priestess whose ancestors are said to have formerly lived at the historic pueblo of Awatobi. This slab is attached to the uprights of an altar, by means of flat slabs of wood, some arranged vertically, others horizontally. On it is depicted, among other symbolic figures, a representation of a bird.

The design in figure 63 represents one of the simplest forms of bird symbols. A hornlike appendage is attached to the sky-band, on each side of an elongate vertical body from which depends a

FIG. 63.—Conventionalized bird form hanging from sky-band; top view.

FIG. 64. — Conventionalized bird form hanging from sky-band; top view.

number of parallel lines representing tail feathers. The identification of this design as that of a bird is based on comparative studies of designs less conventional in character, to which attention has been and will later be called.

FIG. 65. — Conventionalized bird form hanging from sky-band; top view.

FIG. 66. — Conventionalized bird form hanging from sky-band; top view.

A modification of the pendent body on the sky-band[1] appears to have introduced the new element shown in figure 64 in which the body is drawn. Although considerable variation exists in the form of the other parts, a morphological identity exists in all these figures. In figure 65, in which the feathers differ somewhat from those of the

---

[1] The author has seen in the American Museum of Natural History, New York, a single specimen of doubtful provenance, bearing a similar design.

last design, the parallel lines representing the bird's tail are really seen. The design shown in figure 66 is still more elaborate than the last, especially in the anterior semicircle,[1] opposite that in which the tail feathers are depicted.

FIG. 67. — Conventionalized bird form hanging from sky-band; top view.

FIG. 68.—Conventionalized bird form hanging from sky-band; top view.

The portion of the design situated in the anterior semicircle of figure 67 has no resemblance to a bird's head, being destitute of eyes or beak. The backward extending appendages on each side of the tail and the tail itself has a projection on each side.

FIG. 69.—Conventionalized bird form hanging from sky-band; top view.

In figure 68 the whole anterior part of the design above the sky-band is colored, the head appearing as a still darker semicircle. The tail feathers are here reduced to simple parallel lines. The general form of figure 69 is birdlike, but its affinity to the bird figures, pendent from a sky-band, is closer than to any others. The homologous parts—tail feathers, lateral body extensions, sky-band, and head—may be readily recognized; the last mentioned is an ornamented rectangle. The whole anterior hemisphere of this design is occupied by representations of feathers arranged in two clusters, while in the surrounding area their triple lines are crossed similarly to that occurring in other hanging bird figures. It is but a step from this figure to the group of unattached bird designs already considered.

---

[1] For convenience this may be designated the anterior in distinction to that on the other side of the sky-band which may be termed the posterior semicircle.

The wings of figure 70 are outspread and the head consists of two terraced bodies conventionally placed. The body and the tail of this figure are not exceptional, but dragon flies are also represented.

FIG. 70.—Conventionalized bird form hanging from sky-band; top view.

Figure 71 presents a conventionalized bird seen in profile, and a broad sky-band to which are attached representations of feathers and other organs suggesting a bird.

An animal depicted in figure 72 is one of three similar figures from the neck of the same vase, which are connected by a line or band. The design shown in figure 73 represents a highly conventionalized bird hanging from the sky-band with head and wings on one side and tail feathers below.

BIRDS ATTACHED LONGITUDINALLY TO SKY-BAND

The designs shown in figure 74 represent the simplest forms of birds attached lengthwise to the sky-band. The parallel lines on the left hand of the observer are supposed to represent tail feathers and the curve on the right, the heads, or possibly the wings.

One of the best designs representing a bird attached to a sky-band is shown in figure 75, taken from a bowl in the Wattron collection now owned by the Field Columbian Museum, of Chicago. The interior surface of this bowl is considerably worn by use, and the figure a little indistinct, but the

FIG. 71.—Conventionalized bird form hanging from sky-band; top view.

extremities of a band appear. There is a fairly realistic figure on each side of a bird with head and wings above and tail below a diametrical band. There are zigzag markings, supposed to represent lightning, on the under side of the wing. The tail is spread out amply enough to show the different feathers which compose it; and at the bases or on its under side corresponding in position with like symbols on the wing there appear two zigzag figures. The significance of two curved bodies hanging from the sky-band, one on each side of the tail of this

FIG. 73. — Conventionalized bird form hanging from sky-band; top view.

FIG. 72. — Conventionalized bird form hanging from sky-band; top view

figure, can not be satisfactorily interpreted, but the bird design shown in figure 76 has four tail feathers, a prolongation on the opposite side representing a head, and a curved extension comparable with a wing in other figures. The so-called wing terminates in a triangular feather.

The two designs, figures 76 and 77, have parts which evidently correspond, the latter being one of the most beautiful in the collection. Both represent from the side an unknown bird hanging from a band extending across the middle of the bowls. Although the details of organs are more carefully depicted in the latter, there can hardly be a doubt that similar animals were intended in both designs.

It requires some imagination to discover a conventionalized bird in figure 78, but we may

FIG. 74.—Lateral view of bird hanging from sky-band.

regard it as such. We have in this figure a good example of a change in outline that may be produced by duplication or by representing both sides of the body or its organs and appendanges in the same place. Three tail feathers are here apparent; the body is square, with zigzag white lines, and the head, here twisted into a vertical position, has a triangular form. The two crescentic appendages, one on

the right side, the other on the left, represent halves of wings which are theoretically supposed to have been slit longitudinally and folded backward[1] in order that both sides may be shown on the same plane; the two bodies arising from the concave edges of these crescents—one to the left, the other to the right of the s q u a r e b o d y—represent legs. Their unusual form is brought about by a twisting of body and tail, by which feathers of the latter are brought to longitudinal

FIG. 75.—Lateral view of bird hanging from sky-band.

position, and one of the legs is twisted to the right side and the other to the left. If the two appendages supposed to represent the legs or the two parts shaped like crescentlike knives were brought together, the two crescents would likewise merge into one, and we would then have a highly conventionalized bird with three tail feathers and a triangular head, the body being represented by a square design crossed diagonally by zigzag figures each in its own rectangular inclosed field.

DECORATIONS ON EXTERIORS OF FOOD BOWLS

The exterior surface of almost every bowl from Sikyatki is decorated with lines or geometrical designs. Many of these designs may represent animals, probably birds highly conventionalized or so aberrant that the avian form can be recognized only by comparative or morphological studies. They are confined to one side of the bowl; there appears to be little resem-

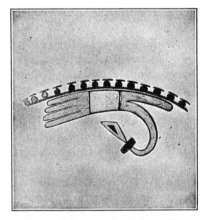

FIG. 76.—Lateral view of bird with extended wing.

blance and no connection between them and the figure depicted on the inside of the same bowls. Although linear in form, one end is sometimes so crooked or bent at an angle, not curved, as to form a head, while the other bears parallel lines, representations of the tail feathers, terraces, or triangles.

---

[1] See also *Seventeenth Ann. Rept. Bur. Amer. Ethn.*, pl. CL, *a*, and CXLVI, *d*.

In plate 80, *a*, we have a characteristic example of one of these exterior decorations. The crooked end is supposed to represent a bird's head; to the other end, or tail, are appended six feathers like those already considered. A row of five stars is strung along the band. A likeness to a bird is very obscure in *b*, while *c* shows several simple triangles with stepped figures in the middle and triangles at the ends. Design *d* has a square form and two triangles appended to each opposite angle. The appendages on the remaining opposite angles have four parallel lines. Design *e* consists of two highly conventionalized bird symbols, united to a third which forms the interior design.

FIG. 77.—Lateral view of bird hanging from sky-band.

The design *f* recalls the sky-band described in the preceding pages. The extremities of this so-called band are enlarged into round spots from which arise parallel lines and triangular designs. From it hang terraced and crooked figures, while strung along one side at equal intervals are five stars, a common accompaniment of sky symbols. The bird symbol comes out clearly in *g*, where the crook design with terraces is repeated.

FIG. 78.—Lateral view of bird hanging from sky-band.

All crooked figures have a similarity in general form, some more closely resembling birds than others, and it is taken for granted that the intention of the artist was to represent a bird in plate 81, *a*, notwithstanding the avian form is highly conventionalized. Design *b* is composite, consisting of a rectangular figure, to the angles of which are attached feathers. Terraced and triangular figures of unknown significance, stars, and other designs cover the rectangle. Design *c* is made up of a triangle with notched borders and a central rectangle with a dot characterizes this design; it has also two triangular extensions that may represent feathers. Design *d* resembles previous figures identified as feathers and terraces hanging from a sky-band.

The most prominent part of the design *e* is a crook and parallel lines. In *f* are variously combined triangles with appended feathers, crooks, and terraced designs, so united as to make up a compound decoration of geometric character.

The geometrical designs in the series, plate 82, *a–f*, may be interpreted as representing birds in flight or with extended wings. Considered in this way, it appears that we have in the figure on each side a highly conventionalized wing forming triangles with extensions at one angle, ending in terraces, crooks, or other designs. In these figures we constantly have a line that may be likened to the sky-band, each end generally terminating in a dot to which parallel lines are attached.

Design *a* has two triangular bodies resembling the letter W, and the line terminating in two dots has two crossbars, while in *b* there is a union of designs. Elongated triangles terminate in lines which are enlarged into dots. These triangles are modified on one side into crooks with smaller triangles.

From remote resemblances rather than similarity of form, *c* is placed near the preceding. Here a band is enlarged at the end representing the knots with attached parallel lines or feathers. The triangular pendants of *b* and the line with terminal dots of *a* are here represented. On the middle vertical of this figure is a trapezoidal design with notched edges.

The elements of *d* form a compound in which triangles predominate. Two W-shaped designs, *e* and *f*, have a form quite unlike *a*, *b*, *c*, and *d*. Of these, *f* is the more complicated, but the similarity of the two is apparent.

Plate 83, *a*, represents two triangles with serrate margins hanging to a horizontal band, one end of which terminates in dots and lines, the other with two parallel notched feathers.

Plate 84, *a–c*, have the W shape shown in plate 82, *e*, *f;* the approach to the conventional bird form with extended wings and tail being most marked in *a*. Design *d* on plate 84 recalls plate 83, *f*, with modifications that are apparent.

The above-mentioned geometrical figures from the exteriors of Sikyatki food bowls show considerable variety of form but all can be reduced to a few elemental designs throughout in which the curved line is absent. The rectangular design is always dominant, but it will be seen from the following plate that it is not omnipresent, especially on the interiors of bowls.

PLATE 80

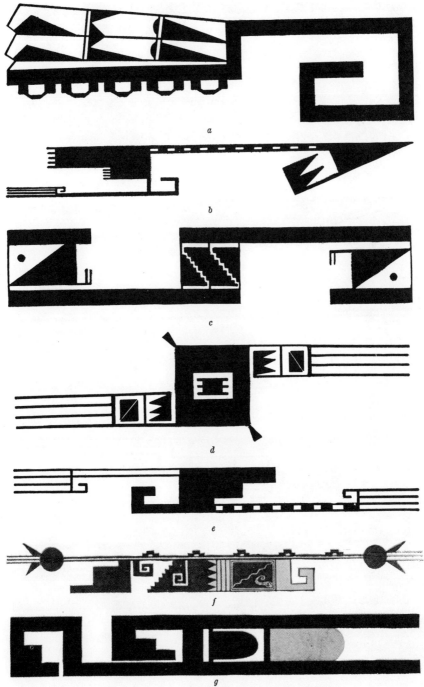

GEOMETRICAL FIGURES ON OUTSIDE OF BOWLS

PLATE 81

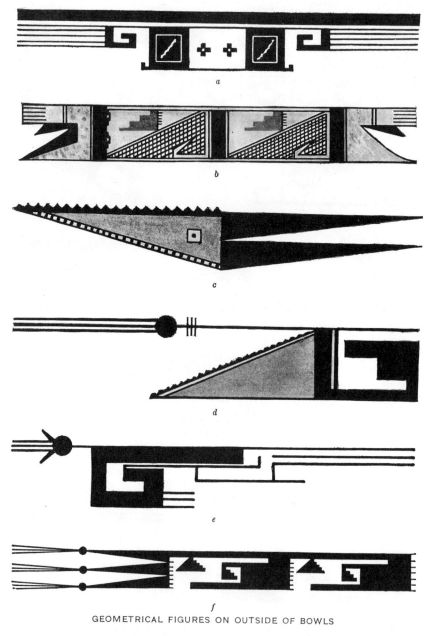

a

b

c

d

e

f

GEOMETRICAL FIGURES ON OUTSIDE OF BOWLS

PLATE 82

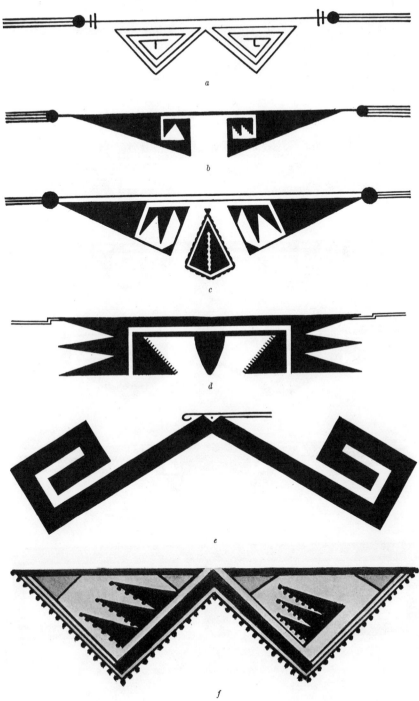

GEOMETRICAL FIGURES ON OUTSIDE OF BOWLS

PLATE 83

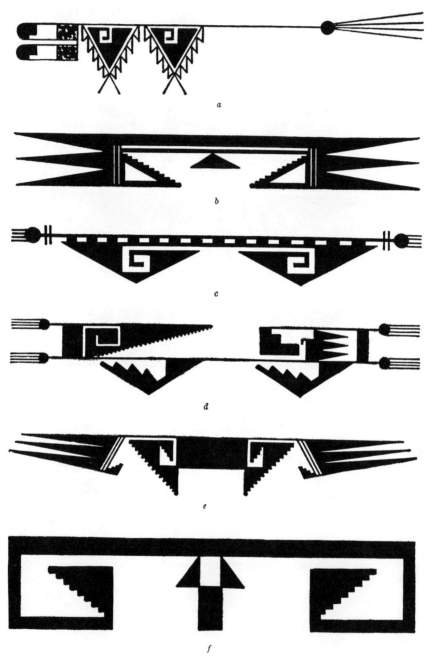

GEOMETRICAL FIGURES ON OUTSIDE OF BOWLS

PLATE 84

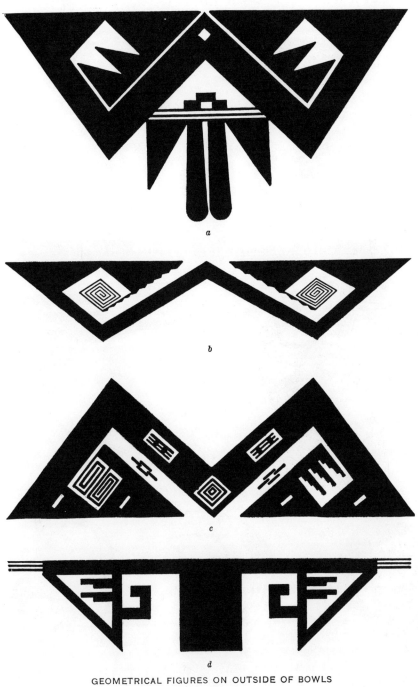

GEOMETRICAL FIGURES ON OUTSIDE OF BOWLS

PLATE 85

E

F

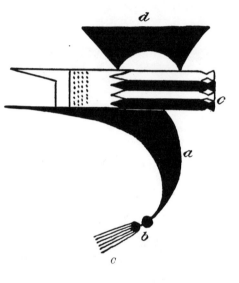

G

C

A

B

D

CONVENTIONALIZED BIRD DESIGNS

PLATE 86

A

B

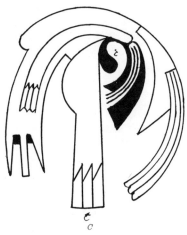

C

D

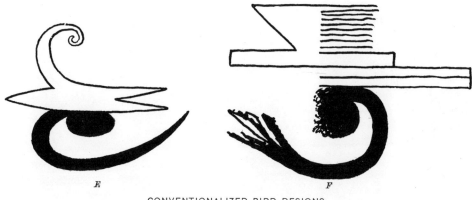

E

F

CONVENTIONALIZED BIRD DESIGNS

CURVED FIGURE WITH ATTACHED FEATHERS

The curved spiral figures shown in plates 85 and 86 are combinations of simple and complicated designs, among the most conspicuous of which are feathers. When these figures are placed in the same position it is possible to recognize three or four components which are designated (a) spiral, (b) appendage to the tip of the spiral, (c) a bundle of feathers recalling a bird's tail, and (d) and (e) other parts of unknown homology occasionally represented. In plate 85, A the appendage b to the spiral a is two triangles and two supplemental spirals arising from their attachments. There is no representation of c, d, or e in this figure.

In B of the same plate the elements a, b, c, and d are represented. The appendage b attached to the tip of the spiral a has the form of a feather of the first type (see pl. 76), and four parallel lines, c, indicating feathers, are attached to the body. The two toothlike appendages e, of unknown significance, complete the figure. In plate 85, C, the design a has two dots b on the distal tip, from one of which arises a number of lines. The fact that b in figure B is a feather leads to the belief that b in figure C is the same design.

Plate 85, D and E, have a resemblance in form, a and c being represented in both; b and e are wanting in E. The different elements in these designs can be readily seen by comparing the same lettering in F and G, and in plate 86, A and B, where a new element, t, is introduced.

Plate 86, B and E, are highly conventionalized designs; they suggest bird form, examples of which have been already considered elsewhere, but are very much modified.

There can be no doubt that it was intended to represent birds or parts of birds as feathers in many of the above figures, but the perspective is so distorted that their morphology or relative position on the bird to which they belong can not be made out. In plate 86, A, for instance, the bird's body seems to be split in two parts and laid on a flat plane. The pendent body, t, in the middle would be a representation of a bird's tail composed of three feathers and with a double triangle terminating in dots from which arise lines of would-be feathers.

Two of the parts, a and t, that occur in the last mentioned, are found in plate 86, B, in somewhat modified form. Thus the position of the tail feathers, t, figure C, is taken by feathers of a different form, their extremities being cut off flat and not curved. The bundles of feathers in B and C are here reversed, the left side of B corresponding to the right of C, and the appendage on the left of the tail of *B* being represented by the appendage on the right of *C*. There are other remote likenesses between them.

Spider and Insects

Other flying animals, like bats and insects, are depicted on Sikyatki pottery, but not as constantly as birds. The spider, and insects like the dragon fly, moth, and butterfly, are the most common. In Hopi mythology the spider[1] and the sun are associated, the former being the symbol of an earth goddess. Although no design that can be referred to the spider has yet been found on Sikyatki pottery, it is not wanting from Hopi (pl. 87, *c*).

The symbol of the dragon fly, which occurs on several bowls from ancient Hopi ruins, is a line often enlarged at one end to form a head, and always with two crossbars near this enlargement to indicate wings. As this insect lives near springs and is constantly associated in modern symbolism with water it is probable that its occurrence on ancient Hopi pottery has practically the same significance as in modern conceptions.

Butterfly and Moth

Five typical figures that may be referred to the butterfly or moth occur on Sikyatki pottery. These figures have in common a triangular body which suggests a highly conventionalized picture of a bird. Their wings are, as a rule, extended horizontally, assuming the attitude of moths while at rest, there being only one of the five examples where wings are folded above the back, the normal position of these organs in a butterfly. With one exception, all these conventional butterfly figures bear two curved rows of dots on the head, probably intended to represent antennæ.

Fig. 79.—Butterfly and flower.

The figure of a moth in figure 79 has a body of triangular form, and the extremities of the wings are shown on each side of a medially placed backward-extending projection, which is the posterior end

[1] The Kokyan, or Spider, clan is not made much of in Hopi legends gathered at Walpi, but Kokyanwügti, the Spider woman, is an important supernatural in the earliest mythologies, especially those of the Snake people. She was the mentor of the Snake youth in his journey to the underworld and an offering at her shrine is made in the Oraibi Snake dance. The picture of the spider with that of the sun suggests that the Spider woman is a form of the earth goddess. No personation of Spider woman has been seen by the author in the various ceremonies he has witnessed.

of the abdomen. These wings bear white dots on their posterior edges suggesting the markings on certain genera of butterflies.[1] There arises from the head, which here is circular, a single jointed appendage curved at the end, possibly the antenna, and an unjointed appendage, like a proboscis, inserted into a figure of a flower, mounted on a stalk that terminates at the other extremity in five parallel extensions or roots. A row of dots about the periphery of the flower suggests petals. The figures are accompanied by crosses representing stars.

The second moth design (fig. 80) has even a closer resemblance to a bird than the last, for it also has a single antenna or row of dots connected by a curved line. It likewise has several curved lines resembling a crest of feathers on top of the head, and lines recalling the tail of a bird. The head this figure bears is a cross suggesting a female butterfly or moth.[2]

FIG. 80.—Butterfly with extended proboscis.

The body in figure 81 is crossed by five lines converging at one angle, imparting to it the appearance of having been formed by a union of several spherical triangles on each of which appear rectangular spaces painted black. A head is not differentiated from the body, but at the point of union of the five lines above mentioned there arise two rows of dots which have the form of circles, each inclosing a dot. From analogy these are supposed to represent antennæ. The middle of wing-shaped extensions recalling butterfly designs are marked by circular figures in figure 82, but the absence in this figure of a head with jointed appendages renders it doubtful whether it represents an insect. The shape of the body and its

FIG. 81.—Highly conventionalized butterfly.

---

[1] Except that the head bears a jointed antenna this figure might be identified as a bird, the long extension representing the bird's bill.

[2] The figures of serpents on the sand mosaic of the Antelope altar at Walpi bear similar crosses or diagonals, crossing each other at right angles. The Antelope priests interpret this marking as a sign of the female.

appendages resembling feathers indicate, so far as they go, that this design represents some bird.

It will be noted that in one of the above-mentioned figures, identified as a moth, flowers are indicated by dotted circles, while in another similar circle, figures, also surrounded with dots, are represented on the wings. One pair of wings is represented in the last-mentioned figure, but a second pair placed behind the larger may have been confounded with the tail feathers. In one of these figures from Sikyatki there is a row of dots around the margin of the wings—a common but not universal feature in modern pictures of butterfly figures. None of the butterfly figures have representations of legs, which is not strange considering how inconspicuous these appendages are among these insects.

Fig. 82.—Moth.

A most striking figure of a butterfly is represented by six drawings on the so-called "butterfly vase" (fig. 83). These, like the above-mentioned, resemble birds, but they all have antennæ, which identify them as insects. These six figures (pl. 90) are supposed to be connected with the six cardinal points which in modern Hopi belief have sex—the butterfly corresponding to the north, male; to the west, female; to the south, male; to the east, female; to the above, male; and to the below, female. The wings of all these insects are represented as extended, the anterior pair extending far beyond the posterior, while both have a uniform color and are without marginal dots. The appendages to the head are two curved rows of dots representing antennæ, and two parallel lines are the mouth parts or possibly the proboscis. The markings on the bodies and the terminal parallel lines are like

Fig. 83.—Moth.

tail feathers of birds. The heads of three figures, instead of having diagonal lines, are covered with a crosshatching, b, b, b, and are supposed to represent the males, as the former, a, a, a, are females.[1]

---

[1] Rain, lightning, animals, plants, sky, and earth, in the modern Hopi conception, are supposed to have sex.

A moth with a conventionalized geometric form is represented in figure 84 with outstretched wings, a rounded abdomen, and a spotted rectangular body recalling designs on the upper embroidered margin of modern ceremonial blankets. A like figure has been elsewhere described by the author as a butterfly.[1] It occurs on the

FIG. 84.—Moth or geometrical form.

stone slab which once formed one side of an Awatobi altar.[2] We have more complicated forms of butterflies represented in figures 85–87, the identification of which is even more doubtful than the last. Figure 86 reproduces in its several parts figure 85, being composed of a central design, around which are arranged six triangles, one of the last being placed above, another below, the main figure, and there are

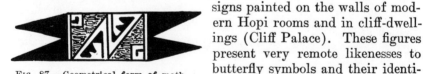

FIG. 85.—Geometrical form of moth.

FIG. 86.—Highly conventionalized butterfly.

two on each side. The design, figure 88, is circular, the alternately colored quadrants forming two hourglass combinations. The double triangle, shown in figure 84, resembles a butterfly symbol, having a close likeness to a figure of this insect found on the Awatobi tablet above mentioned. This figure also resembles triangular designs painted on the walls of modern Hopi rooms and in cliff-dwellings (Cliff Palace). These figures present very remote likenesses to butterfly symbols and their identification as such is difficult.

FIG. 87.—Geometrical form of moth.

GEOMETRICAL DESIGNS

The geometrical designs on the pottery from Sikyatki consist of two well-recognized groups: (1) Purely ornamental or nonsymbolic geometrical figures, and (2) highly conventional life forms. Some of the figures of the second group may be geometrical representations of birds or other animals; but the former are simply embellishments used to beautify the objects on which they are painted. Purely decorative designs, not being symbolic, will not be specially considered, as they do not come within the scope of the present treatise. An

FIG. 88. — Circle with triangles.

interpretation of the significance of many of the second group of geometrical designs is not possible, although they probably represent animal forms.

---

[1] The Butterfly in Hopi Myth and Ritual, fig. 61, f.
[2] Ibid., p. 586.

The strictly geometrical figures so frequently found on pottery from Sikyatki recall the linear decorations almost universal in ancient southwestern ware.

No one who has carefully compared specimens of decorated pottery from Sikyatki with examples from any other southwestern region could fail to be impressed with the differences in some of the geometrical designs from the two localities. Such designs on the Sikyatki ware are almost always rectangular, rarely curved. As compared with pottery from cliff-dwellings there is a paucity or entire absence of terraced designs in the ancient Hopi ware, while zigzags representing lightning are comparatively rare. The characteristic geometrical decorations on Sikyatki pottery are found on the outside of the food bowls, in which respect they are notably different from those of other ceramic areas. Designs on Sikyatki pottery show few survivals of preexisting materials or evolution from transfer of those on textiles of any kind. Such as do exist are so masked that they shed little light on current theories of art evolution.

The designs on ancient Hopi pottery are in the main mythological, hence their true interpretation involves a knowledge of the religious ideas and especially of such psychological elements as sympathetic magic, so prevalent among the Hopi of to-day. The idea that by the use of symbols man could influence supernatural beings was no doubt latent in the mind of the potter and explains the character of the symbols in many instances. The fact that the bowls on which these designs are painted were found with the dead, and contained food for the departed, implies a cult of the dead, or at least a belief in a future life.

RAIN CLOUDS

The most constant geometric designs on Pueblo pottery are those representing the rain cloud, and from analogy we would expect to find the rain-cloud figures conspicuously on ancient Hopi pottery. We look in vain on Sikyatki ware for the familiar semicircular symbols of rain clouds so constant among the modern Hopi; nor do we find the rectangular terraced form which is equally common. These modifications were probably lately introduced into Hopiland by those colonists of alien clans who came after the destruction of Sikyatki, and consequently are not to be expected on its pottery. Their place was taken by other characteristitc forms closely allied to rectangular terraced figures from which hang parallel lines, representing falling rain in modern symbolism.[1] The typical Sikyatki rain-cloud symbol is terraced without rain symbols and finds its nearest relative on pottery derived from the eastern pueblo region.

---

[1] Introduced into the Hopi pueblos by colonists from the Rio Grande; its most conspicuous variant can be seen on the tablets worn in a masked dance called Humis (Jemez) Kachina.

The form of rain-cloud symbol on Sikyatki pottery may be regarded
as characteristic of the Kokop clan which, according to legends,
settled this ancient pueblo. Modified variants of this form of rain-
cloud symbol occur on almost every specimen in the Sikyatki collection, and can be seen hanging from "sky-bands" with appended
star signs or without such connections.

The most common Sikyatki symbol of a rain cloud is shown in figure 89 and plate 90, *f*, *g*. These rain-cloud designs rarely occur singly,
being more often six in number, as if
intended to represent the six cardinal
points recognized in Hopi ceremonies.
We find the Sikyatki rain-cloud symbols
resembling somewhat those of the modern Zuñi, or figures of clouds found on
the characteristic designs on Little

FIG. 89.—Rain cloud.

Colorado ceramics. Somewhat similar angular terraced forms are
almost universally used in eastern pueblos as rain-cloud symbols, but
the semicircular forms (fig. 90) of modern Hopi ceremonials, being
apparently a highly specialized modification, rarely occur on Sikyatki
pottery.

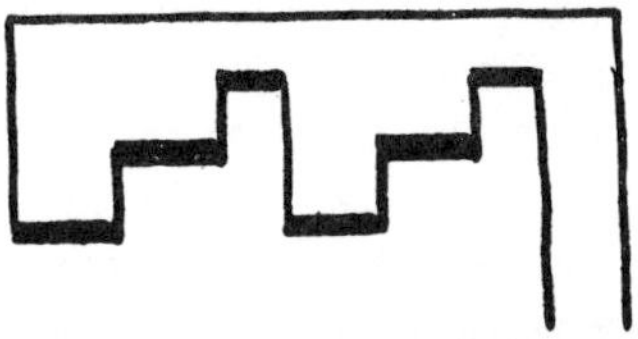

STARS

The star sign occurs as an equal armed cross formed by the approximation of four squares, leaving a central uncolored area. It is

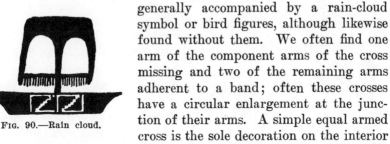

FIG. 90.—Rain cloud.

generally accompanied by a rain-cloud
symbol or bird figures, although likewise
found without them. We often find one
arm of the component arms of the cross
missing and two of the remaining arms
adherent to a band; often these crosses
have a circular enlargement at the junction of their arms. A simple equal armed
cross is the sole decoration on the interior
of numerous food bowls, and there are several examples of St.
Andrew's crosses, the triangular arms of which have been interpreted as representing four conventionalized birds; no example of a cross with unequal arms has yet been found on Sikyatki
pottery.

These crosses, like that with four arms representing the Sky god
in modern Hopi symbolism, probably represent the Heart of the Sky.
A similar cross is figured on paraphernalia used in modern Hopi
rites or on altar slabs; when it is represented by a wooden frame, it
is called *tokpela*, and hangs before the altar. The same object is
sometimes attached horizontally to the top of the helmet of the

personification of the Sky god.[1]   The swastika is rare in ancient pottery and was not found at Sikyatki, although a single example was dug up at Awatobi and a few others were obtained from the Little Colorado ruins.

A multiple cross, formed of three parallel lines crossing three others at an angle, generally accompanies certain conventionalized figures of birds and in one example there are two multiple crosses, one on one side and one on another of a moth or butterfly symbol. The multiple cross is supposed to represent six canes used in a game, and on a prehistoric decorated bowl from ancient Shongopovi,[2] we find what appears to be a highly conventionalized bird figure occupying one-half of the interior of the bowl, while four figures representing these canes appear on the other. The bird figure, in this instance, is interpreted as a gambler's god, or a representation of the god of chance.

SUN EMBLEMS

The most conventionalized sun emblem is a circle or ring with attached feathers. The Sikyatki design (pl. 87, b) is a circle bearing on its periphery appendages believed to represent feathers, with accompanying lines, generally painted red, to represent the rays of the sun.[3]

FIG. 91.—Ring with appended feathers.

The identification of the bird whose feathers are used in sun emblems has not yet been made, although the position of similar feathers on the body of other bird designs suggests that they represent eagle feathers. The feather of the eagle is commonly associated with both ancient and modern pictures representing the sun. Thus we have on a vessel from Sikyatki in figure 91 a design bearing four feathers arranged at intervals a quadrant apart alternating with radiating lines. If we interpret this figure in the light of modern symbolism the circle

---

[1] One symbol of the Sky god has the form of a Lightning god. It has a single curved horn on the head, lightning symbols on the legs, and carries a wooden framework in one hand and a bull-roarer in the other.

[2] *Twenty-second Ann. Rept. Bur. Ethn.*, pt. 1, fig. 74.

[3] In modern Hopi symbolism the sun is a disk with representations of eagle feathers around the periphery and radial lines at each quadrant, symbolic of the sun's rays. In disks worn on the back where real feathers are used the radial lines, or the sun's rays, are represented by horsehair stained red. In ceremonials the Sky god is personated by a bird whose figure occurs on Sikyatki pottery.

PLATE 87

BIRD, SUN, AND SPIDER AND SUN SYMBOLS

PLATE 88

CONVENTIONALIZED BIRD FIGURES

would be regarded as the sun and the feathers would be identified as eagle feathers, while the lines might be considered to represent the red rays of the four cardinal points.

In a bowl found at old Shongo-povi, a ruin inhabited at the same epoch as Sikyatki, the sun takes the form of a sky bird. In this design the ring figure is replaced by a bird with wings, tail, and a beak, evidently the sun bird, hawk, or eagle (pl. 88, *a*).

FIG. 92.—Two circles with figure.

A theoretical interpretation of plate 88, *b*, is facilitated by a comparison of it with the design painted on a bowl from the Wattron collection, now in the Field Columbian Museum. As this has all the parts represented in figure 75, the conclusion would naturally be that the intention of the artist was to represent a bird figure.

FIG. 93.—Sun with feathers.

Ring or circle shaped figures are found on several bowls from Sikyatki, and in one case (fig. 92) we find two circles side by side separated by a rectangular figure. The meaning of these rings and the accompanying design is not known. Concentric circles diametrically accompanied with two figures, one with a head and two lateral feathers, the other with the form of a hash-knife figure, are shown in figure 93.

In figure 94 the appendages of the ring design or sun emblem is much more complicated than any of the preceding. Each of the four quadrants has two appendages, a cluster with two feathers, and a curved body with a sickle-shaped extension, the whole giving a swastika-like appearance to the design. The interior of the circle is

FIG. 94.—Sun symbol.

likewise complicated, showing a structure difficult to interpret. From comparisons with preceding figures this is likewise regarded as a sun emblem.[1]

---

[1] In the Hopi ceremony, Powatawu, as performed at Oraibi, a picture representing the sun composed of a number of concentric circles of four different colors is made of sand on the kiva floor.

The ring or circle shown in figure 95 hangs from a band that may be likened to the sky-band of previous description.[1] A tri-

angle[2] is attached to the upper side of this band, while appended to the ring itself there is a featherlike object corresponding to a bird's tail and wing. This figure is unique in the Sikyatki collection of ancient Hopi pictography.

In figure 96 we find a leg appended to the lower side of the ring balanced by three wing feathers above or on the opposite side, two

FIG. 95. — Ring with appended feathers.

curved or crescentic extensions projecting from the rear, diametrically opposite which arises a curved body (head) with terminating sickle-shaped prolongation. This figure may be considered a bird design, having the tail twisted from a

FIG. 96.—Ring figure with legs and appended feathers.

lateral to a vertical position and the wing raised from the body.

In figure 97 we find a similar ring still further modified, the appendages to it being somewhat different. The ring is here broader than the last, inclosing an area crossed by two lines forming a cross, with short parallel lines at the ends of each arm. There is a head showing a circular face with dots indicating eyes and mouth. The head bears a crest of feathers between two horns. Here we have in place of the appendage to the lower side an elongated curved projection extending to the left, balanced by a short, stumpy, curved appendage on the right, while between these appendages hang four parallel lines

FIG. 97.—Sun emblem with appended feathers.

suggesting the highly conventional feathers of a tail. The horns with the crest of feathers between them recall the crest of the Sun

---

[1] If we interpret the sky-band as the path of the sun in the zenith the solar emblem hanging to it is significant.

[2] Some of the significant sun masks used by the Hopi have the mouth indicated by a triangle, others by hourglass designs.

god, of the Kachina clan, called Tunwup, a Sky god who flogs the children of modern Walpi.

The ring design in figure 98 has a bunch of three feathers in each quadrant, recalling the feathers of a sun emblem so well shown with other kinds of feathers in plate 76, *b*.

In figure 99 we have a circle with four appended bifurcated geometrical extensions projecting outward on the periphery, and recalling featherless tails of birds. This is also a highly conventionalized sun emblem reduced to a geometrical figure.

FIG. 98.—Sun symbol.

In connection with all these circular figures may be considered that shown in figure 92, the form of which is highly suggestive. In the various modifications above mentioned we detect two elements, the ring and its peripheral appendages, interpreted as feathers, head, feet, and other bird organs. Sometimes the ring predominates, sometimes the feathers, and sometimes a bird figure replaces all, the ring being lost or reduced in size. This variation is primitive and quite consistent with the Pueblo concep-tions and analogies known to occur in Hopi ceremonial paraphernalia. This variation illustrates what is elsewhere said about the influence of the magic power on the pictorial art of Hopi.[1]

FIG. 99.—Sun symbol.

The sun, to the Hopi mind, is likewise represented by a bird, or a compound of both becomes a Sky-god emblem; the horned serpent is the servant of the Sky god.

We find among the modern Hopi several disks with markings and decorations of such a character that they are identified as representations of the sun. One of these is worn by the leader of the kachinas in a ceremony called the Powamû, an elaborate rite, the purpose of which is to purify from evil influences. This Sun god[2]

<hr />

[1] Pictures made by prehistoric man embody, first, when possible, the power of the animal or thing represented, or its essential characteristics; and second, the realistic form, shape, or outline.

[2] Several Hopi clans celebrate in a slightly different way the return of their Sun god, which is known by different names among them. The return of the Sun god of the Kachina clan at Walpi, commonly called Ahül, is elsewhere described. Shalako, the Sun god of the Patki clans, was derived from the Little Colorado region, the same source from which the Zuñi obtained their personage of the same name. His return is celebrated on the East Mesa of the Hopi at Sichomovi, the "Zuñi pueblo among the Hopi." Pautiwa is a Sun god of Zuñi clans at Sichomovi and is personated as at Zuñi pueblo. Kwataka, or the Sun god whose return is celebrated at Walpi in the winter solstice, Soyaluna, is associated with the great plumed serpent, a personation derived from the peoples of the Gila or some other river who practice irrigation. Eototo is a Sikyatki Sun god, derived from near Jemez, and is celebrated by Keres colonists.

is called Ahül, and the symbolism of his mask, especially feathers attached to the head, suggests some of the Sikyatki designs considered above.

Rectangular Figures Representing Shrines

The word *pahoki*, prayer-stick house or " shrine," is applied by the modern Hopi to the receptacle, commonly a ring of stones, in which prayer offerings are deposited, and receives its name from the special supernatural personage worshiped. These shrines are regarded as sacred by the Hopi and are particularly numerous in the neighborhood of the Hopi mesas.[1] They are ordinarily simply rude inclosures made of stones or flat stone slabs set on edge, forming boxes, which may either be closed or open on one side. The simplest pictographic representation of such a shrine is the same as that of a house, or a circular or rectangular figure. A similar design is drawn in meal on the floor of the kiva or traced with the same material on the open plaza when the priest wishes to represent a house or shrine. Elaborate pictures made of different colored sands to represent gods are often inclosed by encircling lines, the whole called a house of the gods. Thus the sand picture on the Antelope altar of the Snake dance is called the house of the rain-cloud beings.[2] When reptiles are washed on the ninth day of the Snake dance they are said to be thrown into the house, a sand picture of the mountain lion. It is customary to make in some ceremonies not only a picture of the god worshiped, but also a representation of his or her house. The custom of adding a picture of a shrine to that of the supernatural can be seen by examining a series of pictures of Hopi kachinas. Here the shrine is a rain-cloud symbol introduced to show that the house of the kachina represented is a rain cloud.

Sikyatki bowls decorated with figures identified as supernaturals often bear accompanying designs which may, from comparative reasoning, be interpreted as shrines of the supernatural being depicted. They have at times a form not unlike that of certain sand pictures, as in the case of the curved figure accompanying a highly conventionalized plumed serpent. A great variety of figures of this kind are found on Sikyatki bowls,[3] and often instead of being a rectangular figure they may be elongated more like a prayer offering.

The rectangular figure that accompanies a representation of a great horned serpent (fig. 100) may be interpreted as the shrine house of that monster, and it is to be mentioned that this shrine appears to be surrounded by radial lines representing curved sticks

---

[1] Fewkes, Hopi Shrines Near the East Mesa, Arizona, pp. 346–375.

[2] The sand picture made by the Antelope priest is regarded as a house of the rain gods depicted upon it.

[3] *Seventeenth Ann. Rept. Bur. Amer. Ethn.*, pt. 2.

like those set around sand pictures of the Snake and Antelope altars of the Snake ceremonies at Walpi.[1]

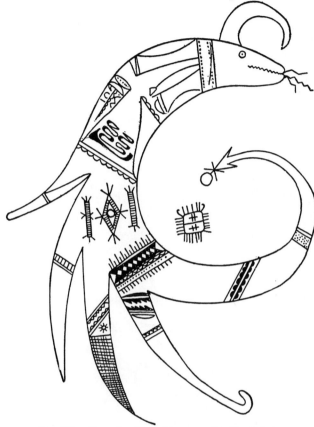

It is suggested that the figure below the mountain sheep (see fig. 18) and the circles with dots accompanying the butterfly and bird designs may also represent shrines. Attention is also called to the fact that each of the six animal figures of the elaborate butterfly vase (pl. 90, *c*) is accompanied by a rectangular design representing a shrine in which feathers are visible.

FIG. 100.—Horned snake with conventionalized shrine.

The general forms of these shrines are shown in figures 101 and 102. The one shown in figure 103 is especially instructive from its association with a highly conventionalized animal.

a

b

FIG. 101.— Shrine.

The Sikyatki epoch of Hopi ceramics is more closely allied to early Keresan[2] than to ancient Tanoan, and has many likenesses to modern Keresan pottery. In fact, none of the distinctive figures have yet been found on true Tanoan ware in any great numbers. There appear also no evidences of incre-

[1] The author has a drawing of the Snake altar at Michongnovi by an Indian, in which these crooks are not represented vertically but horizontally, a position illustrating a common method of drawing among primitive people who often represent vertical objects on a horizontal plane. An illustration of this is seen in pictures of a medicine bowl where the terraces on the rim normally vertical are drawn horizontally.

[2] In using this term the author refers to an extreme area in one corner of which still survive pueblos, the inhabitants of which speak Keres.

ments peculiar to the Little Colorado culture center of which Zuñi is the modern survival; consequently we look in vain for evidence of early communication between these two centers; possibly Sikyatki fell before Zuñi attained any prominence in the Little Colorado area.[1]

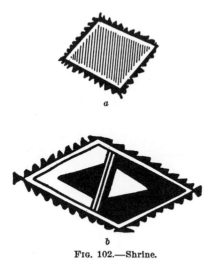

a

b

FIG. 102.—Shrine.

SYMBOLS INTRODUCED FROM SAN JUAN RIVER SETTLEMENTS

Although the majority of Hopi priests declare that the earliest clan to settle Walpi was the Bear, coming from the east, by far the largest number of early colonists are said to belong to the Snake people which came from Tokonabi and other great settlements on tributaries of the San Juan in northern Arizona. The route of their migration is fairly well known from legendary sources supported in late years by some limited excavations that have been made in ruins along its course, so that we know something of the character of the Snake pottery and the symbols, which these early colonists brought to the Bear settlement at the base of the East Mesa. These are not unlike those found along the San Juan and its tributaries from the Mesa Verde to Wukoki near the Black Falls on the Little Colorado, west of the Hopi Mesa.

This ware is commonly either black and white, or

FIG. 103. — Conventionalized winged bird with shrine.

red, and can be readily distinguished from that of Sikyatki by the wealth of geometrical decorations and the poverty of such animal figures as birds, reptiles, and insects. The designs of that early epoch appear to be uniform and hardly distinctive from those that occur in all parts of the Southwest.

---

[1] There is no published evidence in Zuñi legends that Sikyatki received increments from that pueblo.

We may judge of the character of the symbols and designs on pottery from the San Juan and from the ruins of Wukoki on the Black Falls of Little Colorado. It is characterized by an abundance of geometric figures and an almost total absence of life forms or painted figures of men and animals. The pottery is thin, well made, and sometimes colored red, but the majority of specimens are gray or black-and-white ware not especially different from a widespread type occurring pretty generally throughout the Southwest. Coiled and incised ware is more abundant than smooth painted, but these are not as varied in form as later examples. There is no evidence available that there was any very great difference between the Hopi pottery decorations of the first epoch and that of contemporary time in the Southwest. When the Snake clans arrived at Walpi they found the village of Bear people living on the terrace at the base of the East Mesa, possessed of a symbolism like that of Sikyatki. The combined clans, Bear and Snake, were later joined by the Horn and Flute, and it is not unlikely that some of the likenesses between the pottery symbols of the settlement on the terrace below Walpi and Sikyatki may have developed about this time.[1]

The designs on the ceramics of the Snake clans are best illustrated by the prehistoric pottery from ruins and cliff-dwellings in Utah and along the San Juan area, where geometrical patterns far outnumber those representing life forms. This does not deny that many of the pieces of pottery from this region are finely made, equal in technique perhaps to some of the Sikyatki, but the geometric designs on San Juan pottery and that from Sikyatki are radically different. This difference conforms with tradition that the Snake clans left their homes at Tokonabi, in the San Juan region, and came to Hopi after the foundation of Sikyatki, which had probably developed its beautiful ceramic art before Walpi was settled. There is no evidence that the potters of the Snake clan ever introduced any modification in the symbolic decoration of pottery by the women of Sikyatki.

SYMBOLS INTRODUCED BY THE SNAKE PEOPLE

The designs on pottery taken from prehistoric ruins of pueblos or villages once inhabited by the Snake clans claim the archeologist's especial attention. These clans were the most important early additions to the Hopi villages and no doubt influenced early Hopi symbolism. There is little trace in early pottery that can be recognized as peculiar to the Snake. The Snake clans formerly lived at Betatakin, Kitsiel, and neighboring ruins.

---

[1] Since the author's work at Sikyatki, excavations have been made by the Field Columbian Museum at this ruin, but nothing bearing on the relations of symbols has been published so far as known to the writer.

Among many significant differences that occur between the designs on pottery from the ruins in Navaho National Monument and those of Sikyatki may be mentioned the rarity of bird designs and the conventional feathers above described. Parallel lines and triangles have been found on the pottery from Kitsiel and Betatakin. Terraced figures are common; spirals are rare. Pottery designs from this region are simpler and like those of the Mesa Verde cliff-houses and the ruins along the San Juan River. Not only do the designs on prehistoric Sikyatki pottery have little resemblance to those from Tokonabi, a former home of the Snake clan, but the pottery from this region of Arizona is of coarser texture and different color. It is the same as that of the San Juan area, the decorations on which are about uniform with those from the Mesa Verde and Chelly Canyon. The best vases and bowls are of red or black-and-white ware.

In the pottery symbols of the clans that lived at Tokonabi (Kitsiel, Betatakin, etc.) the archaic predominated. The passage architecturally from the fragile-walled dwelling into Prudden's pueblo "unit type" had taken place, but the pottery had not yet been greatly modified. Even after the Snake clans moved to Wukoki, near the Black Falls of the Little Colorado, we still find the survival of geometrical designs characteristic of the prepuebloan epoch. Consequently when the Snake clans came to Walpi and joined the Hopi they brought no new symbols and introduced no great changes in symbols. The influence of the clans from the north was slight—too small to greatly influence the development of Hopi symbolism.

TANOAN EPOCH

The Tanoan epoch in the chronology of Hopi pottery symbolism is markedly different from the Keresan. It began with the influx of Tanoan clans, either directly or by way of Zuñi and the Little Colorado, being represented in modern times by the early creations of Hano women, like Nampeo. It is clearly marked and readily distinguished from the Sikyatki epoch, being well represented in eastern museums by pottery collected from Hano, the Tewan pueblo on the East Mesa.

Migrations of Tanoan clans into the Hopi country began very early in Hopi history, but waves of colonists with Tanoan kinship came to Walpi at the close of the seventeenth century as a result of the great rebellion (1680), when the number of colonists from the Rio Grande pueblos was very large. The Badger, Kachina, Asa, and Hano clans seem to have been the most numerous and important in modifying sociological conditions, especially at the East Mesa of the Hopi. Some of these came directly to Walpi, others entered by way of Zuñi, and still others by way of Awatobi. They brought with them Tanoan and Keresan symbolism and Little Colorado elements, all of which were incorporated. The Tanoan symbols are very difficult to differentiate individually but created a considerable modification in the artistic products, as a whole.

The symbolism that the colonists from the Little Colorado settlements brought to Walpi was mixed in character, containing certain Gila Valley elements. Among the last-mentioned were increments derived directly from Zuñi, as shown in the symbolism of their pottery. Among the most important thus introduced were contributions of the Asa, Kachina, Badger, and Butterfly clans. The most important element from the Little Colorado clans that originally came from the Gila Valley (Palatkwabi) are those connected with the plumed serpent.[1] It is possible to trace successive epochs in the history of ceramic decoration in the Little Colorado ruins and to identify, in a measure, the clans with which these epochs were associated, but to follow out this identification in this paper would take me too far afield and lead into a discussion of areas far distant from the Hopi, for it belongs more especially to the history of ceramic decorations of Zuñi decoration and composition.[2] In the present article all the Little Colorado influences are treated as belonging to the Tanoan epoch, which seems to have been the dominant one in the Little Colorado when emigration, comparatively modern in time, began to Hopi.

SYMBOLS INTRODUCED FROM THE LITTLE COLORADO

After the destruction of Sikyatki there was apparently a marked deterioration in the excellence of Hopi ceramics, which continued as late as the overthrow of Awatobi, when the Sikyatki epoch ceased. Shortly before that date and for a few years later there was a notable influx of foreigners into Hopiland; a number of southern clans from the Little Colorado successively joined the Hopi, bringing with them cultural conceptions and symbolic designs somewhat different from those existing previously to their advent. Among these clans are those known in migration legends as the Patki peoples. Although we can not distinguish a special Patki epoch in Hopi ceramics, we have some ideas of the nature of Patki symbolism from large collections from Homolobi, Chevlon, and Chavez Pass.

---

[1] The Tanoan people (clans) also introduced a horned snake, but different in symbolism from that of the Patki clans.

[2] The oldest pottery in the Zuñi Valley belongs to the same group as that of the oldest Little Colorado ruins and shows marked Gila Valley symbolism. The modern pottery of Zuñi is strongly influenced by Tanoan characters. As these have been transmitted to Hopi they are considered under the term "Tanoan epoch," derived from Little Colorado settlements to which Zuñi culturally belongs.

From traditions and ceremonial objects now in use we also know something of the nature of the objective symbols they introduced into Walpi, and we can detect some of these on pottery and other objects used in ceremonies at Walpi. Some of these symbols did not come directly from the Little Colorado ruins, but went first to Awatobi and from there to Walpi[1] after the destruction of the former pueblo in the autumn of the year 1700. The arrival of southern clans at the East Mesa with their characteristic symbols occurred approximately in the seventeenth century, about 200 years after the date of the discovery of Hopi by Tovar. Awatobi received the Rabbit, Tobacco, and other clans from this migration from the south between the years 1632 and 1700, and Walpi received the Patki shortly after or at the same time the Hano clans came from the far east. The similarities in ancient pottery from the Little Colorado and that belonging to the Sikyatki epoch can not be ascribed to anything more profound than superficial contact. It is not probable that the ancient pottery of Awatobi or that of Kawaika and other Keres pueblos on the Awatobi mesa or in the adjacent plain was modified in any considerable degree by incoming clans from the south, but survived the Sikyatki epoch a century after Sikyatki had been destroyed.

The advent of the clans from the Little Colorado into the Hopi country was too late to seriously affect the classic period of Hopi ceramics; it appears also not to have exerted any great influence on later times. Extensive excavations made at Homolobi, Chevlon, and Chavez Pass have revealed much pottery which gives a good idea of the symbolism characteristic of the clans living along this valley, which resembles in some respects the classic Hopi pottery of the time of Sikyatki, but several of these likenesses date back to a time before the union of the Hopi and Little Colorado clans. As a rule the bird figures on pottery from Homolobi, Chevlon, Chavez Pass, and other representative Little Colorado ruins are more realistic and less conventionalized and complex than those from Sikyatki. The peculiar forms of feathers found so constantly in the latter do not occur in the former, nor does the sky-band with its dependent bird figure ever occur on Little Colorado ware. We are here dealing with less-developed conventionalism, a cruder art, and less specialized symbolism. Even if the colors of the pottery did not at once separate them, the expert can readily declare whether he is dealing with a bowl from Sikyatki or Homolobi. There are, to be sure, likenesses, but well-marked differences of local development. The resemblances and differences in the case of bird figures on prehistoric Hopi ware and that from the ruins on the Little Colorado can be readily shown by considering figures 105, 106, and 107, found at Homolobi and Chevlon, and

---

[1] Pakatcomo in the plain below Walpi was their first Hopi settlement.

the corresponding preceding bird figures. It may be interesting to instance another example. Figure 104 shows a lateral view of a bird with wings extended, bearing marginal dentations representing feathers on the breast and a tail composed of four triangular feathers and two eyes, each with iris and pupil. The upper and lower jaws in this figure are extended to form a beak, as is customary in bird designs from the Little Colorado ruins, but never found at Sikyatki. In figure 105 we have another lateral view of a characteristic bird design

FIG. 104.—Lateral view of bird with double eyes.

from the Little Colorado region, and figures 106 and 107 show hourglass bodies, a special feature of the same region.

In the same way many other distinctive characteristics separating figures of animals from the two regions might be mentioned. Those above given may suffice to show that each is distinctive and in a way specialized in its development, but the main reason to believe that the clans from the Little Colorado never affected the symbolism of Sikyatki is the fact that the latter ruin was destroyed before these clans joined the Hopi villages.

The ruins Homolobi and Chevlon were probably inhabited well into historic times, although there is no archeological evidence that artifacts from them were modified by European influences. The symbolism on pottery shows that their culture was composite and seems to have been the result of acculturation from both south and east. Some of the clans, as the Tobacco, that peopled these settlements joined Awatobi before its overthrow, while others settled at Pakatcomo, the ruins of which near Walpi are still visible, and later united with the people of the largest village of the East Mesa. So far as known, Sikyatki had been destroyed before any considerable

FIG. 105.—Lateral view of bird with double eyes.

number of people had entered the Hopi country from the Little Colorado,[1] the event occurring comparatively late in history.

The pottery from the Little Colorado differs from prehistoric Hopi ware much less with respect to geometrical designs than life forms. The break in the encircling line, or, as it is called, the life gate, which is almost universally found on the ancient Hopi vases, bowls, dippers, and other objects, occurs likewise on pottery from Little Colorado ruins. Some of the encircling lines from this region have more than one break, and in one instance the edges of the break have appendages, a rare feature found in both prehistoric Hopi and Little Colorado ware.[2]

The influence of Keres culture on Zuñi may be shown in several ways, thus: A specimen of red ware from a shrine on Thunder Mountain, an old Zuñi site, is decorated with symbolic feathers recalling those on Sikyatki ware ascribed to eastern influence. The nonappearance of Keres and Tewa symbols on ancient pottery from the Zuñi Valley ruins, Heshotauthla and Hálonawan, and their

[1] As has been pointed out, the designs on ancient Zuñi ware are closely related to those of ruins farther down the Little Colorado, and are not Hopi. Modern Zuñi as well as modern Hopi pueblos were influenced by Keres and Tewa culture superimposed on the preexisting culture, which largely came from the Gila.

[2] No invariable connection was found in the relative position of this break and figures of birds or other animals inclosed by the broken band. The gaps in different encircling bands on the same bowl are either diametrically opposite each other or separated by a quadrant, a variation that would appear to indicate that they were not made use of in a determination of the orientation of the vessel while in ceremonial use, as is true of certain baskets of modern Navaho.

existence in the mountain shrine above mentioned, implies that the latter settlement is more modern, and that the eastern clans united with preexisting Little Colorado clans comparatively late in its history. The first settlements in Zuñi Valley were made by colonists from the Gila. There are several ceremonies in the Walpi ritual which, like the New Fire, although immediately derived from Awatobi, came originally from Little Colorado pueblos, and other cere-

FIG. 106.—Bird with double eyes.

monies came directly to Walpi from the same original source. Among the former are those introduced by the Piba (Tobacco) clan, which brought to Walpi a secret fraternity called the Tataukyamu. This brotherhood came directly from Awatobi, but the Tobacco clan from which it was derived once lived in a pueblo on the Little Colorado, now a ruin at Chevlon, midway between Holbrook and Winslow.[1] The identification of the Chevlon ruin with the historic

---

[1] The author has the following evidence that the inhabitants of the village at Chevlon were the historic Chipias. The Hopi have a legend that the large ruin called Tcipiaiya by the Zuñi was also situated on a river midway between Walpi and Zuñi. The Hopi also say that the Chevlon pueblo was inhabited by the Piba (Tobacco) clan and that the Awatobi chief, Tapolo, who brought the Tataukyamu fraternity to Walpi from Awatobi, belonged to the Tobacco clan. The Tewa name of the Tataukyamu is Tcipiaiyu, or "men from Tcipia."

Chipias has an important bearing on the age of the Little Colorado ruins, for Padre Arvide, a Franciscan missionary, was killed in 1632 by the Chipias, who lived west of Zuñi. In other words, their pueblo was then inhabited.

We know that the Piba joined Awatobi before 1700, or the year it was destroyed; consequently the desertion of the Chevlon ruin (Chipiaya, or Tcipiaiya) evidently occurred between 1632 and 1700,

FIG. 107.—Two birds with rain clouds.

not so much on account of Apache inroads as from fear of punishment by the Spaniards.[1] As no clans from the other large pueblo on the Little Colorado or Homolobi joined Awatobi, we can not definitely fix the date that this group fled to the north, but it was probably not long after the time the Chevlon clans migrated to Awatobi, from which it follows that the Little Colorado settlements were inhabited up to the middle of the seventeenth century. While the

[1] It is known from an inscription on El Morro that a punitive expedition to avenge the death of Father Letrado was sent out under Lujan in the spring of 1632, hence the guilty inhabitants may have abandoned their settlement and departed for Hopi at about that time.

Little Colorado clans did not influence the Sikyatki pottery, they did affect the potters of Awatobi to a limited extent and introduced some symbols into Walpi in the middle of the seventeenth and eighteenth centuries. Among these influences may be mentioned those derived from Awatobi after its destruction in 1700. It is not possible to state definitely what modifications in pottery symbols were introduced into Walpi by the potters of the clans from Awatobi and the Little Colorado. Possibly no considerable modification resulted from their advent, as there was already more or less similarity in the pottery from these geographical localities. The southern clans introduced some novelties in ceremonies, especially in the Winter Solstice and New-fire festivals and in the rites of the Horned Serpent at the Spring Equinox.

SYMBOLS INTRODUCED BY THE BADGER AND KACHINA CLANS

As the clans which came to the Hopi country from Zuñi were comparatively late arrivals of Tewa colonists long after the destruction of Sikyatki, their potters exerted no influence on the Sikyatki potters. The ancient Hopi ceramic art had become extinct when the clans from Awatobi, the pueblos on the Little Colorado, and the late Tewa, united with the Walpi settlement on the East Mesa. The place whence we can now obtain information of the character of the symbolism of the Asa, Butterfly, Badger, and other Tewan clans is in certain ceremonies at Sichomovi, a pueblo near Walpi, settled by clans from Zuñi and often called the Zuñi pueblo by the Hopi. One of the Sichomovi ceremonies celebrated at Oraibi and Sichomovi on the East Mesa, in which we may find survivals of the earliest Tewa and Zuñi symbolism, is called the Owakülti. The Sichomovi variant of the Owakülti shows internal sociologic relation to the Butterfly or Buli (Poli) clan resident in Awatobi before its fall. This statement is attested by certain stone slabs excavated from Awatobi mounds, on which are painted butterfly symbols. The Walpi Lalakoñti, first described by the author and Mr. Owens in 1892, has also survivals of Awatobi designs. It appears that while it is not easy to trace any of the rich symbolism of Awatobi directly into Walpi pottery, it is possible to discover close relations between certain Awatobi symbols and others still employed in Walpi ceremonials. Sikyatki and Awatobi were probably inhabited synchronously and as kindred people had a closely allied or identical symbolism; there is such a close relation between the designs on pottery from the two ruins that Awatobi symbols introduced into Walpi have a close likeness to those of Sikyatki.[1]

---

[1] The Buli (Poli) clan is probably Tewa, as the word indicates, which would show that Tewa as well as Keres clans lived at Awatobi. No legend mentions Buli clans at Sikyatki, but several traditions locate them at Awatobi.

The natural conservatism in religious rites of all kinds has brought it about that many of the above-mentioned designs, although abandoned in secular life of the Hopi, still persist in paraphernalia used in ceremonies. It is therefore pertinent to discuss some of these religious symbols with an idea of discovering whether they are associated with certain clans or ruins, and if so what light they shed on prehistoric migrations. In other words, here the ethnologists can afford us much information bearing on the significance of prehistoric symbols.

One great difficulty in interpreting the prehistoric pictures of supernaturals depicted on ancient pottery by a comparison of the religious paraphernalia of the modern Hopi is a complex nomenclature of supernatural beings that has been brought about by the perpetuation or survival of different clan names for the same being even after union of those clans. Thus we find the same Sky god with many others all practically aliases of one common conception. To complicate the matter still more, different attribual names are also sometimes used. The names Alosaka, Muyinwu, and Talatumsi are practically different designations of the same supernatural, while Tunwup, Ho, and Shalako appear to designate the same Sky-god personage. Cultus heroines, as the Marau mana, Shalako mana, Palahiko mana, and others, according as we follow one or another of the dialects, Keres or Tewa, are used interchangeably. This diversity in nomenclature has introduced a complexity in the Hopi mythology which is apparent rather than real in the Hopi Pantheon, as their many names would imply.[1] The great nature gods of sky and earth, male and female, lightning and germination, no doubt arose as simple transfer of a germinative idea applied to cosmic phenomena and organic nature. The earliest creation myths were drawn largely from analogies of human and animal birth. The innumerable lesser or clan gods are naturally regarded as offspring of sky and earth, and man himself is born from Mother Earth. He was not specially created by a Great Spirit, which was foreign to Indians unmodified by white influences.

As the number of bird designs on Sikyatki pottery far outnumber representations of other animals it is natural to interpret them by modern bird symbols or by modern personations of birds, many examples of which are known to the ethnological student of the Hopi.

In one of a series of dances at Powamû, which occurs in February, men and boys personate the eagle, red hawk, humming bird, owl, cock, hen, mocking bird, quail, hawk, and other birds, each appropriately dressed, imitating cries, and wearing an appropriate mask

---

[1] A unification of names of these gods would have resulted when the languages of the many different clans had been fused in religions, as the language was in secular usage. The survival of component names of Hopi gods is paralleled in the many ancient religions.

of the birds they represent. In a dance called Pamurti, a ceremony celebrated annually at Sichomovi, and said to have been derived from Zuñi, personations of the same birds appear, the men of Walpi contributing to the performance. Homovi, one of the Hopi Indians who took part, made colored pictures representing all these birds, which may be found reproduced in the author's article on Hopi katcinas.[1]

In the Hopi cosmogony the Sky god is thought to be father of all gods and human beings, and when personations of the subordinate supernaturals occur they are led to the pueblo by a personator of this great father of all life. The celebrations of the Powamû, at the East Mesa of the Hopi, represent the return of the ancestors or kachinas of Walpi, while the Pamurti is the dramatization of the return of the kachinas of Sichomovi whose ancestors were Zuñi kin.

Life figures or animal forms, as birds, serpents, and insects, depicted on Little Colorado pottery differ considerably from those on Sikyatki ware. Take, for instance, bird designs, the most abundant life forms on ancient pueblo pottery on the Little Colorado, as well as at Sikyatki. It needs but a glance at the figures of the former to show how marked the differences are. The leader of the kachinas in the Powamû, which celebrates the return of these ancestral gods to the pueblo, Walpi, wears an elaborate dress and helmet with appended feathers. He is led into the village by a masked man personating Eototo.[2]

SYMBOLS INTRODUCED FROM AWATOBI

The women saved at Awatobi in the massacre of 1700, according to a legend, brought to Walpi the paraphernalia of a ceremony still observed, called the Mamzrauti. Naturally we should expect to find old Awatobi symbolism on this paraphernalia, which is still in use. The cultus heroine of the Mamzrauti is the Corn-mist maid, known by the name of Shalako mana or Palahiko mana.[3] We have several representations of this maid and their resemblance to the pictures of Shalako mana depicted by Hano potters would imply a common Tanoan origin.

SHALAKO MANA

The most common figure on the third epoch of Hopi pottery, commonly called modern Tewa and manufactured up to 1895 by Nampeo, a Hano potter, is a representation of the Corn maid, Shalako mana,

---

[1] *Twenty-first Ann. Rept. Bur. Amer. Ethn.*

[2] Ibid., p. 76. Eototo, also called Masauû, was the tutelary of Sikyatki, as Alosaka or Muyinwu was of Awatobi.

[3] A somewhat similar personage to Shalako mana in Aztec ceremonies was called Xalaquia (Shalakia).

who, as shown, is the same personage as Marau mana and Palahiko mana in the festival of the Mamzrauti derived from Awatobi. The symbol of this goddess is instructive and easily recognized in its many variations. Her picture on Hano pottery is shown in figure 108.

The most striking features of her symbolism, brought out in plate 89, are terraced bodies representing rain clouds on the head, an ear of maize symbol on the forehead, curved lines over the mouth, chevrons on the cheeks, conventionalized wings, and feathered garment. It is also not uncommon to find carved representations of

FIG. 108.—Head of Shalako mana, or Corn maid.

squash blossoms occupying the same positions as the whorls of hair on the heads of Hopi maidens.

The Shalakotaka male is likewise a common design readily recognized on modern pottery. Particularly abundant are figures of the mask of a Kohonino god, allied to Shalako, which is likewise called a kachina, best shown in paraphernalia of the Mamzrauti ceremony.

It sometimes happens in Hopi dramatization that pictures of supernatural beings and idols of the same take the place of personations by priests. For instance, instead of a girl or a woman representing the Corn maid, this supernatural is depicted on a slab of wood or represented by a wooden idol. One of the best-known figures of the Corn maid (Shalako mana) is here introduced (pl. 89) to

PLATE 89

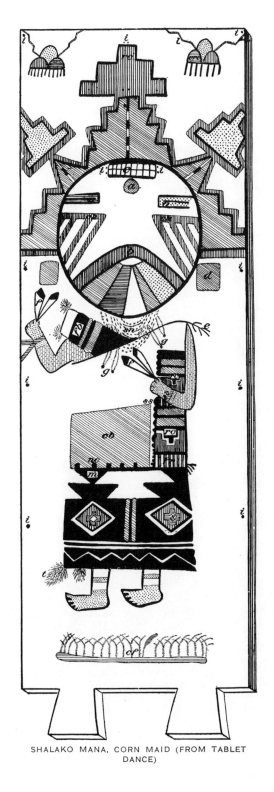

SHALAKO MANA, CORN MAID (FROM TABLET
DANCE)

PLATE 90

TOP OF BUTTERFLY VASE

illustrate the relation of old Awatobi and existing Hopi symbolism; a modern figure (108) of this Corn maid, painted on a wooden slab, is sometimes carried by the Walpi women in their dance. Figures of the Awatobi germ god, Alosaka, otherwise called Muyinwû,[1] are depicted on the slabs used by most of the women at that time.

The different designs on the slab under consideration (pl. 89) are indicated by letters and explained as follows: *a* represents a circular fragment of the haliotis or abalone shell hanging midway from a figure of an ear of corn, *c*. The cheeks are tattooed or painted with characteristic figures, *cb*, the eyes rectangular of different colors. The letter *d* is a representation of a wooden ear pendant, a square, flat body covered on one side with a mosaic of turquoise sometimes arranged in figures. The letter *e* is the end of a string by which the ceremonial blanket is tied over the left shoulder, the right arm being free, as shown in the illustration. Over the right shoulder, however, is thrown a ceremonial embroidered kilt, *fb*.

The objects in the hands represent feathers and recall one type of the conventional feathers figured in the preceding pages. The letters *fr* represent falling rain embroidered on the rim of the ceremonial blanket and *rc* the terraced rain clouds which in *arc* become rounded above; *g* represents a turquoise at the end of a string of turquoise suspended from shell necklaces *sn*; *m* represents the butterfly and is practically identical with the decorations on dados of old Hopi houses; *s* represents a star; *sb* represents shell bracelets, many examples of which occur in ruins along the Little Colorado; *ss* is supposed to have replaced the key patterns which some authorities identify as sprouting beans. There are commonly nine rectangular markings, *nc*, on the upper border of the embroidered region of ceremonial blankets and kilts, each of which represents either a month or a day, by some said to refer to ceremonial or germ periods.[2]

The Shalako mana figures have not yet been found in the unmodified Little Colorado ware, but homologous figures have been found in the Rio Grande area.

The design (pl. 88, *d*) with a horn on the left side of the head and a rectangle on the right, the face being occupied by a terrace figure from which hang parallel lines, reminds one of the " coronets " worn on the head by the *Lakone* maids (manas) in the Walpi Basket dance of the Lalakonti. The horn in the coronet is without terminal appendages, although a feather is tied to it, and the rectangle of plate 88, *d*, is replaced by radiating slats spotted and pointed at

---

[1] An account of this dance with details of the nine days' ceremony as presented in the major or October variant will be found in the *American Anthropologist*, July, 1892. The minor or Winter ceremony, in which the Corn maids are personated by girls, is published in the same journal for 1900. The Corn maid has several aliases in this ceremony, among which are Shalako mana, Palahiko mana, and Marau mana.

[2] This Corn maid is one of the most common figures represented by dolls.

their ends, said to represent the sunflower. The whole design in plate 88, *d*, represents a bird,[1] recalling that of the figure Marautiyo on one of the appended slabs of the altar of the Walpi Marau ceremony. In this altar figure we find not only a horn on the left side of the head, but also a rectangular design on the right.

On the corresponding right-hand side of this altar we have a picture of Marau mana (Shalako mana). It will thus appear that when compared with the Lakone coronet the figure on the Shongopovi bowl represents a female being, whereas when compared with the figure on the Marau altar it resembles a male being. There is, therefore, something wrong in my comparison. But the fact remains that there survive in the two woman's festivals—Lakone maid's coronet and Marau altar—resemblances to prehistoric Hopi designs from Shongopovi. Moreover, it is known that the Marau fetishes are stated by the chief Saliko to have been introduced from Awatobi into Walpi by her ancestor who was saved at the massacre of that town in 1700.

The life figures of the Tanoan epoch, or that following the overthrow of Sikyatki, can be made out by a study of modern Hano pottery. Perhaps the most complex of these is that of the Corn maid, Shalako mana. Shalako mana plays a great rôle in the Mamzrauti, a ceremony derived from Awatobi, and figures representing her are common designs made on Hano pottery. Designs representing this being are common on the peculiar basket plaques made at the Middle Mesa and dolls of her are abundant. The constant presence of her pictures on basket plaques at the Middle Mesa would also seem to show an ancient presence in the Hopi country, and indicate an identity of pottery designs from ancient Shumopavi with those from the East Mesa and Awatobi.[2]

One of her modern Walpi ceremonies has such pronounced Awatobi symbolism that it may be instanced as showing derivation; viz, the New-fire festival.[3] The women of the Marau and the men of the Tataukyamû regard themselves kindred, and taunt each other, as only friends may without offence, in this festival, and the Tataukyamû often introduce a burlesque Shalako mana into their performances.

---

[1] The two parallel lines on the two outside tail feathers recall the markings on the face of the War god Puükoñghoya.

[2] A personation of Shalako mana at Oraibi, according to Mr. H. R. Voth, came from Mishongnovi. This conforms exactly with the legends that state the Mamzrauti may have been introduced into Mishongnovi from Awatobi, for at the division of the captive women at Maski many of the women went to that pueblo.

[3] See Fewkes, The New-fire Ceremony at Walpi, pp. 80–138. The New-fire rites at Walpi are celebrated in November, when four societies, Aaltû, Wüwütcimtû, Tataukyamû, and Kwakwantû, take part. As in all new-fire ceremonies, phallic or generative rites are prominent, the Wüwütcimtû and Tataukyamû who kindle the fire being conspicuous in these rites. Their bodies have phallic emblems painted on them and the latter bear Zuñi symbols.

The designs painted on the bodies and heads of several modern dolls representing Corn maids are symbols whose history is very ancient in the tribe. For instance, those of feathers date back to prehistoric times, and terraced designs representing rain clouds are equally ancient. The dolls of the Corn maid (Shalako mana) present a variety of forms of feathers and the headdresses of many dolls represent kachinas, and show feathers sometimes represented by sticks on which characteristic markings are painted, but more often they represent symbols.[1]

SYMBOLS OF HANO CLANS

Hano, as is well known, is a Tewan pueblo, situated on the East Mesa, which was the last great body of Tewa colonists to migrate to Hopiland. While other Tewa colonists lost their language and became Hopi, the inhabitants of Hano still speak Tewa and still preserve some of their old ceremonies, and consequently many of their own symbols. Here were found purest examples of the Tanoan epoch.

The potters of clans introduced symbols on their ware radically different from those of Sikyatki, the type of the epoch of the finest Hopi ceramics, and replaced it by Tewan designs which characterize Hopi pottery from 1710 to 1895, when a return was suddenly made to the ancient type through the influence of Nampeo. At that date she began to cleverly imitate Sikyatki ware and abandoned *de toto* symbols introduced by Hano and other Tewa clans.

Fortunately there exist good collections of the Tewa epoch of Hopi ceramics, but the ever-increasing demand by tourists for ancient ware induced Nampeo to abandon the Tewa clan symbols she formerly employed and to substitute those of ancient Sikyatki.[2]

The majority of the specimens of Hano pottery, like those of the Tanoan epoch to which it belongs, are decorated with pictures of clan ancients called kachinas. These have very little resemblance to designs characteristic of the Sikyatki epoch. They practically belong to the same type as those introduced by Kachina, Asa, and Badger peoples. One of the most common of these is the design above dis-

---

[1] The designs on the wooden slats carried by women in the dance known as the Marau ceremony are remarkably like some of those on Awatobi and Sikyatki pottery.

[2] Much of the pottery offered for sale by Harvey and other dealers in Indian objects along the Santa Fe Railroad in Arizona and New Mexico is imitation prehistoric Hopi ware made by Nampeo. The origin of this transformation was due partly to the author, who in the year named was excavating the Sikyatki ruins and graves. Nampeo and her husband, Lesou, came to his camp, borrowed paper and pencil, and copied many of the ancient symbols found on the pottery vessels unearthed, and these she has reproduced on pottery of her own manufacture many times since that date. It is therefore necessary, at the very threshold of our study, to urge discrimination between modern and ancient pottery in the study of Hopi ware, and careful elimination of imitations. The modern pottery referred to is easily distinguished from the prehistoric, inasmuch as the modern is not made with as much care or attention to detail as the ancient. Also the surface of the modern pottery is coated with a thin slip which crackles in firing.

cussed representing Shalako mana, the Corn maid, shown in figure 109. In this figure we have the face represented by a circle in the center and many lenticular figures arranged in rows attached to the

FIG. 109.—Head of Kokle, or Earth woman.

neck and shoulders corresponding to the appendages explained in figure 108. It is said in the legends that when the Corn maid appeared to men she was enveloped in fleecy clouds and wore a feathered garment. These are indicated by the curved figures covered with dots and the parallel lines on the body. Feather symbols recalling those of the Sikyatki epoch hang from appendages to the head representing rain clouds.

In figure 109 we have a representation of the head with surrounding clouds, and portions of the body of a kachina, called Kokle, who is personated in Winter ceremonies. It is instructive to note that this figure has symbols on the head that recall the Sikyatki epoch. The ancient Tewan

FIG. 110.—Head of Hahaiwugti, or Earth woman.

earth goddess, Hahaiwugti, is represented in figure 110. She appears also in figure 111, where her picture is painted on a ladle, the handle of which represents an ancient Tewan clown called by the Hano people Paiakyamû.

The War god, Püükon hoya, also a Tewan incorporation in the Hopi pantheon, appears frequently on pottery of the Tanoan epoch, as shown in figure 112. This figure, painted on a terra-cotta slab, is identified by the two parallel marks on each cheek.

CONCLUSION

In the preceding pages an attempt has been made to trace the chronological sequence of pottery symbols in Hopiland by pointing out distinct epochs in cultural history and correlating the sociology of the tribe. This takes for granted that the pottery symbols characteristic of this people are directly connected with certain clans. There have from time to time been sudden changes in symbols, or previous designs have suddenly disappeared and others have taken their places, as well as a slow development of existing symbols into more com-

FIG. 111.—Ladle with clown carved on handle and Earth woman on bowl.

plicated forms. There persist everywhere survivals of old prepuebloan symbols inherited from the past and a creation of new products of Hopi environment not found elsewhere.

FIG. 112.—Püükon hoya, little War god.

The author will close this paper with a brief theoretical account of the unwritten culture history of Hopi, part of which explains certain pottery symbols. If we take that segment of southwestern history extending from the earliest to the present, we find evidences of the existence of a prepuebloan culture existing before terraced houses were built or circular kivas had been used for ceremonial purposes. This epoch was antecedent to the construction of the great walled compounds of the Gila, illustrated by Casa Grande. At that epoch known as the prepuebloan there extended from Utah to the Mexican boundary and from the Colorado to the Rio Grande a culture architecturally characterized by small fragile-walled houses not united or terraced. These houses were sometimes like pit dwellings, either partially or wholly subterranean. When above ground their walls were supported by upright logs in which canes or brushes were woven and covered with mud, the roofs being made of cedar bark or straw overlaid with adobe.

The pottery of this early prehistoric epoch was smooth, painted mainly with geometric patterns, corrugated, or indented. Rectilinear or curved lines constituted the majority of the superficial decorations and life designs were few or altogether wanting. In addition to these architectural and ceramic characteristics, this prepuebloan cultural stage was distinguished by many other features, to mention which would take us too far afield and would be out of place in this article. Evidences of this stage or epoch occur everywhere in the Southwest and survival of the archaic characters enumerated are evident in all subsequent epochs.

The so-called "unit type" or pure pueblo culture grew out of this early condition and was at first localized in northern New Mexico and southern Colorado, where it was autochthonous. Its essential feature is the terraced communal house and the simplest form of the pueblo, the "unit type," first pointed out by Dr. T. Mitchell Prudden—a combination of dwelling houses, with a man's house or kiva and a cemetery. The dwellings are made of stone or clay and are terraced, the kiva is subterranean and circular, embedded in or surrounded by other rooms. The "unit type" originated in Colorado and, spreading in all directions, replaced the preexisting houses with fragile walls. Colonists from its center extended down the San Juan to the Hopi country and made their way easterly across the Rio Grande and southerly to the headwaters of the Gila and Little Colorado, where they met other clans of specialized prepuebloan culture who had locally developed an architecture of Great House style characteristic of the Gila and Salt River Valleys.

The essential differences between the terraced pueblo and the previously existing fragile-walled house culture are two: The terraced architecture results from one house being constructed above another, the kiva or subterranean ceremonial room being separated or slightly removed from the secular houses.

An explanation of the origin of the terraced pueblo is evident. This form of house implies a limited site or a congestion of houses on a limited area. An open plain presents no limitation in lateral construction; there is plenty of room to expand in all directions to accommodate the enlargement which results as a settlement increases in population. In a cave conditions are otherwise; expansion is limited. When the floor of the cavern is once covered with rooms the only additions which can possibly be made must be vertically. In protection lies the cause of the development of a terraced architecture such as the pueblos show, for the early people con-

structed their fragile-walled habitations in a cavern, and as an enlargement of their numbers occurred they were obliged to construct
the terraced pueblos called cliff-dwellings, with rooms closely approximated and constructed in terraces. In the course of time these
cliff-dwellers moved out of their caverns into the river valleys or to
the mesa summits, carrying with them the terraced architecture,
which, born in caverns, survived in their new environment. This
explanation is of course hypothetical, but not wholly without a basis
in fact, for we find survivals of the prepuebloan architecture scat-
tered throughout the Southwest, especially on the periphery of the
terraced house area, as well as in the area itself. The ancient terraced house architecture is confined to a limited area, but around its
ancient border are people whose dwellings are characterized by
fragile-walled architecture. These are the survivals of the prepuebloan culture.

The environmental conditions along the San Juan and its tributaries in Colorado and New Mexico render it a particularly favorable
culture center from which the pure pueblo type may have originated,
and although observations have not yet gone far enough to prove
that here was the place of origin of the unit type, and therefore of
pueblo culture, there are strong indications that a fable of the
Pueblos, that they came from the caves in the north, is not without
legendary foundation so far as their origin is concerned.

The term "cliff-dwelling," once supposed to indicate a distinct
stage of development, refers only to the site and is a feature inadequate for classification or chronology. All cliff-dwellings do not
belong to the same structural type. There is little similarity save in
site between Spruce-tree House on the Mesa Verde, and Montezuma
Castle in the Verde Valley; the former belongs to the "pure pueblo
type," the latter to another class of buildings related to " compounds "
of the tributaries of the Gila and Salt River valleys.

AUTHORITIES CITED

FEWKES, JESSE WALTER. Snake ceremonials at Walpi. *Journal of American Ethnology and Archæology*, vol. IV, pp. 1–126. Boston and New York, 1894.

———. Archeological expedition to Arizona in 1895. *Seventeenth Annual Report of the Bureau of American Ethnology*, pt. 2, pp. 519–742. Washington, 1898.

———. Winter solstice altars at Hano pueblo. *American Anthropologist*, n. s. vol. I, no. 2, pp. 251–276. New York, 1899.

———. The New-fire ceremony at Walpi. *American Anthropologist*, n. s. vol. II, no. 1, pp. 80–138. New York, 1900.

———. The lesser New-fire ceremony at Walpi. *American Anthropologist*, n. s. vol. III, no. 3, pp. 438–453. New York, 1901.

———. Hopi katcinas. *Twenty-first Annual Report of the Bureau of American Ethnology*, pp. 13–126. Washington, 1903.

———. Two summers' work in Pueblo ruins. *Twenty-second Annual Report of the Bureau of American Ethnology*, pt. 1, pp. 17–195. Washington, 1904.

———. Hopi ceremonial frames from Cañon de Chelly, Arizona. *American Anthropologist*, n. s. vol. VIII, no. 4, pp. 664–670. Lancaster, 1906.

———. Hopi shrines near the East Mesa, Arizona. *American Anthropologist*, n. s. vol. VIII, no. 2, pp. 346–375. Lancaster, 1908.

———. The butterfly in Hopi myth and ritual. *American Anthropologist*, n. s. vol. XII, no. 4, pp. 576–594. Lancaster, 1910.

MALLERY, GARRICK. On the pictographs of the North American Indians. *Fourth Annual Report of the Bureau of Ethnology*, pp. 13–256. Washington, 1886.

A CATALOG OF SELECTED
DOVER BOOKS
IN ALL FIELDS OF INTEREST

A CATALOG OF SELECTED DOVER BOOKS IN ALL FIELDS OF INTEREST

CONCERNING THE SPIRITUAL IN ART, Wassily Kandinsky. Pioneering work by father of abstract art. Thoughts on color theory, nature of art. Analysis of earlier masters. 12 illustrations. 80pp. of text. 5⅜ × 8½. 23411-8 Pa. $2.50

LEONARDO ON THE HUMAN BODY, Leonardo da Vinci. More than 1200 of Leonardo's anatomical drawings on 215 plates. Leonardo's text, which accompanies the drawings, has been translated into English. 506pp. 8⅜ × 11¾. 24483-0 Pa. $10.95

GOBLIN MARKET, Christina Rossetti. Best-known work by poet comparable to Emily Dickinson, Alfred Tennyson. With 46 delightfully grotesque illustrations by Laurence Housman. 64pp. 4 × 6¾. 24516-0 Pa. $2.50

THE HEART OF THOREAU'S JOURNALS, edited by Odell Shepard. Selections from *Journal*, ranging over full gamut of interests. 228pp. 5⅜ × 8½. 20741-2 Pa. $4.50

MR. LINCOLN'S CAMERA MAN: MATHEW B. BRADY, Roy Meredith. Over 300 Brady photos reproduced directly from original negatives, photos. Lively commentary. 368pp. 8⅜ × 11¼. 23021-X Pa. $14.95

PHOTOGRAPHIC VIEWS OF SHERMAN'S CAMPAIGN, George N. Barnard. Reprint of landmark 1866 volume with 61 plates: battlefield of New Hope Church, the Etawah Bridge, the capture of Atlanta, etc. 80pp. 9 × 12. 23445-2 Pa. $6.00

A SHORT HISTORY OF ANATOMY AND PHYSIOLOGY FROM THE GREEKS TO HARVEY, Dr. Charles Singer. Thoroughly engrossing non-technical survey. 270 illustrations. 211pp. 5⅜ × 8½. 20389-1 Pa. $4.95

REDOUTE ROSES IRON-ON TRANSFER PATTERNS, Barbara Christopher. Redouté was botanical painter to the Empress Josephine; transfer his famous roses onto fabric with these 24 transfer patterns. 80pp. 8¼ × 10⅞. 24292-7 Pa. $3.50

THE FIVE BOOKS OF ARCHITECTURE, Sebastiano Serlio. Architectural milestone, first (1611) English translation of Renaissance classic. Unabridged reproduction of original edition includes over 300 woodcut illustrations. 416pp. 9⅜ × 12¼. 24349-4 Pa. $14.95

CARLSON'S GUIDE TO LANDSCAPE PAINTING, John F. Carlson. Authoritative, comprehensive guide covers, every aspect of landscape painting. 34 reproductions of paintings by author; 58 explanatory diagrams. 144pp. 8⅜ × 11. 22927-0 Pa. $5.95

101 PUZZLES IN THOUGHT AND LOGIC, C.R. Wylie, Jr. Solve murders, robberies, see which fishermen are liars—purely by reasoning! 107pp. 5⅜ × 8½. 20367-0 Pa. $2.00

TEST YOUR LOGIC, George J. Summers. 50 more truly new puzzles with new turns of thought, new subtleties of inference. 100pp. 5⅜ × 8½. 22877-0 Pa. $2.25

SMOCKING: TECHNIQUE, PROJECTS, AND DESIGNS, Dianne Durand. Foremost smocking designer provides complete instructions on how to smock. Over 10 projects, over 100 illustrations. 56pp. 8¼ × 11.   23788-5 Pa. $2.00

AUDUBON'S BIRDS IN COLOR FOR DECOUPAGE, edited by Eleanor H. Rawlings. 24 sheets, 37 most decorative birds, full color, on one side of paper. Instructions, including work under glass. 56pp. 8¼ × 11.   23492-4 Pa. $3.95

THE COMPLETE BOOK OF SILK SCREEN PRINTING PRODUCTION, J.I. Biegeleisen. For commercial user, teacher in advanced classes, serious hobbyist. Most modern techniques, materials, equipment for optimal results. 124 illustrations. 253pp. 5⅜ × 8½.   21100-2 Pa. $4.50

A TREASURY OF ART NOUVEAU DESIGN AND ORNAMENT, edited by Carol Belanger Grafton. 577 designs for the practicing artist. Full-page, spots, borders, bookplates by Klimt, Bradley, others. 144pp. 8⅜ × 11¼.   24001-0 Pa. $5.95

ART NOUVEAU TYPOGRAPHIC ORNAMENTS, Dan X. Solo. Over 800 Art Nouveau florals, swirls, women, animals, borders, scrolls, wreaths, spots and dingbats, copyright-free. 100pp. 8⅛ × 11.   24366-4 Pa. $4.00

HAND SHADOWS TO BE THROWN UPON THE WALL, Henry Bursill. Wonderful Victorian novelty tells how to make flying birds, dog, goose, deer, and 14 others, each explained by a full-page illustration. 32pp. 6½ × 9¼. 21779-5 Pa. $1.50

AUDUBON'S BIRDS OF AMERICA COLORING BOOK, John James Audubon. Rendered for coloring by Paul Kennedy. 46 of Audubon's noted illustrations: red-winged black-bird, cardinal, etc. Original plates reproduced in full-color on the covers. Captions. 48pp. 8¼ × 11.   23049-X Pa. $2.25

SILK SCREEN TECHNIQUES, J.I. Biegeleisen, M.A. Cohn. Clear, practical, modern, economical. Minimal equipment (self-built), materials, easy methods. For amateur, hobbyist, 1st book. 141 illustrations. 185pp. 6⅛ × 9¼.   20433-2 Pa. $3.95

101 PATCHWORK PATTERNS, Ruby S. McKim. 101 beautiful, immediately useable patterns, full-size, modern and traditional. Also general information, estimating, quilt lore. 140 illustrations. 124pp. 7⅞ × 10¾.   20773-0 Pa. $3.50

READY-TO-USE FLORAL DESIGNS, Ed Sibbett, Jr. Over 100 floral designs (most in three sizes) of popular individual blossoms as well as bouquets, sprays, garlands. 64pp. 8¼ × 11.   23976-4 Pa. $2.95

AMERICAN WILD FLOWERS COLORING BOOK, Paul Kennedy. Planned coverage of 46 most important wildflowers, from Rickett's collection; instructive as well as entertaining. Color versions on covers. Captions. 48pp. 8¼ × 11.
20095-7 Pa. $2.50

CARVING DUCK DECOYS, Harry V. Shourds and Anthony Hillman. Detailed instructions and full-size templates for constructing 16 beautiful, marvelously practical decoys according to time-honored South Jersey method. 70pp. 9¼ × 12¼.
24083-5 Pa. $4.95

TRADITIONAL PATCHWORK PATTERNS, Carol Belanger Grafton. Cardboard cut-out pieces for use as templates to make 12 quilts: Buttercup, Ribbon Border, Tree of Paradise, nine more. Full instructions. 57pp. 8¼ × 11.
23015-5 Pa. $3.50

THE RIME OF THE ANCIENT MARINER, Gustave Doré, S.T. Coleridge. Doré's finest work, 34 plates capture moods, subtleties of poem. Full text. 77pp. 9¼ × 12.   22305-1 Pa. $4.95

SONGS OF INNOCENCE, William Blake. The first and most popular of Blake's famous "Illuminated Books," in a facsimile edition reproducing all 31 brightly colored plates. Additional printed text of each poem. 64pp. 5¼ × 7.
22764-2 Pa. $3.50

AN INTRODUCTION TO INFORMATION THEORY, J.R. Pierce. Second (1980) edition of most impressive non-technical account available. Encoding, entropy, noisy channel, related areas, etc. 320pp. 5⅜ × 8½.   24061-4 Pa. $4.95

THE DIVINE PROPORTION: A STUDY IN MATHEMATICAL BEAUTY, H.E. Huntley. "Divine proportion" or "golden ratio"in poetry, Pascal's triangle, philosophy, psychology, music, mathematical figures, etc. Excellent bridge between science and art. 58 figures. 185pp. 5⅜ × 8½.   22254-3 Pa. $3.95

THE DOVER NEW YORK WALKING GUIDE: From the Battery to Wall Street, Mary J. Shapiro. Superb inexpensive guide to historic buildings and locales in lower Manhattan: Trinity Church, Bowling Green, more. Complete Text; maps. 36 illustrations. 48pp. 3⅞ × 9¼.   24225-0 Pa. $2.50

NEW YORK THEN AND NOW, Edward B. Watson, Edmund V. Gillon, Jr. 83 important Manhattan sites: on facing pages early photographs (1875-1925) and 1976 photos by Gillon. 172 illustrations. 171pp. 9¼ × 10.   23361-8 Pa. $7.95

HISTORIC COSTUME IN PICTURES, Braun & Schneider. Over 1450 costumed figures from dawn of civilization to end of 19th century. English captions. 125 plates. 256pp. 8⅜ × 11¼.   23150-X Pa. $7.50

VICTORIAN AND EDWARDIAN FASHION: A Photographic Survey, Alison Gernsheim. First fashion history completely illustrated by contemporary photographs. Full text plus 235 photos, 1840-1914, in which many celebrities appear. 240pp. 6½ × 9¼.   24205-6 Pa. $6.00

CHARTED CHRISTMAS DESIGNS FOR COUNTED CROSS-STITCH AND OTHER NEEDLECRAFTS, Lindberg Press. Charted designs for 45 beautiful needlecraft projects with many yuletide and wintertime motifs. 48pp. 8¼ × 11.
24356-7 Pa. $2.50

101 FOLK DESIGNS FOR COUNTED CROSS-STITCH AND OTHER NEEDLE-CRAFTS, Carter Houck. 101 authentic charted folk designs in a wide array of lovely representations with many suggestions for effective use. 48pp. 8¼ × 11.
24369-9 Pa. $2.25

FIVE ACRES AND INDEPENDENCE, Maurice G. Kains. Great back-to-the-land classic explains basics of self-sufficient farming. The one book to get. 95 illustrations. 397pp. 5⅜ × 8½.   20974-1 Pa. $4.95

A MODERN HERBAL, Margaret Grieve. Much the fullest, most exact, most useful compilation of herbal material. Gigantic alphabetical encyclopedia, from aconite to zedoary, gives botanical information, medical properties, folklore, economic uses, and much else. Indispensable to serious reader. 161 illustrations. 888pp. 6½ × 9¼. (Available in U.S. only)   22798-7, 22799-5 Pa., Two-vol. set $16.45

READY-TO-USE BORDERS, Ted Menten. Both traditional and unusual interchangeable borders in a tremendous array of sizes, shapes, and styles. 32 plates. 64pp. 8¼ × 11. 23782-6 Pa. $3.50

THE WHOLE CRAFT OF SPINNING, Carol Kroll. Preparing fiber, drop spindle, treadle wheel, other fibers, more. Highly creative, yet simple. 43 illustrations. 48pp. 8¼ × 11. 23968-3 Pa. $2.50

HIDDEN PICTURE PUZZLE COLORING BOOK, Anna Pomaska. 31 delightful pictures to color with dozens of objects, people and animals hidden away to find. Captions. Solutions. 48pp. 8¼ × 11. 23909-8 Pa. $2.25

QUILTING WITH STRIPS AND STRINGS, H.W. Rose. Quickest, easiest way to turn left-over fabric into handsome quilt. 46 patchwork quilts; 31 full-size templates. 48pp. 8¼ × 11. 24357-5 Pa. $3.25

NATURAL DYES AND HOME DYEING, Rita J. Adrosko. Over 135 specific recipes from historical sources for cotton, wool, other fabrics. Genuine premodern handicrafts. 12 illustrations. 160pp. 5⅜ × 8½. 22688-3 Pa. $2.95

CARVING REALISTIC BIRDS, H.D. Green. Full-sized patterns, step-by-step instructions for robins, jays, cardinals, finches, etc. 97 illustrations. 80pp. 8¼ × 11. 23484-3 Pa. $3.00

GEOMETRY, RELATIVITY AND THE FOURTH DIMENSION, Rudolf Rucker. Exposition of fourth dimension, concepts of relativity as Flatland characters continue adventures. Popular, easily followed yet accurate, profound. 141 illustrations. 133pp. 5⅜ × 8½. 23400-2 Pa. $3.00

READY-TO-USE SMALL FRAMES AND BORDERS, Carol B. Grafton. Graphic message? Frame it graphically with 373 new frames and borders in many styles: Art Nouveau, Art Deco, Op Art. 64pp. 8¼ × 11. 24375-3 Pa. $3.50

CELTIC ART: THE METHODS OF CONSTRUCTION, George Bain. Simple geometric techniques for making Celtic interlacements, spirals, Kellstype initials, animals, humans, etc. Over 500 illustrations. 160pp. 9 × 12. (Available in U.S. only) 22923-8 Pa. $6.00

THE TALE OF TOM KITTEN, Beatrix Potter. Exciting text and all 27 vivid, full-color illustrations to charming tale of naughty little Tom getting into mischief again. 58pp. 4¼ × 5½. (USO) 24502-0 Pa. $1.75

WOODEN PUZZLE TOYS, Ed Sibbett, Jr. Transfer patterns and instructions for 24 easy-to-do projects: fish, butterflies, cats, acrobats, Humpty Dumpty, 19 others. 48pp. 8¼ × 11. 23713-3 Pa. $2.50

MY FAMILY TREE WORKBOOK, Rosemary A. Chorzempa. Enjoyable, easy-to-use introduction to genealogy designed specially for children. Data pages plus text. Instructive, educational, valuable. 64pp. 8¼ × 11. 24229-3 Pa. $2.50

Prices subject to change without notice.

Available at your book dealer or write for free catalog to Dept. GI, Dover Publications, Inc., 31 East 2nd St. Mineola, N.Y. 11501. Dover publishes more than 175 books each year on science, elementary and advanced mathematics, biology, music, art, literary history, social sciences and other areas.